When Labor Votes

A Study of Auto Workers

WHEN LABOR VOTES

VOTES

A STUDY OF AUTO WORKERS

Arthur Kornhauser
Harold L. Sheppard
Albert J. Mayer

Wayne University

GREENWOOD PRESS, PUBLISHERS
WESTPORT, CONNECTICUT

Library of Congress Cataloging in Publication Data

Kornhauser, Arthur William, 1896-
   When labor votes.

    Reprint of the ed. published by University Books,
New York.
    Includes index.
    1. Automobile industry workers--Michigan--Detroit
metropolitan area--Political activity. 2. Voting--
Michigan--Detroit metropolitan area. 3. Interna-
tional Union, United Automobile, Aircraft and Agri-
cultural Implement Workers of America. I. Sheppard,
Harold L., joint author. II. Mayer, Albert J.,
joint author. III. Title.
[HD8079.D6K67 1976]   324'.2   76-2533
ISBN 0-8371-8787-7

Originally published in 1956 by University Books, New York

Reprinted with the permission of Lyle Stuart Inc.

Reprinted in 1976 by Greenwood Press,
a division of Williamhouse-Regency Inc.

Library of Congress Catalog Card Number 76-2533

ISBN 0-8371-8787-7

Printed in the United States of America

Preface

This study was made possible by a research grant to Wayne University from the automobile workers' international union, the UAW-CIO. No strings were attached to the union's gift. It was clearly understood that we would have complete freedom in the conduct of the research and in the publication of our results.

The union's purpose, as stated in a letter from Walter Reuther to the University, was "to contribute to better understanding, and thus to improved functioning, of our democratic political system as an instrument for meeting the needs and fulfilling the legitimate aspirations of Americans in all walks of life." He added: "In order to serve its purpose effectively, the survey must be as objective and free from bias as it is humanly possible to make it." It was also specified that the union would receive the same report that would be made available to others.

These facts may be as important as the content of the study itself. Industrial and political organizations have been reluctant to support research into their own activities under conditions of the kind described. The UAW's decision to do so offers evidence of increased security and self-confidence on the part of the union and bespeaks respect and trust in regard to university social research that we find most encouraging.

The research reported here aims to have practical significance in reference to the current political scene; it provides useful information for persons concerned with the participation of

5

organized labor in politics—whether they are *for* it or *against* it. But the study is by no means limited to immediate applications. The results, it is hoped, will help provide deeper understanding of working people's motivations and feelings as these affect their political outlook and behavior. The findings furnish a basis for challenging speculation about what lies ahead. In our final chapter we attempt to define this larger frame of reference within which data of the kind turned up in our survey need to be examined.

In weighing the results of the study, it is necessary constantly to bear in mind that our generalizations are based on a particular sample of people and on particular questions addressed to them. All the data refer to members of the auto workers union in the Detroit area and to comparisons among sub-groups of these workers. Except in the matter of voting, we do not have comparable figures for other parts of the population. The study, then, is not an evaluation of these Detroit workers in contrast to others; it is an analysis of certain politically significant characteristics of this one group.

However, this is an extremely important group—both because of its own political impact (it includes large numbers of unionists in a union that is unusually active politically) and because these people are probably not very different politically from millions of other industrial workers (as they are, or as they may become if unions continue to step up their political action programs). Conclusions regarding these auto workers, consequently, have suggestive value that transcends the limitations of the particular sample.

Within the population of Detroit area UAW members, we attempted to interview a random sample. In fact, however, not all workers are equally available; many cannot be located or cannot be found at home. Consequently our results are not fully representative—particularly not of the most transient, the very young, those having short periods of employment, etc. It is best to think of all generalizations in this report as pertaining primarily to the more settled, less mobile parts of the union membership—which includes the great majority.

Due to the limited number of interviews, moreover, it is

necessary to recognize that statistical results are all subject to a margin of error. We have tried to avoid drawing definite conclusions wherever the numerical relations are such that they could easily have occurred by chance. Nevertheless, since the directions of such differences are often suggestive, we do point to certain of them as indicating interesting tendencies. For the statistically inclined reader, a table is given in Appendix B to aid him in roughly estimating the reliance that can be placed on percentage comparisons of different size.

On the matter of whether we asked the right questions—and precisely what the questions meant to the people interviewed— we can only emphasize that these are serious problems for all survey research and that we have sought to keep the dangers clearly before us. A principal safeguard against unjustified interpretations of responses lies in full reporting of the questions. Accordingly, we have provided the reader with this type of information, thus enabling each to judge for himself whether our conclusions are reasonable and permitting him to draw his own alternative inferences.

The preceding comments are not intended as apologies. While the limitations are to be kept in mind, the results presented throughout the report appear to us to justify significant conclusions—conclusions that contribute to a better understanding of working people's relations to union political activities.

We wish to express our sincere appreciation to the UAW-CIO for their support of this research and for the fine spirit with which the union staff has cooperated with us in the course of the study. Our hearty thanks go, too, to the officials of Wayne University who have aided with the resources of the University and the encouragement of our independent research endeavors. We are also grateful to Dr. Angus Campbell and his staff at the University of Michigan Survey Research Center for generously making available to us the plans and interview schedules of their own extensive national study of the 1952 election. Professors Peter Blau, Morris Janowitz, William Kornhauser, and Harold Wilensky read a preliminary draft and offered valuable critical comments. Finally, we are glad to acknowledge the help of our assistants in the research and we offer a special word of thanks to the hundreds of auto workers who were willing to sit down with our interviewers and answer the long list of questions that provided the indispensable data for this report.

A. K.
H. L. S.
A. J. M.

Contents

CHAPTER 1

Introduction: The Union and the Study

This is a study of labor union members in an industrial metropolis. It is a study of how Detroit auto workers voted in 1952, why they voted as they did, how they feel about labor's political action and, above all, what basic attitudes are associated with their political views and behavior.

Why, it may be asked, single out labor union members for special study? Briefly, the answer is that unions are becoming new centers of power on the American political scene; that consequently, great importance attaches to the question whether their current political activities are mere flashes in the pan, top-level maneuverings and manipulations without mass following, or whether they are built on rank and file support and are aimed at goals genuinely popular among the members. This is the most direct, practical answer. Society needs whatever knowledge can be accumulated concerning unions in national politics, including knowledge of how the organizations' participation in politics is viewed by their members.

When the inquiry deals with one of the largest and most dynamic unions in the nation, the findings take on special significance as a basis for interpreting political trends and for assessing the changing role of organized labor in politics.

But the research also serves a more general purpose. It aims to add a little to our slowly growing understanding of sociopolitical processes in industrialized mass society. What are the shifting and the stable elements of motivation and outlook that characterize modern political man in his varied roles and group attachments, under the impact of the diverse economic and social pressures that play upon him? What is the meaning of voting in present-day America? How do people at the grass roots—or on the shop floor—perceive society, its patterns of power, and their own interests? Whom do they trust? What leadership do they follow? What is happening to "mass man"?

The present study is carried on with full awareness of these grand questions though it can hope to contribute to their answers only in the most limited manner. Nevertheless, the results of our inquiry need to be viewed in the larger context. The political behavior of Michigan auto workers in the 1950's has to be seen against the background of America's changing social structure and the conditions of the contemporary world.

The Changing Social Scene

The powerful influences of a constantly changing technology have vastly altered our way of life. The farm, the village, the close-knit primary group, have been replaced by metropolitan living with its attendant rush, atomization, congestion, and apparent disregard of the individual. Vast corporations, trade associations, and labor organizations dominate the economic scene. We are living in the midst of an "organizational revolution." The political structure has become correspondingly big and impersonal. Candidates for office seldom kiss babies any more.

At the same time, the average citizen's education and plane of living have risen spectacularly. And profound changes have been occurring in American society as a result of lengthening life, drastic curtailment of immigration, increased leisure and new forms of communication, entertainment, and travel. The world picture has likewise been transforming itself before our eyes—with the surge of Communism, the intensified national independence movements, the polarization of the world into East and West, and the fateful harnessing of atomic energy with all its dreadful and wonderful potentialities.

Into this rapid whirl of change men everywhere bring their traditional loyalties and aversions, their personal problems, phil-

osophies, and distinctive group interests. The political behavior
that emerges inevitably assumes varied shapes and directions
for people differently constituted and differently situated. The
more we examine the proverbial "average citizen," the more he
vanishes—to become an interested voter or an apathetic non-
voter; a politically sophisticated member of this wealthy, well-
educated business group or of that liberal, intellectual circle; a
wavering follower of extremist leaders or a dedicated and
undeviating party member; a satisfied, successful farmer or dis-
contented migratory laborer—and on through innumerable such
contrasts.

The citizens upon whom the present study focuses comprise
one highly significant segment of the electorate. Organized
urban industrial workers exercise an influence in American
politics that is already powerful and that *could* grow, or be
forged into, a vastly more potent force. Few, if any, groups
offer more interesting evidence of what is happening along these
lines than do Detroit auto workers. Here is an urban industrial
population concentrated in a type of mass-production manufacturing that has become a symbol over the world of large-scale,
specialized, "de-humanized" operations. At the same time these
men and women are joined together in a young and vigorous
labor union that strongly stresses political and social goals
along with its economic aims. Our study concerns itself with
the political involvement and motivations of this challenging
section of the mass society.

The UAW[1] and Political Action

No one labor union is typical of American unionism. It has
long been recognized that there are unions and unions—and this
variety is nowhere better illustrated than in the political action
dimension. The auto workers' union, though emphatically not
representative of unionism as a whole, is worthy of study in its
own right. Many thoughtful observers believe that it provides a

[1] The official name of the union is International Union, United Automobile, Aircraft and Agricultural Implement Workers of America. It is commonly known as the UAW-CIO or simply the UAW. We shall ordinarily
use this last briefest designation.

major part of the impetus for labor's expanding activities on the political scene. A glance at the union's history and dynamics lends substance to the opinion, as indicated by the following sketch of a few facts concerning the organization. At the same time this account will furnish a useful setting for the data and interpretations to be reported in subsequent chapters.

The UAW has been called a "lusty youngster" among American unions. This is to emphasize its youth, its strength, its vigor. The union was born during the depression 30's and grew up with the New Deal. It expanded at a phenomenal rate until it now numbers a million and a quarter members employed mostly in the automobile, aircraft, and agricultural implement industries in 38 states and Canada. By just about any standard of measurement, the union has proved remarkably successful in achieving its goals—in its economic gains and job-related improvements won from powerful and resistant managements; in unifying and stabilizing its organization while still preserving democratic union government to an unusual degree; in establishing flourishing health services, pension plans, educational programs, publications, and community relations activities; in combatting discrimination; in developing imaginative and effective leadership at all levels, as well as staff departments of exceptional competence to deal with technical problems. And most directly important for our present purposes, the union has been in the forefront of organized labor's political efforts.

Within the whole of American labor, the UAW is probably the union most fully committed to political action on the national level and most influential in the use of its political arm in relation to broad economic and social policies. From the beginning of the CIO-created Political Action Committee in 1944, the Auto Workers were among the strongest supporters of the movement. The union had established a Washington office in 1943, which kept in close touch with legislative proposals and other governmental actions of interest to labor. This office has functioned ever since as a clearinghouse for labor political information and as an initiating point for many of the union's educational and propaganda activities in the political sphere.

By the time of the 1948 election, the UAW was fully embarked on a determined political course, to be maintained as a vital and integral part of the organization's work. The UAW did not stand alone, of course; CIO-PAC and the newly formed AF of L's Labor League for Political Education, also tackled political problems with new energy, stimulated and provoked by the shock of seeing the Taft-Hartley law enacted over labor's united opposition and a Presidential veto. The years since 1948 have been utilized by the UAW for a steady expansion and strengthening of political efforts. These efforts have been devoted largely to grass-roots education and to organizing for political action at the local union and local community levels. We shall return shortly to a more detailed statement concerning these activities as exemplified in the 1952 campaign in the Detroit area.

But first it is important to mention the point of view of the political program we have been describing. The top levels of the union expound the philosophy of *general* economic and social advancement to be gained *both* through collective bargaining and through governmental actions. Fused with practical, "bread-and-butter" objectives are persistent reiterations of idealistic views carried forward from the earlier turbulent years of ideological struggle in the union. A recurrent theme in the educational activities of the union is an emphasis on the close interrelatedness of the economic problems of the individual worker with the political process. To use the UAW's own expression, "the single stroke of a pen in Lansing or Washington can wipe out all the progress gained around the collective bargaining table or through the grievance process." In one of its discussion manuals on political action, the union further attempts to convey to its members the notion that the function of their organization is limited only by the range of the problems facing them, and not merely by what can be done in the shop. In its program for greater political participation, the leadership attempts to convince the members that its approach to politics is a "natural development of problem solving"; moreover, that the problems to be solved politically are not just union problems; they are public problems.

This attempt to equate the auto workers' interests with the public interest is a key element of the union's political efforts. In line with this policy, the union concerns itself with a wide range of vital public issues, whether economic or non-economic; whether local, state, national, or international. This is not to say that the interests of society as a whole are so clear and agreed upon that a political course can be followed that commends itself to all parts of the society—or even to all members of the union. If this were so, there would be no need for political action. From the standpoint of other groups, of course, the interests of auto workers and their union are frequently considered far from identical with the public interest. But by and large, the union seeks to take on the role of spokesman for the "common people"; it pictures itself as working for the advancement of their interests, the protection of their democratic rights, the increase of their influence. This frequently places the union in opposition to the existent power elites of business, wealth, and traditional high status groups. It means a continuation and extension, in the political arena, of the oppositions that exist in direct economic dealings between the union and management.

None of the foregoing is to be construed as signifying "class warfare." The union is not socialistic, not against the present economic system, nor even seriously in favor of establishing a third, "labor party." It believes in independent political action carried on within the two-party system—predominantly, of course, through the Democratic Party. It aims not at overthrowing private capitalism nor at preventing the exercise of business influence on opinion and government, but at *balancing* and *offsetting* what it judges to be one-sided pressures in these areas. It tries to expose and criticize self-interested moves of other power groups that run counter to its own goals and to advocate alternative policies, with analyses of pro's and con's from the standpoint of the workingmen and citizens it represents.

But this description of the "countervailing" function of the UAW neglects other more positive, initiating aspects of the union's political efforts and accomplishments. For example, the union has initiated and vigorously supported measures which, according to its views, will insure stable economic growth and full employment; it has steadily worked for extensions of social security and unemployment compensation (along with its drive for pension plans and guaranteed annual wages by companies), and improvements of governmental provisions for health, education, and welfare; it has exerted its influence in behalf of reforms in taxation, protection of civil rights, development of national resources in the public interest, and a wide range of other economic and social objectives. In international affairs, too, the union has participated actively in moves to strengthen the free nations of the world and the non-Communist labor movements of those countries; to aid underdeveloped countries, and to build healthier world economic conditions.

The sketch of union political activities and philosophy in the last few pages suggests the context within which the present study has its significance. However, an appreciation of the more concrete setting and specific purposes of the research require a few additional words about the special place occupied by the UAW in the Detroit region and particularly about the recent political history of the union in this area where the study was conducted.

The Union's Political Role in the Detroit Area

The ethos of the UAW, the prevailing spirit of the entire union through later as well as earlier years, has been profoundly influenced by the character of the organization as it originally took shape in the environment of Detroit and nearby communities. Here it was that the germ of automotive industrial unionism first sprouted, shortly spread through surrounding regions, ultimately to reach from coast to coast. The continued presence of the union's headquarters and central staff in Detroit, along with the heavy concentration of its membership here, has stimulated and facilitated active involvement in local and state politics, from elections for the local municipal positions to those for the highest state offices. Along with the state CIO organization, the UAW was the nucleus of the 1952 campaign for re-apportionment of state legislative districts. These two organizations have systematically attempted to influence the selection of Democratic Party candidates, to find and run candidates where Democrats have rarely or never run before, and generally, they have helped to create a vigorous on-going party structure in the state and have participated within the party organization to push toward goals compatible with the union's political objectives.

In truth, the UAW in Michigan, at the present time, works in close cooperation with the Democratic Party. But it is only one element in the coalition that makes up that party. Besides the UAW (which is itself a coalition of smaller groups and factions with varying interests that require reconciliation and compromise), there are the other CIO unions, the AF of L (which also contains its divergent elements), the liberal, business, and professional groups, minority and nationality groups, as well as the professional party "regulars." In view of the union's numerical strength in Michigan and in view of the money and manpower expended by the union in its political activities, it is not surprising that it has achieved a significant degree of influence.

Perhaps the role of the UAW in politics can be further clarified by noting the nature of the political structure in Michigan, and some of the points at which the union enters it. For one thing, the general electorate is involved in the process of voting for party precinct delegates. These delegates constitute the representatives to the state and national conventions, and are the lowest and broadest level of party officials. Anyone who can muster twenty signatures of registered voters in his precinct may run for such a position. It is at this level that internal party factions compete with each other most directly. The UAW often enters into these contests by backing someone friendly to labor's views who is willing to serve as a delegate. It was actually through this means that the UAW and other allied groups were able, in 1948, to win a significant voice in the Democratic Party in the Detroit area.

Another way in which the union enters into the political process takes place when representatives of the UAW, along with those of other factions in the party, are actively consulted in the process of considering candidates to support in the primary elections. In the case of the UAW, these choices are partly made through informal communications within its local ranks, and also are presented for official endorsement by, for example, the Wayne County CIO-PAC[2] which is made up of representatives of local unions.

Once such organizational choices are made (on occasion

---

[2] Congress of Industrial Organizations—Political Action Committee.

they are not the choices finally approved by the party), the union further participates in obtaining signatures, usually several thousand, required on nominating petitions. Such operations involve many persons at several levels; they are not performed merely by a small, centralized elite.

In the final phases of the political process, during the election campaign itself, the indispensable role of money, personnel resources, and central planning is apparent. And here the sound trucks, the billboards, the mass meetings at local union halls, the political discussions introduced into the union's radio and television programs, all seek not only to win votes directly but, perhaps even more important, they aim to stimulate and inform labor's grass-roots opinion leaders—the members who already see eye to eye with the union leadership and who carry on the indispensable and influential, informal, person-to-person political process. The political effectiveness of any large-scale organization turns in great measure on the extent to which enthusiasm is aroused and maintained among these active members and, at the same time, the extent to which they are provided with convincing ammunition. The wisdom of practical politicians, as well as careful research studies, indicates that the efforts of these face-to-face influencers probably go a long way to determine the union's success or failure in election campaigns. We shall need to have a particularly close look at these politically loyal and interested union members in a later chapter.

In this connection, some "veteran" observers within and around the UAW have made the point that the union has come a long way in its efforts to stimulate and maintain an interest in political affairs among its members, and to obtain their sanction for participation in political action by the unon itself. Ten or fifteen years ago, they say, in union meetings or workers' education classes, there could always be found sizable numbers of workers expressing in no uncertain terms their opposition to *any* participation by the union ("keep politics out of the union and the union out of politics"); and what is equally important, such remarks would be enthusiastically applauded by other workers present. Such remarks are rarely witnessed today, according to these "veterans." How typical or reliable these reported changes are, we do not know. We hope, however, that this study, with its information as of 1952, will provide a bench-mark against which future trends may be measured.

The political activities we have sketched provide background for the present study. Inevitably the broad purposes and the extensive action programs of the union lead to the question: How do the members feel? How fully do they support such activities? Has the typical auto worker expanded his conception of the union's functions to a point where he approves the accent on political action? Do the members want increased political power for the union? Or is it true, as so often charged, that union leaders are using the organization resources without the approval of their members; that the members are mere pawns who feel no personal involvement and who are not "on side" in respect to political action? How much agreement is there on such matters among the diverse elements that comprise the UAW? Do they vote alike? Do they share identical political philosophies? If not, what characteristics distinguish those who stand strongly with the union from those who do not? These are the issues on which we shall marshall whatever evidence can be extracted from our interviews.

Beyond these questions pertaining to a particular labor group, moreover, stretch the endless challenges referred to in the opening pages of this chapter, vistas of increased general understanding of socio-political processes in an industrialized mass society. While final and conclusive answers will surely not be expected, even on the limited, local questions, it may be hoped that the study can contribute something, in its very small way, to present knowledge of both the specific and the general problems.

Methods Used in the Study

The data needed to carry out the aims of the study were obtained by means of interviews. The study design provided for a pre-election and a post-election interview with a cross-section sample of UAW members in the Detroit metropolitan area. The union members were interviewed at their homes by interviewers who followed a prescribed procedure and a fixed schedule of questions. The question schedules are shown in Appendix A. They combine free-response questions with others that are answerable by a simple checkmark, a rating, or a single word. The range of content of the questions will become clear as we proceed to analyze the findings.

Pre-election interviewing continued from October 20, 1952 to November 3, the day before election. The more detailed post-election interviews were carried on from late November until early February. The pre-election interviews required about a half-hour each, on the average, while the post-election interview averaged an hour. The interviews made no mention of the union's connection with the study and gave no indication of special interest in the respondents as union members. The interview was introduced simply as a public opinion study conducted at Wayne University.

The problem of securing a representative sample of UAW members in and around Detroit proved troublesome. Details of the sampling procedure and examination of the obtained sample are dealt with in Appendix B. Here we note simply that the sample cannot claim to constitute a highly accurate representation of the entire UAW membership in metropolitan Detroit. This is due especially to shortcomings of the mailing list of members; to the shifting, mobile nature of parts of the auto-workers population; and to the difficulty of finding many of the men at home.

Despite the margin of error due to these sampling problems, however, the results can be considered true indications of the behavior and attitudes typical of the main body of UAW members in Detroit—apart from the above-mentioned extremely transient workers and those rarely at home—and about ten per cent or so who refused to be interviewed.

The sample may be briefly described as follows: We began by drawing 1499 names as a systematic random sample from mailing lists of all local unions in the Detroit area. Some 330 of these persons could not be located by interviewers (due to moving, wrong addresses, absence on long vacations, death, etc.) and 341 others either could not be found at home even on repeated call-backs or refused to be interviewed. This left a total of 828 pre-election interviews which were completed (55 per cent of the total sample of names, but 71 per cent of those actually living at the addresses given). A small number of additional post-election interviews (67), obtained from persons missed on the first interview, proved useful in testing certain figures from the main sample. But the results reported on the following pages are all based on the 828 pre-election interviews and the 351 post-election interviews.

Characteristics of UAW Members in the Detroit Area

At the time the study began (Autumn, 1952) there were approximately 290,000 persons on the mailing lists of UAW local unions in the Detroit Metropolitan area. We can proceed from this figure to some estimates of the relationship between UAW membership and the total population. There were about 2¼ million persons living in the area sampled and about 980,000 persons in the labor force. UAW members represented approximately 30 per cent of this labor force. Although precise figures are not readily available, a fairly careful estimate indicates that UAW members comprise about 30 per cent of the eligible voters as well.

Auto workers are not distributed equally throughout the Metropolitan area but tend to live more in some sections than in others. To show this, we spotted the 1,499 persons drawn in the sample on a map according to their mailing address. The distribution of these addresses per 100,000 of population was then calculated. (Figure 1.) In general, areas of lowest income status did not contain the heaviest concentration of auto workers. Rather, UAW members tended to live in neighborhoods with a somewhat higher economic rating. The East side of Detroit, in general, has a much greater proportion of auto workers than does the West side. In addition, the heaviest concentrations occur down-river, in and around Dearborn and in Hamtramck, Ferndale, and Highland Park; the lightest proportion occurs in the large northwest (white collar) section of the city.

A number of the principal characteristics of the union members interviewed in this survey are summarized in Table 1.1. Appendix B compares certain of the results for our sample with those obtained in other population surveys. On the whole the comparisons show satisfactory agreement between our sample and other data for the principal characteristics. This is less true in respect to age than other variables, however. Our sample contains too few young workers (7 per cent under 25 compared to 13 per cent by census figures) and an excess of older workers (22 per cent past 55 as compared to 16 per cent by census figures). As explained earlier, the survey encountered special

FIGURE 1
Distribution of UAW Members in the Detroit Area

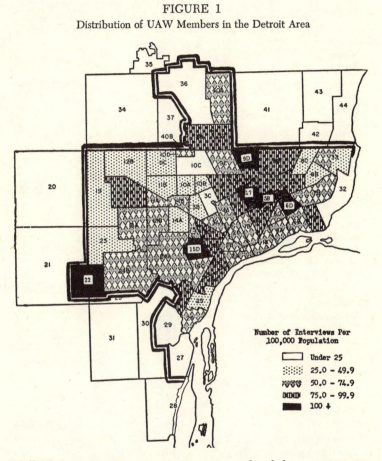

difficulty in securing a proportionate sample of the younger auto workers who are more transient and less frequently to be found at home. In this respect the sample, and such figures as those of Table 1.1, are not fully representative of auto workers in the Detroit area.

TABLE 1.1

CHARACTERISTICS OF UAW MEMBERS
IN THE OBTAINED SAMPLE

Sex	*Percent*	
Men	89%	
Women	11	
	100%	(828 cases)
Race		
White	81%	
Negro	19	
	100%	(828 cases)
Age		
Under 25	7%	
25 to 34	25	
35 to 44	25	
45 to 54	21	
55 to 64	17	
65 and over	5	
	100%	(801 cases)
Education		
4 years or less	9%	
5 to 7 years	15	
8 years	21	
9 to 11 years	28	
12 years (H.S. graduate)	21	
Some college or college graduate	6	
	100%	(807 cases)
Occupation		
White collar	7%	
Skilled manual	19	
Semi-skilled and unskilled	74	
	100%	(792 cases)
Religion		
Protestant	51%	
Catholic	42	
Other and none	7	
	100%	(812 cases)
Years in Detroit Area		
Less than 7 years	10%	
7 to 11 years	11	
12 to 22 years	15	
23 years or more (but not all life)	47	
All life	17	
	100%	(815 cases)

The following table (Table 1.2) describes the background of the union members in terms of where they were born, where they grew up, and the national origins of their fathers. This table and all remaining ones in this section differ in an important respect from Table 1.1. All the tables except Table 1.1 are based on data obtained from the more limited sample of the post-election interview. Specifically, this means that they omit auto workers who were ineligible to register—whether by reason of age, non-citizenship, or residence requirements. The figures of Table 1.2 and following tables, then, are representative not of all workers initially interviewed but only of those who could be reached among the 94 per cent of pre-election respondents who were eligible to register and vote.

Slightly over one-third of these members were born in Michigan, and another 23 per cent were born in the Southern states. Of these 23 per cent, 14 per cent are white and 9 per cent Negro. The foreign born were represented in about the same proportion in the UAW as in the general population of Detroit—about 18 per cent. When persons in the sample were asked where they lived when growing up, the figures are somewhat different. These replies probably provide a more valid indication of the cultural forces influencing them in their youth. We find that half the sample lived in Michigan, and 18 per cent lived in the Southern states.

Data on place of birth of the respondent's father also are shown in Table 1.2. About one-half of the union members' parents were foreign born, and half of these were born in Eastern Europe (Poland primarily).

Table 1.2 also reports whether the background of the union members was urban or rural. While a "Big City" background was the most common (44 per cent), farm and small town backgrounds together accounted for another 46 per cent.

Table 1.3 shows total family income level in 1952. This includes income from all sources. Sources other than wages were almost negligible. Ninety-three percent had no other source at all, and five per cent obtained income through renting property. Combined pensions and rents were a source of income for a few persons.

TABLE 1.2

ADDITIONAL SELECTED CHARACTERISTICS OF RESPONDENTS

Place of Birth

United States		82%
Michigan	35%	
Other North Central	13	
Southern	23	
All others	11	
Foreign		18
Europe	15	
West	10%	
East	5	
Canada	3	
Total		100% (346 cases*)

Where Respondent Lived While Growing Up

A. United States		86%
Michigan	50%	
Other North Central	11	
Southern	18	
All others	7	
Foreign		14
Europe	11	
West	8%	
East	3	
Canada	3	
Total		100% (341 cases*)
B. Farm		20%
Small Town		26
Medium Size City		10
Big City		44
Total		100% (344 cases*)

Place of Birth of Respondent's Father

United States		48%
Foreign		52
Europe	47	
West	20%	
East	27	
Canada	4	
Other Foreign	1	
Total		100% (346 cases*)

*Percentages are based on 351 post-election interviews (omitting a few cases of "no answer"), with proper weighting of cases to make them representative of the pre-election sample of eligible voters interviewed. The weighting procedure is described in Appendix B, p. 324.

TABLE 1.3

TOTAL FAMILY INCOME IN 1952,
BY NUMBER OF PERSONS IN FAMILY

	Size of Family					
	1 Person	2 Persons	3 Persons	4 Persons	5 Persons or more	All Families
Median Income	$4054	$4771	$4848	$4804	$4894	$4706

Table 1.4 shows the relationship of the other working adult(s) to the person in our sample and certain additional economic facts. In 36 per cent of the families, at least one other person worked. Most frequently the other working person was a husband or wife (usually a wife as our respondents were mostly male).

The average (median) number of years in automobile plants was 8.8. That is, one-half of the workers had been in the auto industry less than 8.8 years and one-half had worked longer

TABLE 1.4

SELECTED ECONOMIC CHARACTERISTICS OF RESPONDENTS

Other Earners In Family

No other earner	64%	
Wife or husband	22	
Son(s); Daughter(s)	8	
Other Relative(s)	6	
Total	100%	(345 cases*)

Length of Time In This Kind of Work

Under 6 months	7%	
6 months-2 years	10	
2-5 years	19	
6-10 years	25	
11-19 years	19	
20 years or more	20	
Total	100%	(342 cases*)
Median years	8.8	

Own or Rent

Own Home	59%	
Rent (includes "room," etc.)	41	
Total	100%	(345 cases*)

* See note to Table 1.2.

than this. One-fifth of the persons interviewed had been employed over twenty years in this type of work. This of course
does not necessarily mean twenty years at one job, or even at
one plant.

Another economic index is the proportion of home owners as
compared with renters in the sample. Our results indicate that
59 per cent of the workers owned their homes and 41 per cent
rented. This is almost as high as for the population in general
in Detroit. In the latter group, 65 per cent were home owners
and 35 per cent rented.

Nine per cent of the persons interviewed did not mention
union membership when asked about organizations to which
they belong (Table 1.5). We examined these particular interviews and it was evident that it was not usually a matter of
deliberate untruth but rather a failure to think of themselves as
union members. To a few, union dues apparently mean merely
another payroll deduction. Included in the nine per cent, too,
are two per cent who really are not members of the union but
who were on the mailing list. In Chapter 5 we will report more
fully on members' attachment to the union.

TABLE 1.5

PERCENT REPORTING MEMBERSHIP IN FORMAL ORGANIZATIONS

Organization	Percent who report belonging
Unions	91%
Church	51
Lodges; fraternal organizations	17
Veterans	8
Social Groups	7
Church Groups	7
Sports Clubs	5
Neighborhood Groups	4
P.T.A.'s	4
"All Other" Groups	4
Political Groups	2
Combinations of Above Groups	
Union only	29%
Union and church only	25
Union, church, and other	23
Union and others (not church)	14
Church only or church and others (not union)	4
No organizations or no answer)	5
	100% (351 cases)

CHAPTER 2

How They Voted and Why

This chapter is devoted to an analysis of the voting behavior of UAW members in the 1952 presidential election and their reasons for voting as they did.

Number Registered and Voting

Approximately 5 of every 6 *of those interviewed* voted in the 1952 election (Table 2.1). If we omit those not eligible to register, the proportion of actual voters among all eligible voters is somewhat greater (nearly 90 per cent). However, the proportion of non-voters would be considerably increased if we include the

TABLE 2.1

PROPORTION WHO VOTED AMONG PERSONS INTERVIEWED[1]

Voted	83%
Did not vote—	
though eligible to register (5/6 of these were not registered)	10
Not eligible to register	
(Age, citizenship, residence requirements)	6
Not ascertained	1
	100%

[1] These percentages are based on 351 post-election interviews plus 51 cases of persons ineligible for registration, all properly weighted to represent proportions of the total pre-election sample of persons interviewed. Details of weighting procedure are explained on page 324 of Appendix B. Percentages in all the following tables on post-election data are similarly computed from weighted figures.

non-interviewed since larger proportions of them are more mobile
(those unlocated or not found at home) and less likely to vote.
Official registration records tend to support this view and provide a basis for estimating the extent of non-voting for the total
membership, the non-interviewed as well as the interviewed.

The official registration records of persons in the total potential sample were checked.[2] Since in a number of cases these
records were ambiguous,[3] the best we could do was estimate
upper and lower limits of the number registered. These maximum and minimum figures are given in Table 2.2. The estimates
were arrived at first for the persons interviewed and then we
adopted the same ratio of maximum to minimum for the non-
interviewed.[4]

TABLE 2.2

PERCENTAGE REGISTERED AS ESTIMATED FROM INTERVIEWS AND OFFICIAL ELECTION RECORDS

	Minimum	Maximum	No. of Cases
Interviewed	75%	84%	828
Not Interviewed	51	57	671
Total	64	72	1499

The minimum estimate, which is based on actual records,
assumes that the election bureau records are complete and
correct; that the persons interviewed who said they were registered were mistaken or were not telling the truth and that
consequently there are fewer registered than our interviews
indicate. It is unlikely, however, that many of the interview
reports of registration were false or erroneous. In most instances

---

[2] The files of the Detroit and suburban election bureaus were checked
by members of our staff.

[3] We were not able to check the registration status in every instance,
and also in certain interviews the person said he was registered, although
we could find no official registration. It is possible that the election bureau
records were occasionally out of date or in error, or more likely, that some
names were misspelled or changed, making it difficult or impossible to find
them. Further, some persons could have been registered at different addresses or in different cities.

[4] This procedure somewhat overestimates the maximum percentage for
the non-interviewed but the maximum for the total group is not seriously
affected (2 per cent at the most).

the respondent's answers and attitudes as revealed in the further course of the interview told a consistent story of voting and reasons for voting. The *maximum* estimate assumes that the persons interviewed were accurately reporting their registration and that consequently more persons were registered than could be located in the election bureau files. We arrive then at the estimate that 64 per cent to 72 per cent of all UAW members in the Detroit area were registered.[5] Again using the evidence from our interviews we assume that almost all of these persons voted. This leaves approximately one-third of the auto workers who did not vote. Almost two-thirds of these were eligible for registration; the remainder were ineligible because of age, citizenship or length of residence. The conclusion is that about one union member in five who was eligible to vote did not vote.

As the proportion registered and voting in the general adult population of Wayne County was about 67 per cent in 1952, it is highly probable that registration and voting in the two groups, the UAW and the public at large, are very nearly the same. This would indicate that the union's efforts to encourage registration probably did succeed in increasing registration of a working class population since registration is usually found to be less in such a group.

The Vote for President

Table 2.3 shows how UAW members voted for president in the 1952 election. There is no question of the strong Democratic majority of Detroit auto workers. Even though many workers of Democratic leaning voted for Eisenhower, Stevenson still had a majority of 3 to 1. The national totals showed 45 per cent for Stevenson. In Wayne County Stevenson received 58 per cent of the vote, and in the city of Detroit he obtained 61 per cent of the vote. Among the auto workers in our sample who told how they voted, 75 per cent were for Stevenson.[6]

---

[5] When members under 21 are omitted, the minimum to maximum range becomes 62 per cent to 73 per cent, a negligible variation from the figures given.

[6] Negro members of the union were somewhat undersampled on the second interview. If correction is made for this, an increase of one percentage point occurs in the Stevenson proportion, bringing it to 76 per cent.

TABLE 2.3

THE STEVENSON VERSUS EISENHOWER VOTE

For Stevenson	73%*
For Eisenhower	24
Refused to say (Includes one third-party vote)	3
	100%

* Percentages are based on 295 post-election interviews of persons who reported voting. These base figures are weighted to make them representative of the total sample (see note, page 29).

Of the respondents who reported their own vote and who said that their spouses voted, 90 per cent stated that the spouse voted for the same candidate as they did and 10 per cent voted for the opposing candidate. Among the Stevenson voters 9 per cent of the spouses voted for Eisenhower and among Eisenhower voters 14 per cent of the spouses voted for Stevenson. We also asked how other members of the family had voted. Of the respondents who answered this question, 68 per cent said that other family members voted for the same candidate as they did and 32 per cent said that one or more of the family members voted for the opposing candidate. Among Stevenson voters 35 per cent said that one or more family members voted for Eisenhower while among Eisenhower voters 25 per cent said that one or more family members voted for Stevenson.

Intended Vote Compared With Actual Vote

The auto workers' voting *intentions* are reported in Table 2.4. Fifty-nine per cent of all persons interviewed declared their intention to vote for Stevenson, 14 per cent for Eisenhower, and 6 per cent were undecided. However, some persons in both the Stevenson and Eisenhower groups, when further questioned, indicated that they "might change." Computing percentages on the basis of eligible voters only, we find 71 per cent for Stevenson, 17 per cent for Eisenhower, and, 12 per cent undecided, refused, or "other." How does this compare with the actual voting behavior as reported in the post-election interviews? Returning to Table 2.3, we see that 73 per cent did vote for

Stevenson and 24 per cent for Eisenhower. Clearly the *proportion* for Stevenson decreased from the intention figures—from 81 per cent of the Stevenson-Eisenhower *intent* to 75 per cent of the Stevenson-Eisenhower *vote*.

TABLE 2.4

PRESIDENTIAL VOTE INTENTION
(during final two weeks of campaign)*

Stevenson		
Definite	53%	
"Might Change"	6	59%
Eisenhower		
Definite	12	
"Might Change"	2	14
Undecided		6
Refused to say; no answer; other		4
Not registered		17
		100%

* Percentages are based on 828 pre-election interviews.

TABLE 2.5

PRESIDENTIAL VOTE IN RELATION TO VOTE INTENTION*

	Vote Intention				
Actual Vote	Stevenson	Eisenhower	Undecided	Refused to say, etc.	Said not Registered
Voted for Stevenson	94%	1%	45%	54%	4%
Voted for Eisenhower	2	98	45	32	5
Refused to say	2	—	7	14	—
Did not vote	2	1	3	—	91
	100%	100%	100%	100%	100%
No. of cases	(152)	(90)	(31)	(22)	(56)

* Percentages are based on 351 cases, properly weighted.

A detailed comparison of voting intent and actual voting is seen in Table 2.5. Persons who expressed an intention almost all voted as intended (94 per cent of Stevenson intent and 98 per cent of Eisenhower intent). Stevenson lost more of his intended votes (from 4 to 6 percent) as compared with Eisenhower (2 per cent). Because the Stevenson percentage is based on a much larger total, the absolute loss of Stevenson voters was far greater than the loss of Eisenhower voters. Among persons undecided and not expressing a voting intention, Eisenhower ran almost even with Stevenson.

Certainty of Presidential Choice

Several questions were asked of the respondents aimed at eliciting the degree of certainty with which they held their respective presidential vote intentions. One such question asked in the pre-election interview was:

> "Is there a chance you might change your mind and not vote for (Stevenson or Eisenhower)?"

Of the pro-Eisenhower registered voters, 17 per cent said "Yes" to this question, compared to 11 per cent of the pro-Stevenson registered voters. No doubt this is what would be expected within a group of voters who traditionally vote for the Democratic candidate and whose predominant group sentiment continues to favor that candidate.

Another question on this subject of degree of certainty was also asked in the pre-election interview:

> "Has there been any time when you thought you might not vote for (Stevenson or Eisenhower)?"

Here again, the answers suggest a slightly higher percentage of "waverers" among the pro-Eisenhower UAW members than among the pro-Stevenson members, the respective figures being 23 per cent and 17 per cent who answered "Yes" to the question.

Taking those persons who answered "Yes" to this question, and inquiring into the reasons for their previous hesitancy, we find that among the pro-Stevenson workers, some prominence was given to such reasons as:

> "I didn't know Stevenson (or his program) well enough."
> "I was for Kefauver during the Democratic Convention."

"I was waiting for Eisenhower (or the Republicans) to say
something good."

"I didn't know Eisenhower (or his program) well enough."

Among the pro-Eisenhower workers, prominent among the
reasons given were:

"I didn't know Eisenhower (or his program) well enough."

"I was worried at first about his military background."

A few referred to their fears about a depression under a Republican administration, the Nixon affair, and in the case of a small
minority who had intended to vote for a Democratic candidate,
to the treatment of Kefauver at that party's convention.[7]

A direct question was asked during the post-election study:

"Had you ever thought during the campaign that you might
vote for (opposite candidate)?"

About one-fifth of the two groups together replied that they had
thought of doing so, with no difference between the Stevenson
and Eisenhower voters. The similarity in percentages, however,
can be misleading for practical purposes: if those Stevenson
voters who indicated that during the campaign they had thought
of voting for Eisenhower actually had done so, the effect would
have been *numerically* much greater, because of the larger ratio
of Stevenson to Eisenhower voters among the UAW members.[8]

Of the 8 per cent who said before the election that they
might change, 5 per cent indicated in the post-election survey
that they actually did change their minds and vote for the candidate other than the one they had originally mentioned in the
pre-election interview. All of these people had originally intended
to vote for Stevenson, but instead changed their minds and

---

[7] Favorable references to Kefauver and dislike of treatment of him at
the Democratic Convention occur in several of the interviews (both pro-
Stevenson and pro-Eisenhower), even though no question was deliberately
included to elicit any sentiments concerning him.

[8] This same point should be noted with reference to Table 2.5, in which
it is shown that 2 per cent of those intending to vote for Stevenson, as
over against 1 per cent of those for Eisenhower, actually changed their
minds in the election. Although both percentages are very small, the
absolute number of Stevenson-to-Eisenhower voters was much greater than
the number of Eisenhower-to-Stevenson voters.

voted for Eisenhower. In other words, none of the pro-Eisenhower voters in the pre-election "might change" category did
change their original intentions; 7 per cent of the pre-election
pro-Stevenson voters in this category did change their minds.

Time of Decision

In the post-election interview, workers were asked:

"How long before the election did you decide you were
going to vote for (Stevenson or Eisenhower)?"

Answers to the question are summarized in Table 2.6. Approximately half of the voters indicated they had made up their minds
before the nominations. There were differences, however, between the Stevenson and Eisenhower voters: 51 per cent of the
Stevenson voters but only 37 per cent of the Eisenhower voters
replied that they had decided before the nomination.

TABLE 2.6
TIME OF DECISION OF VOTERS

	Stevenson Voters	Eisenhower Voters	Total Sample
Before his nomination	51%	37%	47%
At the time of nomination, or shortly thereafter (June or July)	34	39	35
9-12 weeks before election day (August)	2	3	3
5-8 weeks before election day (September)	5	7	6
2-4 weeks (first half of October)	4 } 15%	5 } 24%	4 } 18%
Last 2 weeks before election day	3	6	4
Election day	1	3	1
	100%	100%	100%
No. of cases	(157)	(111)	(268)

A little less than one-fifth of the total sample made up their
minds after July, 15 percent of Stevenson voters and 24 per
cent of Eisenhower voters. These figures suggest that many of

those who decided to vote for Eisenhower made their decisions late in the campaign and presumably after considerable hesitation. They were a minority group within their own milieu, opposing the prevailing political sentiment. Under such circumstances, it is understandable that they took a longer time to make up their mind.

How Non-Voters Would Have Voted

As previously noted, a small number of persons eligible to register and vote did not vote in the election. Among these union members, Stevenson would have secured a smaller proportion of support than among the voters (Table 2.7). If the statements of these people as to how they would have voted are reliable, the conclusion would be that efforts to persuade more of them to vote would increase the absolute number of Democratic versus Republican voters, but would decrease the total Democratic percentage. That is, additional voters would probably vote for the Democratic candidate but almost as many would vote for the Republican candidate. However, if these people were registered and planning to vote they might well have been more influenced by prevailing opinion around them. Also some may have said Eisenhower in the post-election interview because of the attraction of backing a winner.

TABLE 2.7

HOW NON-VOTERS *WOULD* HAVE VOTED

Non-voters (eligible to register) who say they would have voted—	
For Stevenson	47%*
For Eisenhower	36
Don't know or refuse to say	17
	100%

* Percentages are based on 57 cases.

Party Affiliation and Vote

In the pre-election interview persons were asked if they thought of themselves as Democrats, Republicans or Independents. The question was phrased:

"Generally speaking, do you usually think of yourself as a Republican, a Democrat, an Independent, or what?"

Then if the respondent answered in terms of a party he was asked:

"Would you call yourself a strong (Republican or Democrat) or not very strong (Republican or Democrat)?"

If the respondent answered Independent or "other" he was asked:

"Do you think of yourself as closer to the Republican or Democratic party?"

Results are shown on Table 2.8.

TABLE 2.8

PARTY PREFERENCE

Democrat or strong Democrat	53%	67%*
Not very strong Democrat	14	
Republican or strong Republican	3	7
Not very strong Republican	4	
Independent—Democrat leaning	13	
—Republican leaning	4	26
—Neither Democrat or Republican	9	
		100%
Democrats plus Democratic leaning	80%	
Republicans plus Republican leaning	11	
Independents with no leaning	9	
	100%	

* Percentages are all based on the 678 cases of registered voters answering the question.

There can be no question that the great majority of union members considered themselves Democrats. Only 3 per cent were definitely Republicans, and only 4 per cent thought of themselves as "weak" Republicans. Even when Independents of Republican leanings are added, the Republican group comprised only 11 per cent of the total. Since the Republican presidential candidate received 25 per cent of the votes in our sample, it is abundantly clear that his personal pulling power influenced a number of persons of Democratic leaning to cast their ballots for him. This tendency is observable in greater detail in the following tables.

TABLE 2.9

VOTING INTENTION BY PARTY PREFERENCE
(Registered Voters Only)

	Think of Self as:			
Vote Intention	*Democrat°*	*Republican°*	*Independent*	*Total Sample*
Stevenson	85%	8%	30%	71%
Eisenhower	5	86	41	17
Undecided, refused to say, etc.	10	6	29	12
	100%	100%	100%	100%
No. of cases	(541)	(73)	(64)	(678)

° Includes Independents with Democratic or Republican leaning respectively.

Looking at the voting intent (Table 2.9) it is seen that only a small proportion of persons of declared party affiliation expressed a definite intention of voting for other than their party's candidate. Although approximately the same percentages of Democrats and Republicans intended to vote for the opposite party or were undecided or "not saying" (15 per cent and 14 per cent respectively), these percentages represent a much greater absolute number of potential Democratic defections than of Republicans. Moreover, the Independents were more often for Eisenhower than for Stevenson. This, of course, may have been due to the tendency for union members who intended to vote for Eisenhower to call themselves Independents.

When actual voting behavior is analyzed (Table 2.10), these relationships become still clearer.

Among the Democrats, about the same proportions voted for Stevenson as expressed intention to vote for him, but at the same time, Eisenhower's proportion doubled, increasing from 5 per cent to 10 per cent. Those undecided and "not saying" before the election tended to swing to him. Among Republicans, the same type of relationship was observed; that is, Stevenson received the same proportion as anticipated voting for him, but the "undecided, refused, etc.," apparently voted for Eisenhower when the chips were down. Among the Independents, Stevenson received close to the anticipated 30 per cent, but the pre-election proportion for Eisenhower (41 per cent) increased to 64 per cent when voters actually went to the polls. It is quite possible that many of those who were in the category "undecided, refused to say, etc.," were intending to vote for Eisenhower and did not wish to say so.

TABLE 2.10

PRESIDENTIAL VOTE BY PARTY PREFERENCE

Voting Behavior	Think of Self As:			
	Democrat*	Republican*	Independent	Total Sample
Stevenson	86%	8%	32%	72%
Eisenhower	10	92	64	24
Did not vote or refused to say**	4	—	4	4
	100%	100%	100%	100%
No. of cases	(201)	(46)	(43)	(290)

 * Includes Independents with Democratic or Republican leaning respectively.

 ** All but a few of the persons in this category are non-voters (seven-eighths of all). Since the few others have almost no effect on the percentages, in all subsequent tables this category is labeled simply "did not vote."

A further breakdown, not shown in this table, indicates that of persons declaring themselves "Democrats and Strong Democrats" 5 per cent voted for Eisenhower, whereas among the "not strong" Democrats and "Independent" Democrats 21 per cent voted for Eisenhower. Of Democrats who intended to vote for Stevenson almost all actually did so, while of the undecided Democrats, slightly over half voted for Stevenson. In all groups, the election *intent* represented the maximum of Stevenson support; when the voters not definitely committed to Stevenson went to the polls, they tended to vote for Eisenhower and most of these changes between expressed intent and actual vote occurred among union members who considered themselves Democrats.

This loss of Democratic votes is further illustrated by a comparison of the 1952 votes with the 1948 votes of the auto workers interviewed (Table 2.11).

TABLE 2.11

1952 VOTE IN RELATION TO 1948 VOTE

| | 1952 Vote | | | |
Vote in 1948	Stevenson	Eisenhower	Did not vote*	Total Sample
Truman	82%	41%	26%	65%
Dewey	1	31	5	8
Did not vote	12	21	51	19
Other, don't remember, etc.	5	7	18	8
	100%	100%	100%	100%
No. of cases	(170)	(116)	(65)	(351)

* Includes only persons eligible to register.

According to the way these persons say they voted in 1948, if we consider only the Truman and Dewey votes, 89 per cent were for Truman and 11 per cent for Dewey. This contrasts with their 1952 vote of 75 per cent for Stevenson and 25 per cent for Eisenhower. Again considering only those persons who report voting for Truman or for Dewey in 1948, it is found that 57 per cent of the Eisenhower voters in this UAW sample were for Truman in 1948. Conversely, of those who reported voting for Truman in 1948, 14 per cent voted for Eisenhower in 1952.

Social and Personal Characteristics of UAW Members in Relation to Their Voting

Who are the union members who voted for Eisenhower? How do they differ from the Stevenson voters? In what ways do both these groups differ from the non-voters? And what about the members who remained undecided during the campaign, ones who by virtue of their uncertainty are presumably most susceptible to campaign influences? Data bearing on these questions are summarized in Tables 2.12 and 2.13. Other evidence will be added as we proceed with the analysis.

TABLE 2.12

PRESIDENTIAL VOTE IN RELATION TO PERSONAL AND SOCIAL CHARACTERISTICS

	Voted For		No. of
	Stevenson	Eisenhower	Cases*
Total Sample	75%**	25%**	(286)
Sex			
Men	74	26	(257)
Women	81	19	(29)
Race			
White	73	27	(258)
Negro	91	9	(28)
Occupation			
White Collar	41	59	(24)
Skilled	72	28	(73)
Semi-skilled (and Unskilled)			
$2 or More Per Hour	74	26	(82)
Less Than $2 Per Hour	81	19	(101)
Age			
Under 25	80	20	(10)
25-34	81	19	(64)
35-44	77	23	(74)
45-54	68	32	(68)
55 and Over	68	32	(68)
Years in Detroit			
Less Than 7	83	17	(11)
7-11	82	18	(26)
12-16	66	34	(18)
17-22	73	27	(26)
23 or More (Not All Life)	73	27	(153)
All Life	77	23	(52)
Education			
Under 18 Years	84	16	(51)
8	64	36	(63)
9-11	83	17	(82)
12 or More	66	34	(83)

TABLE 2.12—(*Continued*)

| | Voted For | | No. of |
	Stevenson	Eisenhower	Cases
Religion			
Catholic	81%	19%	(124)
Protestant	71	29	(135)
Other and None	58	42	(26)
Own or Rent			
Own Home	71	29	(190)
Rent	85	15	(75)
Socio-economic Classification			
(Relative Position *Within This Sample*)			
High	65	35	(60)
Medium	78	22	(124)
Low	82	18	(59)
Father's Occupation			
White Collar	60	40	(42)
Farmer	71	29	(61)
Skilled	74	26	(55)
Semi-skilled or Unskilled	81	19	(125)
"Class" Identification (*Workers' Self-labeling*)			
Middle (and Upper†)	63	37	(72)
Working (and Lower†)	79	21	(208)
Early Life			
Farm	79	21	(47)
Small Town	79	21	(71)
Medium-sized City	75	25	(32)
Large City	70	30	(129)
Father's Political Party			
Democrat	84	16	(119)
Republican	49	51	(47)
Don't Know, etc.	73	27	(120)

* The percentages are based on weighted figures computed from the raw counts given in this column. See note on first page of this chapter.

** Percentages reading across each line total 100 per cent since only cases of known votes for one or the other candidate were included.

† Only one member said "upper class"; only four said "lower."

Using the figures of these tables, we shall first compare the Stevenson and Eisenhower supporters. In brief, Stevenson support tends to be especially strong in the following groups:

Negro members. (They were almost solidly for Stevenson.)
Catholics[9]
Younger workers (under 45)
Education either less than 8th grade or some high school (versus 8th grade or high school graduate)[10]

Socio-economic Factors
{
Manual workers versus white collar[11] (and lower paid semi-skilled slightly more than skilled or better paid semi-skilled)
Members whose fathers were manual workers, (particularly semi-skilled or unskilled)
Those who rent their homes versus owning
Socio-economic level relatively low or medium versus high[12]
Those who consider themselves in the "working class" rather than "middle class"
}
Members whose fathers were Democrats

---

[9] The difference between Catholic and Protestant groups is greater than that shown in the table if we consider only white workers, since almost all Negroes are Protestant and voted for Stevenson. Among white members, the figures are: Catholics, 81 per cent for Stevenson; Protestants, 66 per cent.

[10] The relatively high Eisenhower vote among persons having 8th grade schooling as contrasted with those having either less than that or more, short of high school graduation, is puzzling. The relationship is not accounted for by age differences; it holds within each separate age grouping, though most pronounced at ages under 45. Nor is it due to the influence of race differences; it is found when whites are analyzed alone. Further effort to clarify the curious finding by analyzing out other variables has likewise yielded no fully adequate explanation. However, clues are found in these facts: the eighth grade group contains an unusually high proportion of Protestants and these eighth grade Protestants were especially pro-Eisenhower; further, the eighth grade Eisenhower votes tended to occur most among foreign-born voters and those of foreign-born fathers.

[11] White collar workers showed a notably sharp increase in proportion of *votes* for Eisenhower contrasted with the number who expressed *intention* to vote for him.

[12] The socio-economic classification used here is a rating based on three factors: occupation, income-level of the census tract in which the person lives, and whether he owns or rents his home (or room). The index is described on page 328 of Appendix C. The designation "high," "medium," or "low" refers only to relative socio-economic position *within our sample of auto workers*. The strata do not correspond to those of the entire population. This fact should be kept in mind in all later comparisons among these socio-economic groupings.

Also, the following two categories tended to be slightly more pro-Stevenson than the average (for white members alone as well as for the total sample):

Members who have lived in Detroit less than 12 years
Members who grew up in a farm or in a small town rather than in a large city

Supplementary tabulations indicate that Stevenson enjoyed only slightly greater support from UAW members who grew up in the South than from Northerners (86 per cent versus 78 per cent of those expressing definite voting intentions). Those who came from other countries were pro-Democratic in the same proportion as Southerners. Those workers whose fathers were foreign-born similarly expressed pro-Stevenson intention a little more often than did those of American parentage (83 per cent to 76 per cent). However, there is substantial difference among the nationality groups. For example, in the largest ethnic group, the Polish, voting intention ran 90 per cent for Stevenson while among persons of German and Russian origin the figure is only 52 per cent. Apart from the German and Russian groups, in fact, the figure for *all* remaining persons of foreign parentage is 89 per cent.

Summarizing, it is fair to say that none of the personal and social characteristics examined were extremely influential as determinants of voting behavior. Though differences among the groups compared are certainly worthy of note, it is nevertheless true that in every comparison, save the single exception of the small white collar occupational category, even the least pro-Stevenson groups gave him a large majority. But the heaviest majorities occurred among marginal or minority groups—Negroes, Catholics, ethnics of foreign parentage (excepting those of German and Russian nationality); among members below middle age, those who left school before the eighth grade or during high school, those whose fathers were Democrats, and among workers whose socio-economic position is medium or low relative to other auto workers.

Socio-economic differences in voting are clearest in respect to occupation, either of the union member or his father (white collar workers are especially low in Stevenson support), and in respect to home ownership (renters are decidedly more pro-

TABLE 2.13

VOTING INTENTION IN RELATION TO PERSONAL AND SOCIAL CHARACTERISTICS

	Voting Intention		Unde-cided, etc. Refused,	Not Reg-istered but Eligible	Not Eligible to Register	No. of Cases
	Steven-son	Eisen-hower				
Total Sample	59%*	14%	10%	11%	6%	(828)
Sex						
Men	59	14	10	11	6	(745)
Women	60	17	10	8	5	(83)
Race						
White	54	17	11	11	7	(671)
Negro	78	4	7	9	2	(157)
Age						
Under 25	38	8	2	17	35	(52)
25-34	62	12	6	16	4	(205)
35-44	61	13	8	13	5	(200)
45-54	56	19	16	5	4	(166)
55 and Over	59	17	14	5	5	(178)
Education						
Under 8 Years	60	7	12	13	8	(194)
8	60	19	8	11	2	(166)
9-11	65	10	10	9	6	(228)
12 or More	53	23	8	9	7	(219)
Occupation						
White Collar	42	37	10	4	7	(52)
Skilled	64	17	10	8	1	(153)
Semi-skilled (and Unskilled)	60	12	10	12	6	(581)
Religion						
Catholic	62	10	12	9	7	(338)
Protestant	60	18	7	10	5	(414)
Other or None	43	15	13	19	10	(60)
Years in Detroit						
Less Than 7	40	7	3	22	28	(87)
7-11	68	11	7	10	4	(88)
12-16	66	14	8	11	1	(64)
17-22	65	21	7	7	—	(57)
23 or More (But Not All Life)	64	15	13	5	3	(383)
All Life	49	16	7	21	7	(136)

* Percentages reading across each line total 100 per cent.

Stevenson). Income-level of neighborhoods where members live shows less consistent relation to voting, as is evident in Table 2.14. Indeed the relationship disappears completely when we omit Negroes (who are almost all in low income neighborhoods and for Stevenson). Considering white workers alone, the percentages for Stevenson, corresponding to the four figures in the first column of Table 2.14, become: 74 per cent, 82 per cent, 75 per cent, 76 per cent. If we take only semi-skilled and un-skilled white workers the results are actually in the direction of greater Stevenson support in the higher income districts (the four percentages corresponding to the preceding are: 83, 82, 72, 75). These findings throw into question the view that as working people move into better districts they tend to become "middle class" and accordingly to vote Republican.

TABLE 2.14

INTENTION TO VOTE FOR EISENHOWER OR FOR STEVENSON IN RELATION TO INCOME LEVEL OF CENSUS TRACT WHERE WORKERS NOW LIVE

	Vote Intention		Total	No. of Cases
	Stevenson	Eisenhower		
High (relative to total sample)	74%	26%	100%	(115)
Fairly high	82	18	100	(157)
Medium	78	22	100	(135)
Low	86	14	100	(193)

Further analyses of relations among socio-economic position, age, education, race, and religion indicate that the last two (or subcultural characteristics associated with them) are the most influential factors affecting voting differences in our sample. Since Negroes in this sample almost unanimously supported Stevenson, no analysis of variations by economic level, education or other variables is feasible for them. Considering white workers alone, detailed analysis confirms the generally greater Democratic leaning among Catholic auto workers than among Protestants. Consistently in all three occupational categories (skilled, semi-skilled, and white collar) and at all three economic levels, considerably higher proportions of Catholics voted for Stevenson. The contrast is especially great in the upper economic classification, where 78 per cent of Catholics who voted, as against 47 per cent of Protestants were for Stevenson. In fact, we found no significant defections from a strong Democratic position among any subgroupings of Catholics (by age, education, occupation and socio-economic status). Particularly strong pro-Stevenson support was present among *skilled* Catholic workers and among semi-skilled Catholics over 40 years of age with less than eighth grade schooling. Approximately nine out of ten in these groups planned to vote for Stevenson.

Among Protestants, our evidence shows much more relation of voting to economic, age, and educational differences. Stevenson support was substantially greater among Protestants under 40 years of age, at the lower and middle economic levels, than among those older (84 per cent versus 63 per cent). It is thus apparent that these *younger* white Protestants (who grew up under the New Deal and the impact of the depression) voted in accordance with union recommendations just about as fully as did Catholic and Negro workers. The effect of age difference is not due to greater education on the part of younger workers; it is true of those with only eighth grade schooling as well as those with more. Persons who went beyond the eighth grade are more pro-Stevenson than the less educated at the high and low economic levels but less pro-Stevenson in the large middle economic range.

Non-voters and Undecided Voters

In the same manner that we have compared Stevenson and Eisenhower voters we shall now look for distinctive characteristics of non-voters and undecided voters. In what subgroups of auto workers do we find more than the average proportion failing to register and vote though eligible to do so? Since these union members constitute a potential source of additional votes they are of special interest. Likewise, those voters who were still undecided about their presidential preferences during the last weeks preceding election day comprise another group presumably susceptible to political influence. We may dismiss from further consideration members who are ineligible for registration, since such ineligibility stemmed principally from age and citizenship requirements. Passage of time will take care of most of

these non-voters, bringing the young to voting age and gradually reducing the number of immigrant non-citizens (though
efforts to encourage naturalization can also have an effect here).
Of all other workers interviewed—that is, of all who could have
registered and voted—slightly over 11 per cent failed to register.[13]
An additional 6 per cent remained uncertain about their vote
late in the campaign—and half of them ended by voting for
Eisenhower.

A number of the distinguishing characteristics of non-voters
(those eligible to register) may be seen in Table 2.13. Further
detailed analyses of the data lead to the conclusions enumerated
below. *Non-voting* rates are particularly high in the following
groupings:

> Young workers (Of those under 25, one-fourth are not
> registered; of all under 45, one-sixth are not registered
> while of those over 45 only one in twenty failed to regis-
> ter).[14]

> Workers who came to Detroit in recent years—and those
> who lived there all their life (30 per cent non-registered
> among those in Detroit less than 7 years; 11 per cent of
> those 7 to 16 years; 5 per cent of those more than 16
> years (but not all life); 22 per cent of those in Detroit
> all their life).

> Workers of relatively low economic status—

> Non-voting by occupational categories:
> 13 per cent of semi-skilled, 8 per cent of skilled, 4 per
> cent of white collar.

> Non-voting by income level of neighborhood:
> 15 per cent of low, 9 per cent of middle, 9 per cent of
> high. (For whites alone: 18 per cent, 10 per cent, and
> 9 per cent).

---

[13] Earlier in this chapter, it was estimated that one worker in five of
those eligible had failed to register and vote. These figures referred to the
total potential sample, including the *non*-interviewed. The percentage on
this page refers only to that part of the sample reached by interviewers.

[14] All the proportions and percentages in this and following items are
based on the total number of *eligible* voters interviewed. Consequently they
differ from the figures of Table 2.13 which are percentages of all respondents, including those ineligible to vote.

Non-voting by socio-economic rating[15]:
  17 per cent of low, 8 per cent of middle, 3 per cent of high.
Non-voting by own or rent home:
  17 per cent of renters, 5 per cent of owners.

Non-voting is somewhat more closely associated with certain combinations of the above characteristics, as indicated in the following notes:

  Limited schooling is associated with non-voting especially at the low socio-economic level (32 per cent non-voters among those with 8th grade or less and in the low economic classification versus 8 per cent for all other eligible voters). Among white workers this percentage of non-voters goes to 37 per cent and for Protestant white workers it is 52 per cent. Among all white workers under age 40 who have only 8th grade education or less, two-thirds are non-voters (though with these successive sub-divisions the numbers become so small that they are merely suggestive).

  Negro workers have a lower proportion of non-voting than do white workers at comparable economic levels (among semi-skilled, 14 per cent of whites against 7 per cent of Negroes are non-voters; in the low income neighborhoods, percentages are 18 per cent for whites and 11 per cent for Negroes).

  Catholics and Protestants have approximately the same pro-portions of non-voting in the upper and middle economic strata but at the lower level our data show 29 per cent non-voting among Protestants contrasted with only 11 per cent among Catholics.

  The tendency for younger workers to have higher rates of non-voting is most evident at the middle and upper economic levels and, by occupation, among skilled and white collar workers. For example, among semi-skilled the per-

---

[15] See footnote 12, page 44.

centages of non-voting for those under and over age 40 are respectively 15 per cent and 10 per cent; but among skilled and white collar together the corresponding figures by age are 13 per cent and 2 per cent.

In brief, non-voting is greatest among workers of relatively low economic status, especially if they are also of limited education, and this is more pronounced among Protestants than Catholics. Non-voting is also more frequent among younger workers than older, especially at upper and middle economic levels. It is likewise more frequent among workers living in Detroit relatively few years and among native Detroiters.

Turning to the "undecided" voters, we have inquired similarly as to their distinguishing characteristics. Since the number of these persons is small, however, we can derive only suggestive indications; and no comparisons of sub-groupings based on combinations of characteristics appear warranted.

The principal groups that have greater than average proportions of undecided voters are the following:

Older workers (9 per cent of those over age 45; 7 per cent of the 35 to 45; 4 per cent of those under 35).

Residence in low income neighborhoods (among white workers, 12 per cent in low neighborhoods, 7 per cent at all other levels combined).

White workers compared with Negroes (At equivalent low income level of residence, 12 per cent of whites versus 5 per cent of Negroes).

Catholics compared with Protestants (10 per cent of Catholics, 5 per cent of Protestants). This relationship exists at each of the three socio-economic levels.

Campaign Issues and Reasons for Voting

In addition to obtaining the facts of who voted for whom we attempted to find out the reasons behind the vote. The present section is concerned with what the voters considered to

TABLE 2.15
MAIN ISSUES AND ISSUES MOST IMPORTANT TO RESPONDENT AS SEEN BY PERSONS OF DIFFERENT VOTE INTENTIONS

Vote Intention

	Stevenson		Eisenhower		Undecided		Refused; No Answer		Total	
	Main Issues (1)	Most Imp't to Resp. (2)	Main Issues (3)	Most Imp't to Resp. (4)	Main Issues (5)	Most Imp't to Resp. (6)	Main Issues (7)	Most Imp't to Resp. (8)	Main Issues (9)	Most Imp't to Resp. (10)
	Rank %	Rank %	Rank %	Rank %	Rank %	Rank %	Rank %	Rank %	Rank %	Rank %
Korean War	1 (32)	II (24)	1 (45)	I (46)	1 (43)	I (39)	2 (19)	I (32)	1 (32)	I (28)
Employment; economic security; prosperity	2 (26)	I (29)		IV (13)	2 (16)	V (6)	1 (24)	V (5)	2 (23)	II (23)
Civil Rights	3 (14)	IV (15)					4 (11)	II (11)	4 (11)	IV (12)
Taxes	4 (13)	V (10)	4 (17)	II (20)	3 (12)	III (8)	5 (11)	III (8)	3 (13)	V (12)
Labor Problems: interest of working people; labor vs. big business; repeal of Taft-Hartley	5 (12)	III (17)							5 (10)	III (13)
Corruption; mess in Washington			2 (19)	III (14)	5 (10)	IV (8)				
Foreign Policy; defense of of U.S.; world peace; relations with Russia			3 (18)	V (18)		II (12)				
Domestic Communism			5 (14)							
Government economy and finance; waste and inefficiency					4 (12)		3 (19)	IV (8)		
Name Calling, mud slinging; personality battle										

be the main issues in the campaign, their reasons for intending to vote for their candidate, and the reasons they gave after the election for voting as they did.

In the pre-election interview persons were asked, "What would you say are the main issues or things being talked about in the presidential campaign?" and, "What issues or things being talked about are the most important ones to you?" The most frequent responses to these questions are summarized in Table 2.15. More detailed data are given in Tables 2.16 and 2.17.

In Table 2.15 the odd-numbered columns give the five main issues ranked by the percentage of persons considering them to be main issues. The even-numbered columns show corresponding rankings and percentages for the issues considered most important personally by the persons interviewed.

Looking first at those issues which the respondents considered to be the main issues, it is clear that the Korean war was considered the most important. Comparing Stevenson and Eisenhower supporters with respect to the main issues, we find that apart from the Korean war (which was mentioned more often by the Eisenhower people), Stevenson supporters stressed the issues emphasized by the Democrats and by their own union organization (see column 1) while the Eisenhower advocates correspondingly mentioned those issues stressed by the Republicans.

Looking at the main issues as viewed by the undecided (column 5) we see that with the exception of one issue ("name calling, etc.") they named as main issues a mixture partly similar to responses of the Democrats and partly resembling the Republican position. This presumably reflects their political ambiguity and the cross-pressures to which they were subjected. Their views on issues were consistent with their indecision as to candidate. The "refused; no answer" group seemed more like persons of Stevenson intent (column 7). The fact that they, like the undecided group, include "name calling, etc." as a main issue may indicate in both groups some feeling that campaigns fail to deal with real issues—perhaps a spirit of "a plague on both your houses." The uncertainty and indifference in these groups are also shown by the high proportions of "no answer," "don't

TABLE 2.16

MAIN CAMPAIGN ISSUES AS SEEN BY REGISTERED VOTERS OF DIFFERENT VOTE INTENTIONS

(Pre-election Interviews)

What would you say are the main issues or things being talked about in the presidential campaign?

Issues	Vote Intention				
	Steven-son	Eisen-hower	Unde-cided	No answer; refused to say	Total Sample
Korean War	32%*	45%*	43%*	19%*	34%*
Employment; security; prosperity	26	12	16	24	23
Taxes	13	17	12	11	13
Civil rights	14	3	2	11	11
Labor problems; interests of working people; labor vs. big business; repeal of Taft-Hartley	12	5	4	3	10
Corruption; "mess" in Washington	7	19	10	3	9
Name-calling; mud slinging; personality battle	8	6	12	19	8
Foreign policy; defense of U.S.; world peace; relations with Russia	8	18	—	—	8
Domestic Communism	2	14	2	3	4
Government economy and finance; waste and inefficiency	2	14	2	—	4
Democrats vs. Republicans; Stevenson vs. Eisenhower, etc.	4	2	4	—	3
Need a change	1	3	2	—	1
Tidelands oil	1	2	—	—	1
Military vs. civilian control	2	—	—	—	1
Miscellaneous, indefinite and unclassifiable	8	14	18	11	10
No answer; don't know	19	11	22	35	19
No. of cases	(486)	(118)	(49)	(37)	(690)

* Percentages total more than 100%, since some respondents mentioned more than one issue. The sample used here includes all persons who reported that they were registered voters.

TABLE 2.17

CAMPAIGN ISSUES CONSIDERED MOST IMPORTANT BY
REGISTERED VOTERS OF DIFFERENT VOTE INTENTIONS

(Pre-election Interviews)

What issues or things being talked about are the most important ones
to you?

Issues	*Vote Intention*				
	Steven-son	Eisen-hower	Unde-cided	No answer; refused to say	Total Sample
Korean War	24%*	46%*	39%*	32%*	28%*
Employment; security; prosperity	29	13	6	5	23
Labor problems; interests of working people; labor vs. big business; repeal of Taft-Hartley	17	**	6	8	13
Civil rights	15	3	4	11	12
Taxes	10	20	8	5	12
Foreign policy; defense of U.S.; world peace; relations with Russia	7	13	12	5	8
Corruption; "mess" in Washington	2	14	8	—	4
Government economy and finance; waste and inefficiency	2	6	4	8	3
Domestic Communism	3	10	4	5	5
Democrats vs. Republicans; Stevenson vs. Eisenhower	4	3	—	—	3
Miscellaneous, indefinite and unclassifiable	11	14	18	8	12
No answer; don't know	14	8	14	32	14
No. of cases	(486)	(118)	(49)	(37)	(690)

* Percentages total more than 100% since some respondents mentioned
more than one issue.

** Less than 1%.

know," and "indefinite, unclassifiable" responses in respect to issues (Tables 2.16 and 2.17).

When "main issues" are compared with those considered "most important to the respondent" himself (Table 2.15) only small differences are found but the directions of change are of considerable interest. Although Stevenson supporters named the same five issues in both instances (columns 1 and 2), their emphasis on the Korean war issue decreased in terms of personal importance while emphasis on labor problems and on employment and prosperity increased. Eisenhower supporters likewise changed little from the first to the second part of the question but their answers regarding the importance of issues to them personally did tend to place slightly less emphasis on charges of Democratic corruption and on domestic Communism and slightly increased relative emphasis on taxes, economic security, and prosperity.

When workers of undecided vote intention and those who refused to state their intent were asked about issues most important to them, their replies showed a markedly decreased reference to issues of "employment, security, prosperity" as contrasted with the number naming these as main issues and also in sharp contrast to the number of Stevenson supporters who considered these as personally most important. This suggests that one factor tending to differentiate the undecided and "not saying" workers was the existence of individual situations or beliefs that caused them to discount problems of personal job security and fears of bad economic conditions. An increased number of the undecided also emphasized foreign policy as a personally important matter and the "refused to answer" people increased their mention of the Korean war.

These results are all consistent with an interpretation that views the Stevenson supporters as especially inclined to emphasize labor's interests and economic conditions affecting working people; Eisenhower voters as leaning more to an emphasis on Korea and foreign relations and on economic issues as seen by tax-payers; and the undecided and "refusing to say" as persons impressed by the Republican appeals regarding Korea and peace and not strongly moved by Democratic and labor union economic appeals.

Good and Bad Points of the Presidential Candidates;
Reasons for Voting For or Against Them

Union members were asked about the good and bad points of the two candidates in a series of four pre-election questions:

> I'd like to ask you about the good and bad points of the two candidates for president. Is there anything in particular about Eisenhower that might make you want to vote for him? (What is it?)

> Is there anything in particular about Eisenhower that might make you want to vote against him? (What is it?)

> Is there anything in particular about Stevenson that might make you want to vote for him? (What is it?)

> Is there anything in particular about Stevenson that might make you want to vote against him? (What is it?)

Answers to these questions, classified in broad categories for purposes of overall comparison, are summarized in Table 2.18. The results are reported more completely in Tables 2.19 to 2.22.[16]

A number of significant relations are brought to light in Table 2.18. In general, personal qualifications of the candidates are seen to loom large in the voters' thinking compared with the more abstract considerations under the headings of either party references or campaign issues. This was probably influenced somewhat by the form of question, however, since it inquired in terms of "anything about Stevenson (or Eisenhower)" rather than by reference to the party or the party's candidate. Party references and issues were about equally often given as reasons for favoring candidates, though Stevenson supporters gave party

---

[16] Percentages in Table 2.18 do not correspond to those of Tables 2.19 to 2.22 since the latter all show the *proportions of persons* who mention ideas in each category; the percentages in each column may total more than 100 per cent since some persons volunteered two or more ideas. Table 2.18 on the other hand shows the *proportions of all ideas* that fall within each category; the percentages must total 100 per cent as they are based on the total number of ideas expressed. Use of this different percentage base in Table 2.18 is necessary in order justifiably to summate the frequencies of the separate sub-categories to obtain totals for the three broad categories.

references a little more frequently than issues as reasons for voting for him. Party references were definitely more common than issues as reasons for voting against the opposed candidate.

But the most important results in Table 2.18 are the comparisons of Stevenson and Eisenhower advocates. The principal conclusions are these:

1. Workers intending to vote for Stevenson were more committed and unequivocal in their intentions than were those planning to vote for Eisenhower. This is shown in the fact that the Stevenson supporters offer many fewer reasons that might make them vote against him (13 per cent as compared with 32 per cent by Eisenhower supporters regarding *their* candidate). At the same time, Stevenson voters gave *more* reasons for voting against the opposing candidate (79 per cent by Stevenson supporters compared with 61 per cent of Eisenhower voters giving reasons against Stevenson).

2. Workers planning to vote for Eisenhower especially emphasized his personal qualifications as a reason for voting for him whereas Stevenson supporters stressed "party" almost as often as personal qualifications in stating why they would want to vote for Stevenson. The Stevenson people likewise referred to issues and group interests much more, proportionately, than did Eisenhower supporters. In the case of Eisenhower, mention of personal qualifications were decidedly more frequent than references to party and issues combined (59 per cent to 28 per cent); for Stevenson this relation is strongly reversed (34 per cent to 48 per cent).

3. A similar reversal occurs in the reasons given *against* Stevenson and *against* Eisenhower. Against Eisenhower, points regarding personal qualifications exceed other reasons (24 per cent to 8 per cent by Eisenhower supporters and 43 per cent to 36 per cent by Stevenson supporters) while against Stevenson personal qualifications run definitely behind considerations of party and issues (5 per cent to 8 per cent by Stevenson supporters and 16 per cent to 45 per cent by Eisenhower supporters). This finding and the preceding one underscore the large

TABLE 2.18

GOOD AND BAD POINTS OF THE PRESIDENTIAL CANDIDATES AS SEEN BY PERSONS OF DIFFERENT VOTE INTENTIONS

	Persons Intending to Vote for Stevenson		*Persons Intending to Vote for Eisenhower*	
	Reasons might want to vote FOR *Stevenson*	*Reasons might want to vote* AGAINST *Stevenson*	*Reasons might want to vote* FOR *Eisenhower*	*Reasons might want to vote* AGAINST *Eisenhower*
Party References	28%	6%	15%	2%
Issues; Group Interests	20	2	13	6
Personal Qualifications	34	5	59	24
No; No Answer or Unclassifiable	18	87	13	68
	100%	100%	100%	100%
	Reasons might want to vote FOR *Eisenhower*	*Reasons might want to vote* AGAINST *Eisenhower*	*Reasons might want to vote* FOR *Stevenson*	*Reasons might want to vote* AGAINST *Stevenson*
Party References	2%	23%	3%	43%
Issues; Group Interests	3	13	5	2
Personal Qualifications	23	43	24	16
No; No Answer or Unclassifiable	72	21	68	39
	100%	100%	100%	100%

part played by Eisenhower's personal reputation, primarily as a source of support but, among many of these auto workers, also as a basis for negative reactions. By contrast, Stevenson was much more often accepted or rejected on grounds of his party and his stand on issues.

4. Although personal qualifications were much more *salient* concerning Eisenhower, both in a positive and a negative direction, the personal considerations were more *favorably* mentioned, on balance, in the case of Stevenson. That is to say, among these union voters the ratio of

positive to negative references regarding the candidates' qualifications was clearly higher in the case of Stevenson. Specifically, his ratios of favorable to unfavorable personal references were 34 per cent to 5 per cent among those supporting him and 24 per cent to 16 per cent among those opposing him; corresponding figures for Eisenhower were 59 per cent to 24 per cent among his supporters and 23 per cent to 43 per cent among his opponents.

5. Decidedly the most common reason against Stevenson by Eisenhower proponents was opposition to the Democratic party and its performance. In the case against Eisenhower by Stevenson supporters, party was again important but criticisms of his personal qualifications and his position on issues and group interests were also prominent.

The more specific points of approval and disapproval regarding the candidates may be seen by reference to Tables 2.19 to 2.22. In respect to Stevenson, it is apparent that the principal point in his favor besides his party and his personal qualifications (political experience, good record, intelligence, etc.) was the belief that he would best advance the interests of working people (in part through repeal of the Taft-Hartley law). Objections to him consisted mainly of criticisms of the Democratic party, its performance in Washington, and, by Kefauver backers, criticisms of the way Stevenson was nominated. There were also some negative references to Stevenson's political and personal record and his use of humor instead of taking things more seriously. In regard to Eisenhower, the outstanding matters mentioned are his military and leadership qualities—which are strongly stressed as factors both for and against him. His party affiliation and associates and fears of his stand on labor questions and civil rights are stated as other grounds for opposition to him, while in his favor we again have expressions of need for a change from the Democrats and faith that he would end the Korean war.

It may also be observed in these tables that responses of workers who were undecided or not saying how they would vote generally fall between those of Stevenson and Eisenhower

TABLE 2.19

CONSIDERATIONS IN FAVOR OF STEVENSON BY REGISTERED VOTERS OF DIFFERENT VOTE INTENTIONS
(Pre-election Interviews)

Is there anything particular about Stevenson that might make you want to vote for him?

Responses	Steven-son	Eisen-hower	Unde-cided	No answer; refused to say	Total Sample
Party References					
Running on Democratic ticket	31%*	3%*	14%*	19%*	24%*
New Deal platform; liberal; in FDR-Truman tradition	7	—	4	3	6
Don't want change	1	—	—	—	**
Issues; Group Interests					
Better for workers; repeal of Taft-Hartley Act	17	3	6	5	13
Civil Rights	5	2	2	5	4
Employment; security; prosperity	2	—	—	3	2
Other (e.g. Tidelands, Social Legislation)	2	**	—	3	2
For the benefit of the people; for everybody	3	—	—	—	2
Stevenson's Personal Qualifications					
Experienced; qualified for Presidency; knows politics; good record; a leader	24	14	16	8	21
Honest; religious; down-to-earth	9	2	14	5	8
Has ability; intelligent; well-educated	5	5	8	3	5
Good man; better man	4	3	4	5	4
Good talker; sense of humor	3	**	6	3	3
Lawyer; businessman	2	2	—	3	2
Miscellaneous; indefinite and unclassifiable	11	9	14	5	11
No; no answer; don't know; can't say	14	69	35	51	27
No. of cases	(486)	(118)	(49)	(37)	(690)

* Percentages total more than 100% since some respondents gave more than one answer.
** Less than 1%.

TABLE 2.20

CONSIDERATIONS AGAINST STEVENSON BY REGISTERED VOTERS OF DIFFERENT VOTE INTENTIONS

(Pre-election Interviews)

Is there anything in particular about Stevenson that might make you want to vote against him?

Responses	Vote Intentions				
	Steven-son	Eisen-hower	Unde-cided	No answer; refused to say	Total Sample
Party References					
He's a Democrat; I'm voting against Democrats, for Eisenhower; too close to Truman	2%*	31%*	4%*	5%*	7%*
The people backing him	2	5	4	—	2
Time for a change	—	7	2	—	1
Don't like way he was nominated; Kefauver should have been the candidate	2	10	—	3	3
Issues; Group Interests					
Not sure of his stand on Civil Rights; don't like Sparkman	2	2	—	—	1
Stevenson's Personal Qualifications					
Wisecracker; doesn't take himself or issues seriously; name-caller; playboy; divorced man	3	7	6	5	4
Record as Governor; lack of experience; not smart enough; connection with Illinois corruption	2	13	2	3	4
Miscellaneous, indefinite and unclassifiable	4	14	6	14	7
No; no answer; don't know; nothing against him	86	36	76	73	76
No. of cases	(486)	(118)	(49)	(37)	(690)

* Percentages total more than 100% since some respondents gave more than one answer.

TABLE 2.21

CONSIDERATIONS IN FAVOR OF EISENHOWER BY REGISTERED VOTERS OF DIFFERENT VOTE INTENTIONS
(Pre-election Interviews)

Is there anything in particular about Eisenhower that might make you want to vote for him?

Responses	Vote Intentions				
	Steven-son	Eisen-hower	Unde-cided	No answer; refused to say	Total Sample
Party References					
Running on Republican Ticket (or platform); not a Democrat; voting against Democrats	2%*	8%*	—	3%*	3%*
Need a change	**	13	—	—	2
Issues; Group Interests					
Korean War—will solve, end, etc.	2	6	6	5	3
Foreign Policy; Russia fears him	**	5	2	3	1
His stand on domestic issues (e.g., corruption, taxes, inflation, etc.)	1	9	—	—	2
Eisenhower's Personal Qualifications					
Military, war experience; good general	11	23	16	8	13
Leader; independent; picks good advisors; takes job seriously; knows more about being President	2	21	4	—	5
The right man; a great man	4	8	12	—	5
Job he did in Europe; experienced in world affairs	2	15	6	5	5
Honest	3	11	6	3	5
Has ability; intelligent; level-headed	1	5	2	3	2
Clean record; general experience	**	5	2	3	1
Miscellaneous, indefinite and unclassifiable	6	11	20	16	8
No; no answer; don't know; can't say	68	9	45	59	56
No. of cases	(486)	(118)	(49)	(37)	(690)

* Percentages total more than 100% since some respondents gave more than one answer.
** Less than 1%.

TABLE 2.22

CONSIDERATIONS AGAINST EISENHOWER BY REGISTERED VOTERS OF DIFFERENT VOTE INTENTIONS
(Pre-election Interviews)

Is there anything in particular about Eisenhower that might make you want to vote against him?

Responses	Vote Intentions				
	Steven-son	Eisen-hower	Unde-cided	No answer; refused to say	Total Sample
Party References					
Running on Republican Ticket; anti-New Deal	19%*	1%*	6%*	16%*	15%*
Association with Taft	8	1	8	5	7
Association with others than Taft	4	—	6	5	3
Issues; Group Interests					
Anti-Civil Rights	5	2	2	3	4
Will be run by Wall Street; "big shots"; the rich	5	1	—	3	3
Anti-labor	3	3	—	—	3
Will bring depression; anti-social security	2	—	2	—	2
Eisenhower's Personal Qualifications					
Military man; increased chances for war	32	13	12	11	26
Not qualified for civilian leadership; doesn't know domestic problems	17	8	8	11	14
Not independent	4	4	—	—	4
Weak; evasive in stating his policies; not consistent; dishonest	3	2	—	3	2
Miscellaneous, indefinite and unclassifiable	3	7	12	11	5
No; no answer; don't know; nothing against him	23	67	53	51	34
No. of cases	(486)	(118)	(49)	(37)	(690)

* Percentages total more than 100% since some respondents gave more than one answer.

adherents. As compared with Stevenson supporters, those undecided and not answering express more favorable feelings regarding Eisenhower's personal qualifications and decidedly fewer
express negative feelings on this score. As compared with Eisenhower backers, they are much more negative concerning his
Republican party ties and associates and less inclined to favor
him on the basis of his military record and leadership qualifications.

Reasons for Voting for Eisenhower or Stevenson

Many of the foregoing reasons in favor of one or the other
presidential candidate appear more clearly in response to direct
questions that were asked the respondents concerning the reasons

TABLE 2.23

REASONS FOR INTENDING TO VOTE FOR STEVENSON
(Pre-election Interviews)

Would you tell me why you are going to vote for Stevenson?

Party References

Running on Democratic Ticket	39%*
New Deal Platform; liberal; in FDR-Truman tradition	5
Don't want change	5

Issues; Group Interests

Better for workers; repeal of Taft-Hartley	25
Employment; security; prosperity	8
Civil rights stand	4
For the benefit of the people; for everybody	3
Tidelands oil	2
Social legislation (unemployment; pensions)	2

Stevenson's Personal Qualifications

Good man; better man	10
Experienced, knows politics; qualified for Presidency; good record; good administrator, etc.	10
Honest; religious	4
Has ability; intelligent; well-educated	3
Miscellaneous, indefinite and unclassifiable	6
No answer	2
No. of cases	(486)

* Percentages total more than 100% since some respondents gave more
than one answer.

for their vote. The pre-election interview included the question: "Would you tell me why you are going to vote for (Stevenson, Eisenhower)." The post-election questions were as follows: "What would you say was the main reason why you voted for (Stevenson, Eisenhower)?" and "Was there any other important reason why you voted for (Stevenson, Eisenhower)?"

TABLE 2.24
REASONS FOR INTENDING TO VOTE FOR EISENHOWER
(Pre-election Interviews)

Would you tell me why you are going to vote for Eisenhower?

Party References

Running on Republican Ticket	6%*
Need a change	32

Issues

His stand on domestic issues (e.g., corruption, taxes, inflation, etc.)	22
Korean War	12
Foreign policy	5

Eisenhower's Personal Qualifications

A leader; independent; knows more about being President; will pick good advisors, etc.	12
A great man; the right man	13
Job he did in Europe; experienced in World Affairs	8
Military, war experience; a great general	6
Has ability; intelligent	5
Honest	3
Miscellaneous, indefinite and unclassifiable	13
No answer	5
No. of cases	(118)

* Percentages total more than 100% since some respondents gave more than one reason.

Replies to these questions are reported in Tables 2.23 to 2.26. When these reasons are totaled for each of the three broad categories—Party references; Issues and group interests; Personal qualifications—it is again found that among these auto workers support of Eisenhower is ascribed to his personal qualifications more frequently than such reasons are mentioned in support of Stevenson. This is true both before and after the election. Personal qualifications comprise 33 per cent (before the election) and 38 per cent (after the election) of all "main reasons" assigned for Eisenhower votes; corresponding percentages in the case of Stevenson are 22 per cent and 19 per cent. Conversely, voters supporting Stevenson refer more often to party and to issues than do those backing Eisenhower.

TABLE 2.25

REASONS WHY VOTED FOR STEVENSON

What would you say was the main reason why you voted for *Stevenson?*
Was there any other important reason why you voted for *Stevenson?*

	Main Reasons	Other Important Reasons	Total
Party References			
Ran on Democratic Ticket; liked Democratic platform	52%*	17%*	68%*
Didn't want a change	12	3	15
New Deal program; FDR-Truman tradition	3	2	5
Issues; Group Interests			
Better for working man; for unions; backed by labor	27	14	42
Employment; security; prosperity	7	5	12
Civil Rights	2	**	2
Stand on Korea and War	**	1	2
Stevenson's Personal Qualifications			
Able, intelligent; a leader; inspiring, well-educated; good talker; better man, etc.	14	13	27
Good record as Governor; experienced; knows politics	7	6	13
A civilian; not a military man	5	3	8
Miscellaneous, indefinite and unclassifiable	6	6	13
No. of cases	(170)	(170)	(170)

* Percentages total more than 100% since some respondents gave more than one reason. Those who gave no answer are omitted.
** Less than 1%.

The figures of Tables 2.23 to 2.26 make it evident that the most important factors in the minds of Stevenson voters were their loyalty to the Democratic party and its policies; many expressed approval of the preceding Democratic administration and indicated that they did not "want a change"; they believed that a continued Democratic administration would be better for workers and labor unions and that it would insure greater economic prosperity and security. They accepted Stevenson as a capable, experienced leader though there are few signs of over-

TABLE 2.26

REASONS WHY VOTED FOR EISENHOWER

What would you say was the main reason why you voted for *Eisenhower?*
Was there any other important reason why you voted for *Eisenhower?*

	Main Reasons	Other Important Reasons	Total
Party References			
Needed a change	34%*	12%*	47%*
Just voted against Democrats	9	5	14
He ran on Republican ticket; liked his platform	9	2	10
Wanted to get rid of Truman's influence	4	3	7
Issues			
Will end Korean War	14	5	19
Wanted end of waste; corruption; wanted to "clean house"	8	8	16
Stand on domestic issues (e.g., economic policy; lower taxes, etc.)	4	7	11
Eisenhower's Personal Qualifications			
Intelligent; able; a better man; a great man; a leader; honest; sincere, etc.	34	22	55
Military experience; job he did in Europe; experience in world affairs	21	12	33
Miscellaneous, indefinite and unclassifiable	9	9	19
No. of cases	(116)	(116)	(116)

* Percentages may total more than 100% since some respondents gave more than one answer.

whelming enthusiasm for his personal qualifications. Turning to the Eisenhower voters, it is once more apparent that his personal appeal was the outstandingly important factor. In addition, however, large numbers echo the campaign slogan of "time for a change"; they speak of the need for removing the Democrats from power in order to end alleged waste and corruption. Faith that Eisenhower would end the Korean fighting and in general that he would be more effective in foreign affairs also stands out as an important influence. Belief in Republican economic policies is manifested in a smaller segment of replies. It is noteworthy that Republican claims regarding Communists in government and the domestic Communism issue as a whole are scarcely mentioned. Only 2 to 3 per cent of Eisenhower supporters refer to the matter—that is, approximately one-half of one per cent of the total sample.

The Senatorial and Gubernatorial Elections

An assessment of auto workers' voting in 1952 cannot properly stop with their choice for President. It is well known that Eisenhower ran ahead of the Republican ticket as a whole. Conversely, even among the preponderantly Democratic Detroit auto workers, Stevenson received considerably fewer votes than did the Democratic candidates for the United States Senate and the governorship. Defections from straight Democratic voting were to candidate Eisenhower rather than to the Republican party. Since the union strongly endorsed Moody and Williams for the Senate and governorship respectively, the vote for these offices as well as for the Presidency needs to be weighed in judging members' agreement with the organization's position.

Both the declared vote intentions before the election and the reports of voting behavior after the election showed Williams and Moody ahead of Stevenson. In pre-election interviews, of all workers who expressed their voting intent for any of the three offices, 83 per cent and 81 per cent were planning to vote for Williams and Moody respectively, as compared with 76 per cent for Stevenson. The difference increased on election day; the percentages of actual votes reported gave 85 per cent for Williams, 81 per cent for Moody, 75 per cent for Stevenson. (Official returns on all voters in Wayne County show Stevenson receiving 58 per cent of the two-party vote while Williams received 63 per cent.)

Stevenson supporters almost all voted for Williams and

Moody—that is, they voted a straight Democratic ticket for the three offices. By contrast, many Eisenhower voters split their ballots and voted for Williams and Moody. In pre-election interviews, 96 per cent of workers planning to vote for Stevenson also intended to vote for the other Democratic candidates while only 66 per cent of those intending to vote for Eisenhower were also planning to vote for the other Republican candidates.

When it came to actual voting, the corresponding figures were 98 per cent straight Democratic against 55 per cent straight Republican. Only 13 per cent of all UAW voters interviewed voted a straight Republican ticket. It is also significant that among persons undecided or refusing to state their Presidential vote intention shortly before the election, 85 per cent intended to vote for Williams and Moody. These people were apparently Democrats who were wavering on their Presidential choice or were inclined toward Eisenhower.

These findings clearly indicate that auto workers in the Detroit area were decidedly more Democratic than their votes for Stevenson and Eisenhower would suggest. Only about half the union Eisenhower voters also voted for Republican candidates for Governor and Senator. While the ratio of Stevenson to Eisenhower votes was 3 to 1, that for Governor Williams over his opponent was 6 to 1. Both sets of results are significant for any balanced estimate of where auto workers stood politically in 1952.

Vote on a State Reapportionment Proposal

Another test of whether union members voted in agreement with union recommendations was provided by a ballot on proposals for revising the State's voting districts. The union campaigned actively on the reapportionment issue, in support of "Proposal 2" and against "Proposal 3." The alternative proposals bore no party labels; they were somewhat abstract and difficult to grasp; publicity for them lacked the vigor and concrete dramatic appeal of campaigns for candidates. As a consequence many voters remained uninformed, vague, or confused. At the same time the *union's* role in reaching members may be especially clearly reflected in the voting on reapportionment since its efforts were probably less intermingled with the operation of other influences. The pre-election interview asked:

> Have you heard about any proposals to vote on reapportionment in Michigan? (Followed by: Have you heard anything about Proposal 2 or Proposal 3?)

Only 56 per cent of all registered union voters replied affirmatively. When they were asked how they were going to vote on the proposals, with probing questions to see whether they understood the meaning of the vote (see Question 25b, Interview I), only 23 per cent revealed sufficient clarity to be classifiable as for or against one of the Proposals. Of the 23 per cent, 20 per cent were for Proposal 2 (the one approved by the union) and 3 per cent for Proposal 3.

Questions about actual voting on reapportionment (Question 8, Interview II) showed 79 per cent of the registered voters saying "yes" they did vote on the issue. When they were asked how they had voted, 57 per cent gave answers that could be classified as for or against Proposal 2; others were too indefinite or confused to be classified as for or against. This 57 per cent represents a great increase over the 23 per cent who were clear about their position on the issue during the weeks before the election. Evidently many had obtained their information during the last days of the campaign. The 57 per cent divided as follows: 51 per cent voted for Proposal 2; 6 per cent against it. Among Stevenson voters, the reapportionment vote was: 64 per cent for Proposal 2; 3 per cent against it. Among Eisenhower voters, 36 per cent voted for Proposal 2; 21 per cent against it. Thus, a majority of even the Eisenhower voters were in accord with the union's stand on this issue, although not quite as strongly as the Stevenson voters.

The post-election interview asked if the respondent knew what groups or organizations were for Proposal 2 and what ones for Proposal 3. Slightly less than half of all UAW registered voters (46 per cent) could answer correctly that "unions," "CIO," etc. were for Proposal 2. Only 22 per cent gave a correct answer as to groups for Proposal 3 (such answers as "Out-state," "Republicans," "Manufacturers," etc.). Moreover, when those who had voted for Proposal 2 were asked for their reasons for voting as they did, about half indicated that they could give no reason, or they did not remember, or they were simply vague or confused. The only clear reason given by any number of voters, and this was true of both Eisenhower and Stevenson voters (about one quarter of each) was: "gives the cities more representation." When asked whether the fact that Proposal 3 won made any difference to them, in the great majority of cases (about three out of four) both Stevenson and Eisenhower adherents were indifferent or unable to reply.

The foregoing findings tend to support conclusions that are partly positive and partly negative in regard to the union's accomplishments in its campaign on reapportionment. On the unfavorable side, the reapportionment issue remained relatively unfamiliar and poorly understood by large numbers of auto workers during the pre-election period; even at election time many did not vote on it and many others voted without knowing what their vote meant. It appears that the union was none too successful in reaching members on this issue and in acquainting them with the reasons for concern over the question. Nevertheless, on the positive side of the union's accomplishment, it is clear that those workers who did vote cast their ballots overwhelmingly for the recommended Proposal. The union's difficulty apparently lay in the failure to get its message effectively to more of the members. The union voters whom the message did reach and who understood it were nearly unanimous in voting in agreement with the union's position.

Summary

In this chapter we have looked at the voting behavior of auto workers in the 1952 election. Also we have attempted to discern differences in voting behavior between various social and economic groups within the union membership. Lastly, we analyzed some of the reasons for voting for particular candidates. Certain facts stand out from this body of material. These facts are summarized in the following paragraphs.

Union people registered and voted in approximately the

same proportions as the public at large, a phenomenon not usually observed in blue collar groups. This would indicate that union efforts to get out the vote may have had some degree of success. One-third of the membership did not vote, however, even though the great majority of these non-voters were legally eligible.

Of those UAW members who voted, three out of four were for Stevenson. This represented a decrease from the proportion expressing a choice for Stevenson before the election (81 per cent). The loss was produced both by failure of workers who had intended voting for Stevenson to do so and by the relatively large number of Eisenhower votes among those who had been undecided or who had refused to state their preference (almost half of these people voted for Eisenhower).

Only 11 per cent of the union members called themselves Republicans or Independents with Republican leaning; 80 per cent said they were Democrats or had Democratic leaning. Even with the powerful appeal of the Eisenhower candidacy, only 13 per cent voted a straight Republican ticket. Although the percentage of Democrats voting for Eisenhower was only a little greater than the percentage of Republicans for Stevenson, these percentages of course, represent vastly larger absolute numbers in the case of Democrats. "Independents" without party leaning voted two to one for Eisenhower.

Democratic candidates for the governorship and U.S. Senate ran well ahead of the presidential nominee—85 per cent of the UAW vote was cast for Williams and 81 per cent for Moody compared with 75 per cent for Stevenson.

The loss of Democratic votes to Eisenhower is underscored, too, by comparison with the 1948 election. Of the auto workers who reported a 1948 vote for either Truman or Dewey, 89 per cent were in the Truman column, which signifies a 14 percentage-point decline to Stevenson's 75 per cent.

Analysis of personal and social characteristics related to voting uncovered few very strong differentials between various subgroupings of union members. However, the heaviest Stevenson majorities clearly occurred among Negroes, Catholics, persons of foreign parentage, workers of medium or relatively poor socio-economic status, those whose fathers were Democrats, those below middle age (the New Deal generation), and those who left school either before completing the eighth grade or during high school. Younger, white Protestants at middle and lower economic levels voted for Stevenson as fully as did Catholics, Negroes, and other strongly pro-Democratic categories. The small white collar group were the only union members who gave a majority to Eisenhower. Contrary to the opinion of some political analysts, auto workers residing in better income neighborhoods voted Republican no more than those in less favored districts.

Non-voting is greatest among workers of relatively low economic status, especially if they are also of limited education, and this is more pronounced among Protestants than Catholics. Non-voting is also more frequent among younger workers than older, especially at upper and middle economic levels. It is likewise more frequent among workers who have lived in Detroit relatively few years and among native Detroiters.

Greater than average proportions of undecided voters were found among older workers, among Catholics, and among white residents of low income neighborhoods. The numbers of undecided voters are too small, however, to yield very reliable comparisons.

Analysis of workers' replies to questions asking about campaign issues indicates that Stevenson supporters were inclined to emphasize labor's interests and economic conditions affecting working people, while Eisenhower voters leaned more toward an emphasis on Korea and foreign relations and on economic issues as seen by taxpayers. Persons in the undecided and "refusing to say" categories were characterized by the fact that they were impressed by the Republican appeals regarding Korea and peace, and apparently were not strongly moved by Democratic and labor union economic appeals.

Before the election we also asked the people interviewed whether there was "anything in particular about Stevenson (and about Eisenhower) that might make you want to vote for him (and against him)." It was found that workers planning to vote for Stevenson were more committed and unequivocal in their intention than those intending to vote for Eisenhower, as shown by the fact that, as compared with Eisenhower voters, they gave fewer reasons against their own candidate and more reasons against the opposing candidate. Unionists planning to vote for Eisenhower especially emphasized his personal qualifications whereas those for Stevenson stressed "party" almost as often as personal qualifications as a reason for voting for him. The Stevenson supporters likewise referred to issues and group interests much more, proportionately, than did Eisenhower supporters. These same contrasts are apparent in replies to direct questions asking respondents the reason for their voting choices.

One other test of whether union members voted in accord with union recommendations was afforded by a ballot on proposals for reapportionment of voting districts in the State. The UAW conducted a vigorous campaign on this issue. Our results on members' voting and information about the issue indicate that large numbers remained poorly informed and unaware of the importance of the question. Only 57 per cent were able to state how they had voted (21 per cent of registered voters did not vote on the issue). Nevertheless, on the positive side of the union's accomplishment, those workers who did vote cast their ballots overwhelmingly for the proposal supported by the union (51 per cent of the 57 per cent).

CHAPTER 3

Campaign Influences

In this chapter we are concerned with what the members of the UAW could tell us about the political influences to which they were exposed, and how they felt regarding these influences. We are also concerned with the differences between the Stevenson and Eisenhower supporters in these matters. Specifically, we shall concentrate on the following questions:

1. Did the workers discuss the campaign, and with whom?
2. Did they listen to candidates and other political speakers on radio and television? How often, and to whom?
3. Did they listen regularly to news programs and commentators? To which commentators?
4. Did they read about the election in the daily newspapers? Other papers and publications?
5. What kinds of direct communications did they receive from the interested parties, i. e., the union, the Democrats and Republicans, and others? Did they approve or disapprove of such communications?
6. Where did they get most of their information about the election? Which of these sources did they consider most important?
7. Which media of communication are trusted most? Which the least?
8. Were there any particular persons, groups, or organizations whose ideas they wanted to get before deciding how to vote?

Discussion of Politics

According to the responses in the pre-election interview, two-thirds of the union members eligible to register discussed politics with friends and associates during the campaign. This means that a substantial minority indicated during the last two weeks before the election that they had not talked politics with anyone. Slightly more of the pro-Stevenson unionists than of the pro-Eisenhower ones replied affirmatively to the question, which asked: "Within the past few weeks have you talked politics with anyone?" As most of the discussions were with co-workers, the smaller percentage for the Eisenhower supporters is probably a reflection of the reluctance on the part of these particular workers to discuss politics with a group which was predominantly pro-Stevenson.

TABLE 3.1

DISCUSSION OF POLITICS DURING THE CAMPAIGN
(Post-election Question)

	Stevenson Voters	*Eisenhower Voters*	*Did Not Vote*[*]	*Total Sample*
Talked politics—	82%[**]	79%	55%	78%
with co-workers	66%	58%	43%	61%
friends, relatives, and neighbors	14	17	7	14
others; no indication	2	4	5	3
Talked with none	18	21	45	22
	100%	100%	100%	100%
No. of cases	(167)	(116)	(62)	(345)

[*] The "non-voter" category referred to here and elsewhere includes a few cases of persons who refused to answer, as explained in note to Table 2.10.
[**] Percentages are all based on weighted figures as explained at Table 2.1.

By the time the campaign ended, the percentage of union members who had not talked politics with anyone dropped considerably, as indicated by the responses to a similar question asked in the post-election interview, reported in Table 3.1. However, there were still 22 per cent who said they did not talk politics in the weeks before the election. Since 61 per cent mentioned co-workers in the post-election query, but only 45 per cent in the pre-election one, it could be concluded that the difference between the two interviews was largely a result of increased conversations among the workers in the plants as the campaign came to its climax.

Radio and TV Listening

When the auto workers were asked if they listened to radio or TV programs by candidates for office in the last few weeks before the election, 83 per cent of the total sample replied "Yes," with no difference between the Stevenson and Eisenhower voters. However, only 67 per cent of the people who did not vote said "Yes." Over three-fourths of the entire sample heard or watched both Republican and Democratic candidates. Table 3.2 presents the more detailed answers to the question.

TABLE 3.2

LISTENING TO CANDIDATES ON RADIO OR TELEVISION, AND FREQUENCY OF LISTENING DURING LAST WEEKS OF CAMPAIGN

	Stevenson Voters	*Eisenhower Voters*	*Did Not Vote*	*Total Sample*
Listened to radio or TV	85%	85%	67%	83%
At least 3 times a week	45%	44%	36%	43%
Twice a week, or less	26	35	25	28
Not indicated, or vague	14	6	6	12
Did not listen	12	13	26	14
No answer	3	2	7	3
	100%	100%	100%	100%
No. of cases	(170)	(116)	(65)	(351)

When it came to radio and television speeches by non-candidates, the percentage of respondents indicating that they had heard or watched them dropped considerably. Fifty-three per cent of the total sample said "Yes" to the question asking if they had listened to radio or television political talks by persons who were not candidates. Fifty-eight per cent of the Stevenson voters, as compared to 50 per cent of the Eisenhower voters and 33 per cent of all others in the post-election sample, said they listened.

When asked who these non-candidates were, the UAW members mentioned Harry Truman much more frequently than any-one else (Table 3.3). Twelve per cent of the whole sample named him, with very little difference between the Stevenson and the Eisenhower voters. If we restrict ourselves to those respondents who said "Yes" to this question asking whether they heard non-candidates, we find that 23 per cent mentioned Truman, with 27 per cent of the Stevenson voters and 22 per cent of the Eisenhower voters doing so. Alben Barkley, then Vice-President, was the second most frequently mentioned (12 per cent), with Walter Reuther and the late Robert Taft both being named by 9 per cent of the respondents who listened to non-candidates.

TABLE 3.3

NON-CANDIDATES HEARD ON RADIO OR TV DURING LAST WEEKS OF CAMPAIGN

	Stevenson Voters	Eisenhower Voters	Did Not Vote	Total Sample
Did listen	58%	50%	33%	53%
Democrats				
Truman	15%*	11%*	4%*	12%*
Barkley	8	6	1	6
Reuther	6	7	3	5
Kefauver	4	2	3	3
Other National and Local Democrats	11	9	5	7
Republicans				
Taft	6	4	1	5
Dewey	5	3	5	3
Hoover	5	3	—	3
MacArthur	2	2	—	2
McCarthy	2	—	—	1
Other National and Local Republicans	2	5	1	2
No names given	19	17	21	19
Did not listen; no answer	42	50	67	47
	100%	100%	100%	100%
No. of cases	(170)	(116)	(65)	(351)

* Since some respondents listened to more than one speaker, the percentages in these columns total more than the figures in the top row which reports the percentage who listened to anyone.

Apparently, very little "differential selection" in listening prevailed among the Stevenson and Eisenhower voters within the union ranks. That is, Stevenson voters did not tend to listen to pro-Democratic speakers any more than did Eisenhower voters, nor did Eisenhower voters listen to pro-Republican speakers any more than did Stevenson voters. This is not as unusual as it appears. If we were dealing with a sample selected from the entire voting population which included upper levels as well as workers, such a lack of difference would be astonishing indeed.

TABLE 3.4

NEWS PROGRAMS AND COMMENTATORS
LISTENED TO REGULARLY

Program or Commentator	Stevenson Voters	Eisenhower Voters	Did Not Vote	Total Sample
Total who listened	59%	61%	33%	56%
Walter Winchell	18%*	17%*	4%*	15%*
Drew Pearson	13	6	5	10
John C. Swayze	11	14	1	9
Guy Nunn	7	3	1	5
Lowell Thomas	4	6	4	4
Douglas Edwards	5	3	1	3
Gabriel Heatter	3	7	1	3
Edward R. Murrow	3	3	1	2
Fulton Lewis, Jr.	—	5	—	1
Panel Programs (Meet the Press, etc.)	5	6	—	4
Other National Commentators	6	3	3	5
Other Local News Announcers	14	25	15	14
Did not listen; no answer	41	39	67	44
	100%	100%	100%	100%
No. of cases	(170)	(116)	(65)	(351)

* See note to Table 3.3.

But we are dealing here with a particular stratum of the larger electorate, namely, workers who traditionally are overwhelmingly predisposed to Democratic sentiments. This is as true of many of the Eisenhower voters in our sample as it is of the Stevenson voters.

The variations in the percentages within each column (that is, the differences in the frequency by which each non-candidate was mentioned by each voter category) probably reflect the differences in frequency of appearances and participation by the non-candidates in radio and television programs, and not necessarily their popularity.

When it came to listening to news programs and commentators we do find some indication of a certain amount of selection by the Stevenson and Eisenhower voters, as seen in Table 3.4.

Concentrating only on those respondents who indicated they listened regularly to some news program or commentator, we find that the nine most frequently named commentators are mentioned in the following pattern:[1]

Mentioned by Greater per cent of Stevenson than of Eisenhower voters	*Mentioned by Greater per cent of Eisenhower than of Stevenson voters*	*Approximately the same per cent*
Pearson (22% vs. 10%)	Swayze (23% vs. 18%)	Winchell
Nunn (12% vs. 4%)	Heatter (11% vs. 6%)	Thomas
D. Edwards (9% vs. 4%)	Lewis (8% vs. 0%)	Murrow

In other words, the Stevenson voters tended to listen to Pearson, Nunn, and Douglas Edwards more than did the Eisenhower voters; and the opposite was true for Swayze, Heatter, and Lewis. It would require a content analysis of the broadcasts and telecasts of each of these six men to determine exactly their political leanings during the 1952 campaign, in order to make a finer examination of the selective factors involved. In the case of two of the six, we already know their dispositions—Guy Nunn of the UAW's radio department, obviously for the Democratic candidate, and Fulton Lewis, Jr., who, at the time of the campaign, was vigorously for the Republican candidate.

It is worth noting, first, that none of the Stevenson voters said they listened to Fulton Lewis, Jr., even though he immediately preceded Nunn on the same radio station, and second, that Nunn rates the lowest among the Eisenhower voters, along with Douglas Edwards.

---

[1] Percentages are based on the number in each voting group who reported listening to any news program or commentator. Differences of 5 percentage points or more are included in the first two columns; those less than 5 points, in the third column.

Newspaper and Other Reading

When our respondents were asked if they had read about the election in the newspapers during the last weeks of the campaign, 84 per cent indicated that they had, with the percentage for non-voters dropping to 70 per cent. Details of the answers to this question are shown in Table 3.5.[2]

TABLE 3.5

NEWSPAPERS READ DURING 1952 CAMPAIGN

Response	Stevenson Voters	Eisenhower Voters	Did Not Vote	Total Sample
A. Total who read	86%	88%	70%	84%
The News only	25%	14%	8%	20%
The Times only	18	15	35	20
Free Press only	5	5	8	5
News and Times	5	7	5	5
News and Free Press	9	13	6	10
Free Press and Times	15	15	5	14
All 3 papers	9	18	3	10
Did not read any	14	11	25	15
No answer	—	1	5	1
	100%	100%	100%	100%
B. The News	47%	52%	23%	45%
The Times	47	55	49	50
Free Press	38	52	23	39
No. of cases	(170)	(116)	(65)	(351)

Several points are worth noting with regard to the newspaper reading habits of the UAW members. First, the percentage of non-voters reading no paper at all is much higher than for Stevenson and Eisenhower voters, a fact in accordance with the other things we know about this group (lower socio-economic status, etc.). Second, exactly one-half of those non-voters who read any paper at all read *only* the Hearst publication, the *Times;* in fact, this particular paper was read to a much greater extent by the non-voters than either of the other two papers. Third, the proportion of Eisenhower voters reading two or more

---

[2] The percentage of persons who replied that they did not read any newspapers might be partly affected by the large percentage, reported on below, who indicated that they did not trust this source of information (see Tables 3.10 and 3.11).

papers is the highest of the three types of voting groups; indeed, the proportion of Eisenhower voters reading all three is twice as large as that of the Stevenson voters.

Asked if they had read about the election in any magazines or in other papers, 31 per cent of all the respondents replied that they had. The same percentage prevailed among the Stevenson voters; 39 per cent of the Eisenhower voters, and only 14 per cent of the non-voters, gave affirmative answers. The distribution of the magazines or other papers read is shown in Table 3.6.

While the proportion of Stevenson voters who refer to union publications is much greater than that of the Eisenhower voters, the 10 per cent figure for the former group might be considered startlingly low when it is borne in mind that a great deal of campaign news and discussion was carried by the union papers. We shall have more to say on this in a later section of this chapter dealing with the question about organizations whose ideas the workers wanted before deciding how to vote.

TABLE 3.6

MAGAZINES AND OTHER PAPERS READ DURING THE CAMPAIGN*

Magazines or other papers	Stevenson Voters	Eisenhower Voters	Total Sample
Life	8%	11%	8%
Look	5	4	4
American, Colliers, or Sat. Eve. Post	6	12	7
Time or Newsweek	3	8	4
Reader's Digest	4	3	3
Union publications	10	3	7
Ethnic publications	2	2	2
Others	6	7	6
No. of cases	(170)	(116)	(351)

* Because of the small numbers involved, the figures for those who did not vote are not reported. The "Total Sample" column, however, does include them.

The difference in the percentages of Stevenson and Eisenhower voters naming union publications, as well as most of the other differences in Table 3.6, is probably accounted for in large measure by the "differential selection" factor having to do with

the two groups' respective political tendencies, and also by the
part socio-economic factors play in influencing the reading
habits of individuals.

Direct Communications

In both interviews, a series of questions was asked concerning
other campaign communications, what they were about, who
initiated them, the respondents' evaluations, etc. The question
as asked in the second interview was:

> "As you know, many groups and organizations get in touch
> with voters before the election. What ways were any groups
> and organizations in touch with you?
> Did they send you things in the mail? Which party or
> candidate were they for? What people or organizations (sent
> you things in the mail), etc.?
> Did they hand you leaflets?
> Did they phone you?
> Did they talk to you in speeches at meetings?
> Did they talk to you in person?
> Were there any other ways?"

For each kind of contact, the respondent was asked if he thought
it was a good thing or not.

Because of the publicity drive on registration that took place
in the entire Detroit area for some time before the election,
part of the pre-election questioning also asked if the material
received, or the organizational contact, was about registration.
Only 15 per cent said that it was. According to their responses,
only 45 per cent of the registered voters in the pre-election interview had any kind of contact with organizations such as the
CIO, Democrats, Republicans, etc., and/or their representatives,
in the form of being sent things in the mail, handed leaflets,
being phoned, asked to meetings, or talked to in person.

However, by the end of the campaign, as indicated by the
responses to a similar question in the post-election interview,
76 per cent of the sample stated that they had been contacted
by one organization or more. This increase from 45 per cent to
76 per cent probably reflects the augmented spurt in campaign
activities in the "home-stretch" shortly before election day.

The remainder of the discussion on this question will be confined to the responses to the post-election question, because of the larger percentage indicating some contact. Mail and personally distributed leaflets were the only two kinds of contacts mentioned with enough frequency to justify analysis. No more than 10 per cent of the voters mentioned any one of the other kinds.

Fifty per cent of the total sample reported that they received mail about the election. Of the total mail contacts, 56 per cent were about the Democratic candidates, 44 per cent about the Republican candidates. And of the information received through the mail concerning the Democratic candidates, 35 per cent was received from the UAW or CIO, 16 per cent from the Democratic party, 20 per cent from other sources (such as church, veterans, and ethnic organizations), and 29 per cent from unidentified sources (couldn't remember, etc.). If these latter are distributed in a ratio similar to the identified ones, the percentages would be: from UAW or CIO, 49; Democrats, 22; other, 29.

Of the information received through the mail on the Republican candidates, 29 per cent was received from the Republican party, 28 per cent from other sources, and 43 per cent from unidentified sources. Again, if these latter are distributed in a ratio similar to the identified sources, the percentages would be: Republicans, 51; other, 49.

Nearly three-fifths (59 per cent) of the voters in the sample said they had been handed leaflets during the campaign. Of the total contacts through this medium, 74 per cent were about the Democratic candidates, and 26 per cent about the Republican ones. Of the former, 68 per cent were reported from the UAW or CIO, 3 per cent from the Democratic Party, 4 per cent from other sources, and 25 per cent from unidentified ones. If these are distributed in the same proportion as are the identified sources, the percentages would be: UAW or CIO, 91 per cent; Democrats, 4 per cent; and other sources, 5 per cent. These figures, as well as those concerning mail contacts, suggest the extent to which the union is performing campaign tasks, rather than leaving such functions to the party itself. There is also the possibility that the percentage of direct Democratic contacts was actually higher, but that the average worker fails to make a distinction, during election time, between the union and the party, and gives priority in his recollection to his union's role in the campagn.

Of the information received in the form of leaflets about the Republican candidates, 21 per cent were reported by the respondents to have come from the Republican party, 15 per cent from other sources, and 64 per cent from unidentified sources. The adjusted percentages would be: Republicans, 57 per cent; other groups, 43 per cent.

In none of these items discussed so far was there a marked difference between the Stevenson and Eisenhower voters.

In an attempt to get at their approval or disapproval of being sent campaign material in the mail, or handed leaflets, by organizations, we asked the respondents who indicated receiving them, the following question:

"Do you think it is a good thing or not for them to (send you things in the mail) (hand you leaflets)?"

The responses were the following:

	Percentage of Respondents Receiving Mail	*Percentage of Respondents Receiving Leaflets*
Favorable	52%	60%
Unfavorable	27	20
Not clear; no answer	21	20
	100%	100%

If the "Not clear" and "No answer" category is distributed in the same ratio as are the others, the "Favorable" category for mail would be 66 per cent; for leaflets, 75 per cent. The larger percentage for the latter is probably related to the fact that a greater percentage of the leaflets than of the mail was about the Democratic candidates, and was from individuals and organizations known to the recipient.

When these data are broken down into *sources* of the mail or leaflets—in particular, unions, Democrats, or Republicans as sources—we find that: 1) Stevenson voters, as expected, had a substantially more favorable reaction than the Eisenhower voters to mail and leaflets from the UAW or the CIO, and from the Democrats. While the percentages of favorable reactions to mail and to leaflets from the union or the Democrats among the Stevenson voters were at least 80 per cent, among the Eisenhower voters the percentages were 55 per cent in the case of mail from the Democrats, and 45 per cent in the case of leaflets from the UAW or CIO. 2) Somewhat surprisingly, the proportion of Stevenson voters expressing some favorable comment on mail from Republican sources—although lower than the response to mail from unions and Democrats—was about the same as that of the Eisenhower voters, which was slightly less than 60 per cent. The absolute numbers involved here, however, are too small (especially considering the low number of Eisenhower voters reporting any contacts through the mail from Republican sources) to warrant any extended discussion. Of course, this lack of difference in favorable comment might be due to the fact that, in general, people possibly consider any kind of circulation of viewpoints as a desirable thing, that there is no harm in it, one doesn't have to accept the views presented, etc.

One final note, in this connection, about materials which were either sent through the mail or personally distributed: despite the great prevalence of favorable responses to them, no conclusions concerning their importance to the union voter should be made. As we shall see below, leaflets and mail receive a very low rating in terms of the union voter's estimate of their importance in giving him any information or ideas about the candidates and the election, or in terms of their trustworthiness as sources of political information. In fact, none of the voters mentioned such material *spontaneously* when asked before the election where they got most of their information. After the election, only 2 per cent checked leaflets and mail as the most important source of information. Only 1 per cent cited them as a medium trusted *most;* but 32 per cent named them as a medium trusted *least,* second only to newspapers.

Sources of Campaign Information

In the pre-election interview, the 690 registered voters were asked, in the form of a free-response question, where they got most of their information about candidates. The results are summarized in Table 3.7. Slightly more than 4 per cent indicated no source at all. The most frequently mentioned source was the newspapers with television and radio next. As indicated above, no one mentioned leaflets or materials sent through the mail.

TABLE 3.7

SOURCE OF MOST OF INFORMATION ABOUT CANDIDATES

Newspapers	65%*
Television	47
Radio	31
Talking with people, including co-workers	17
The Union	7
Magazines	5
All other sources	6

* The percentages total more than 100% since many persons named more than one source (not more than two sources were recorded for any one respondent).

Only two of the sources differ markedly as between the Stevenson and Eisenhower supporters. The union was mentioned by 8 per cent of the former, and by only 1 per cent of the latter; magazines, by 4 and 9 per cent, respectively.

Most important sources of information. The frequency with which campaign influences are reported, however, is not the same as the evaluations attached to them. When asked in the post-election interview to indicate which of a given list of seven media they considered the *most important* in giving them information about the candidates and the election, the respondents replied as shown in Table 3.8.

Comparing Table 3.7 and 3.8, it can be seen that while newspapers were mentioned more as the source of most of the workers' campaign information, their importance is by no means to be inferred from this fact. For only the Eisenhower voters do newspapers remain relatively important, a fact which is largely explained in terms of the agreement in political choices between these voters and the Detroit papers, all of which were for Eisenhower. More significantly, the two tables reflect the great importance of television as a vital influence in the political process.

Campaign influences trusted most and least. This point about television is borne out even more directly in the responses to the questions asking which sources were trusted *most* and which *least*. After being requested to indicate which of the above seven sources were most important, our respondents were asked:

"Which of these on the list would you say you *trust most?*"
"Which of these do you *trust least?*"

The answers to each of these questions are shown in Tables 3.9 and 3.10.

TABLE 3.8

MOST IMPORTANT SOURCE OF INFORMATION

	Stevenson Voters	Eisenhower Voters	Did Not Vote	Total Sample
Television	60%*	52%*	57%*	58%*
Newspapers	35	55	40	40
Radio	19	22	15	19
Personal talks	10	5	13	10
Speeches at meetings	8	2	3	6
Magazines, etc.	2	8	5	3
Leaflets and mail	3	1	2	2
No. of cases	(156)	(107)	(55)	(318)

* Percentages are based on all eligible voters in the post-election sample who expressed a judgment concerning the media. Percentages total more than 100% since some respondents named more than one item (not more than three were coded for any one respondent).

The responses suggest the small extent to which newspapers are trusted as a source of political information except, again, in the case of the Eisenhower voters. In sharp contrast, television has the highest percentages trusting it the most, and along with radio, the lowest percentages trusting it the least. This confidence in television probably reflects the utilization by this medium of the psychology of "seeing is believing." Television apparently is trusted so highly because the voters also feel that, to date, television constitutes virtually the only medium through which both sides of the political argument can be heard and seen. Unlike the newspapers, which the auto workers (especially the pro-Stevenson ones) distrust most, television is considered as immune from one-sided slanting of current events and political campaigns. The contrast in the reputation of newspapers and television as sources of political information is highlighted further by a comparison of the ratios of trust to distrust. We find that 94 per cent of all workers expressing either trust or distrust of television say that they trust it; in the case of newspapers, only 39 per cent trust it as against 61 per cent on the distrust side. The contrast is even greater in the case of the rating of newspapers by the Stevenson voters, among whom the trust-distrust ratio for newspapers falls to 27 per cent.

TABLE 3.9

MEDIA TRUSTED *MOST* AS SOURCES OF POLITICAL
INFORMATION

	Stevenson Voters	Eisenhower Voters	Did Not Vote	Total Sample
Television	51%*	43%*	52%*	50%*
Newspapers	16	40	32	23
Radio	17	16	13	17
Personal talks	15	9	18	14
Speeches at meetings	9	—	7	7
Magazines, etc.	3	6	4	4
Leaflets and mail	—	4	2	1
No. of cases	(143)	(101)	(50)	(294)

* See note for Table 3.8.

These two tables, as well as the preceding one, Table 3.8, also show how the Eisenhower voters differ in their low ratings of personal talks and speeches at meetings. This group of UAW members was at variance with the majority of their fellow-workers with whom they had the most opportunity to discuss the 1952 campaign, and also at variance with their union which used the occasion of meetings to present political speeches. Their low ratings, therefore, of personal talks and speeches at meetings are probably accounted for by such factors. Conversely, the higher ratings by the Stevenson voters are a reflection of this group's agreement with the views of their fellow-workers and union.

Key individuals and organizations. Much of the foregoing discussion is focused on the role of mass media, such as television, radio, and the printed word. But to what extent did the

TABLE 3.10

MEDIA TRUSTED *LEAST* AS SOURCES OF POLITICAL INFORMATION

	Stevenson Voters	Eisenhower Voters	Did Not Vote	Total Sample
Newspapers	51%*	21%*	29%*	42%*
Leaflets and mail	26	49	38	32
Speeches at meetings	9	25	25	14
Personal talks	11	12	19	12
Magazines, etc.	5	1	4	4
Television	4	4	4	4
Radio	3	1	6	3
No. of cases	(124)	(81)	(42)	(247)

* See note for Table 3.8.

UAW voters feel that they wanted to consult particular persons or groups before deciding how to vote? Two specific questions on this point were directed to the respondents in the post-election interview, worded as follows:

> "Were there any particular people you know personally whose ideas you wanted to hear before you decided how you would vote? (If yes) What people were they?"

> "Were there any particular *groups* or *organizations* whose ideas you wanted to get before you decided how you would vote? (If yes) What groups or organizations were they?"

Only 7 per cent of the entire sample replied "Yes" to the first question, with no marked difference between the Stevenson and Eisenhower voters. The specific persons named (in terms of their relation to the respondent) were too scattered to warrant categorization. The responses to this question should not be confused with those discussed in the previous pages, in which it was pointed out that 17 per cent of the sample considered talking with people a source of most of their campaign information, and that 10 per cent considered this source the most important one.

However, a slightly larger proportion, 12 per cent, indicated that there was some group or organization whose ideas they wanted to get before voting. And here we do find a marked difference between the Stevenson and Eisenhower voters: 16 per cent of the former, as compared to 8 per cent of the latter, said "Yes." These figures probably remain as low as they are because of the respondent's disinclination to admit any lack of independent judgment in political decisions.[3] Keeping this in mind, it is interesting that the only organization named by enough auto workers to justify a separate category was the union. The proportion naming the union was 8 per cent. As would be expected, these were mostly Stevenson voters. Eleven per cent of the latter group, but only 3 per cent of the Eisenhower voters, named the union.

Summary

What can we say by way of summary concerning the various kinds of campaign influences among Detroit's UAW members? The following are among the findings in this chapter:

1. The most impressive item is the extent to which the new medium of mass communication, television, undergoing its first widespread "try-out" in politics in the election covered by this survey, was rated as the most important source of information about the candidates and the election. Moreover, and perhaps this is of greater importance, television far outranked all other media in the degree to which it is *trusted*. Half of all the respondents said they trusted it *most* (among the 7 media listed) and only one in twenty-five named it as trusted least.

2. Even though newspapers were cited as the source of most of their campaign information (not to be confused with workers' *rating of importance*), the UAW members—in particular, the Stevenson voters among them—ranked this source as the one trusted *least*.

3. Understandably, the Eisenhower voters had the highest proportion who trust newspapers the most and who rate them as the most important source. Moreover, they were the heaviest readers of the daily papers.

---

[3] Had we given the respondents a list of organizations when asking this question, we undoubtedly would have obtained much higher percentages. This is what happened, as a matter of fact, when we sought to determine the extent to which particular groups' political recommendations were trusted and not trusted. The results are reported in Chapter 4.

4. The union was mentioned spontaneously by only a very small minority of workers as: 1) a source of most of their information about the campaign; 2) the most important source; 3) a source of publications about the election; and 4) as an organization whose ideas they wanted before election day.

5. There seemed to be no difference between the Stevenson and Eisenhower voters as regards their proportions listening to the candidates and other campaign speakers. However, there were some slight differences in expected directions when it came to listening to certain news commentators.

6. As might be expected, the lack of interest in the election among the non-voters was reflected in their low reading, viewing, and listening patterns.

7. Considering the amount of printed literature that deluges the average voter during political campaigns, it is of no little pertinence to emphasize how poorly this form of campaign influence is valued by the auto workers in our sample, as indicated by the low ratings of leaflets and mailed literature in terms of their importance and their trustworthiness. The fact that a sizable proportion of workers receiving them gave favorable reactions can only be interpreted as meaning that they don't object to getting such materials, and not necessarily that they would encourage a continuation of the practice.

All in all, it appears that in the Detroit area at least, where the newspapers traditionally have taken political stands contrary to the political preferences of the majority of the auto workers, the key influential channel of mass political communication today is television. Its role will probably become even more crucial as its techniques of persuasion are developed, and as conflicting interest groups, seeking to win public favor, become increasingly aware of the positive evaluation of the new medium by that public. From the standpoint of the union, it is already a matter of concern that it have access to television equal to that of other forces with a stake in the political process.

CHAPTER 4

Political Orientation and Political Interest

In this chapter and the following ones we shall look at the voting behavior of UAW members in a more rounded way, as an expression of their total personal and socio-political orientation. Our aim is to gain further understanding of the feelings and attitudes that lead them to vote as they do or not to vote at all. How do the members feel about politics and the union's role in political action? What are the personal motivations and the social influences in their lives that help to account for the political outlook they have? Specific votes in a particular election are, after all, not our chief concern. 1952 is past. We cannot assume that the specific circumstances of that election will occur again. Rather our central interest is to derive insights and tentative conclusions about unionists' political behavior that will have meaning in 1956 and 1966—conclusions that will add a stone here and there to the growing structure of dependable knowledge about labor in politics and about modern political man generally.

It may be well to describe our viewpoint here a little more fully since it governs the entire presentation in these last chapters. Voting behavior, like any other social act, flows from the numberless influences that have played upon each individual from his earliest years as well as from his contemporary social conditions and associations. The lifetime experiences are currently represented by the complex system of dispositions (habits, beliefs, values, feelings, ideals) that each of us carries around

94

with him—his total "personality." For present purposes we are particularly concerned with those components of people's make-up that relate to their political orientation and their voting behavior. What general attitudes lie back of specific election decisions? What beliefs and interpretations has the auto worker accepted regarding his own interests and regarding the groups, organizations and leaders which he thinks have interests that are either the same or opposed? What degree of concern do different persons in the union feel in reference to social and political affairs? How contented or dissatisfied are they with things as they are? What conceptions of society are held; what beliefs about power relations and conflicting group interests, about the way social and economic policies are shaped and whether individuals (working people, for example) can do anything to improve their world? We assume that answers to such questions have bearing on the way people vote and on their attitudes as to whether their union should engage in political action.

We have attempted to obtain samples of UAW members' feelings on a number of questions of this kind. The information will be examined in this and the following chapter with two purposes in view: (1) to provide a better understanding of these union people and their political orientation by describing certain of their general attitudes, and (2) to draw some conclusions —even though rough first approximations—about the way in which their voting and political attitudes are related to several of these more general dispositions.

In a parallel and interrelated manner we assume, too, that objective differences in respect to people's backgrounds—where they grew up, their race, religion and nationality, the amount of education they obtained, the kind of job and amount of income they have—will also influence their political outlook and their votes. Accordingly, in these last chapters we shall further analyze these facts of personal and social characteristics of people in relation to their political interest and voting behavior.

All of this analysis is aimed at helping to throw light on the complex central question: What people (within the UAW in this study) holding what underlying attitudes, under what current conditions and influences can be expected to support what type of political program? Although evidence from the present research goes only a very short distance toward finding answers to the grand overall question, we believe that a significant step is taken simply by formulating the question in this way and by analyzing some illustrative results within this framework. Even tentative and partial answers to the many-faceted question will have practical value in indicating what union members want the union to do; in showing what differences of views divide the membership; in letting people at all levels in the union and outsiders in all relationships to the union know the climate of opinion among the members so that each, according to his lights, can take whatever steps seem to him appropriate to change or intensify prevailing attitudes in one direction or another.

We may now give greater definiteness to the foregoing discussion by referring to the selected general attitudes that we shall deal with here. They are shown in the diagram on page 97. This chart will serve as a guide to the various measures and relationships to be examined in Chapters 4 and 5. Preceding sections of our report have dealt principally with political behavior (Level 1 of the chart) and certain of the objective factors related to voting (items shown in the box at the right of the chart). Attitudes toward parties, candidates and issues (Level 2) have been treated somewhat incidentally as components of current voting behavior. Though these attitudes may be valuably explored for the light they throw on voting decisions their explanatory significance appears to be limited since they remain essentially descriptive aspects of the voters' orientation toward the particular election. We have included them in the large box with political behavior to suggest that they are here conceived as one portion of the election activity itself, to be understood or explained as far as may prove feasible by reference to more general levels of attitudes and by objective social conditions and characteristics.[1]

Within the framework sketched, then, we shall focus attention on the seven sets of attitudes shown at Levels 3, 4 and 5 of

[1] The study of these attitudes regarding party, candidates, and issues forms the core of the voting research conducted by the University of Michigan Survey Research Center in its inquiry into the 1952 election. A. Campbell, G. Gurin, and W. E. Miller, *The Voter Decides,* Evanston, Row Peterson, 1954.

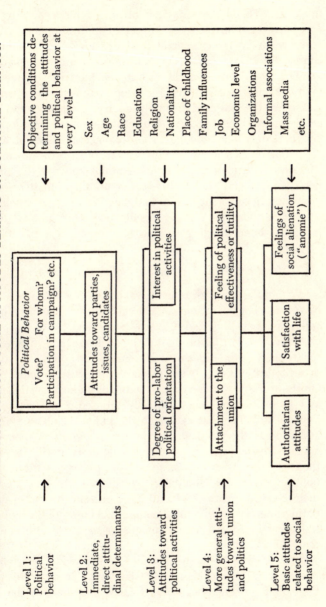

CHART I

SUGGESTED INTERRELATIONS AMONG SOME ATTITUDES BEARING ON POLITICAL BEHAVIOR

Objective conditions determining the attitudes and political behavior at every level—

Sex
Age
Race
Education
Religion
Nationality
Place of childhood
Family influences
Job
Economic level
Organizations
Informal associations
Mass media
etc.

Level 1:
Political behavior

Political Behavior
Vote? For whom?
Participation in campaign? etc.

Attitudes toward parties, issues, candidates

Level 2:
Immediate, direct attitudinal determinants

Level 3:
Attitudes toward political activities

Interest in political activities

Degree of pro-labor political orientation

Level 4:
More general attitudes toward union and politics

Feeling of political effectiveness or futility

Attachment to the union

Level 5:
Basic attitudes related to social behavior

Feelings of social alienation ("anomie")

Satisfaction with life

Authoritarian attitudes

the chart. These categories are obviously not exhaustive; they are, however, illustrative of important motivational dispositions at successively more general or basic levels. One cannot, of course, think of these various attitudes as independent of one another; they are different aspects or foci of single complex motivational systems within the people studied. As this implies, moreover, the attitudes certainly do not arrange themselves in neatly ordered arrays; they have intricate mutual interdependencies that defy the rigid boxes and connecting lines of a chart. Depicting of their interrelatedness is one of the tasks for research. The same is true of the complex relations between the objective determinants and the attitudes. On all these matters we can offer merely some suggestive findings. However, it is our belief that even these preliminary results may contribute a little to increased understanding and possible practical applications.

Members' Attitudes Toward Labor Political Activities

Within the frame of reference sketched above, we shall begin by considering the attitudes at Level 3, attitudes toward political activities. Levels 1 and 2 have been dealt with in previous chapters and will be brought in again from time to time as we relate them to the other attitudes and dispositions. The two sets of attitudes at Level 3 are primary concerns of union political efforts—to have members agree with the union's overall position and to have them feel politically aroused. Our first question, then, is this: To what extent do the union members agree with and support the political position and activities of their organization? Do they perceive their own interests and goals vis à vis those of business groups in a way that points toward a need for political action by labor? Or, by contrast, do they look upon themselves as identical with all other citizens, devoid of differentiating interests, with no inclination to choose politically between the views of employers and unions or to agree with one rather than the other?

The answer to these questions was provided partially and indirectly by the evidence in Chapter 2. It became apparent there that the great majority of UAW members in the Detroit area voted and voiced opinions in a manner that corresponded to the union's recommendations. Although a sizable minority of approximately 25 per cent voted for Eisenhower contrary to the union's stand, the proportion voting Republican for state offices and the number expressing a Republican party leaning was considerably smaller (less than 15 per cent). A still larger majority of those voting on the state reapportionment proposals voted in accordance with the union position (approximately 90 per cent of those who voted on the issue). Examination of the reasons for Stevenson and Eisenhower votes, and feelings expressed about the issues (see pp. 51-69), reveals frequent mention of views that correspond with the content of the union's campaign regarding candidates and issues. The responses contain numerous references to economic interests on which there is believed to be opposition between working people on one side and businessmen and people of wealth on the other side.

Several Key Questions on Attitudes Concerning the Union's Political Activities

It seemed desirable to go beyond the scattered evidence produced by these questions that have been cited in order (1) to secure more definite, direct expressions of opinion in regard to the union's political activities, and (2) to ascertain the degree to which the members' views imply support for one or another type of union political program, or for no such program.

Three key questions are employed here to indicate members' attitudes toward the organization's political activity.

1. The most direct question was:

"During the Presidential campaign, many labor unions were for Stevenson, and many businessmen and business groups were for Eisenhower. Do you think it was all right for the unions to work to get Stevenson elected, or that it was not all right?"

The responses are summarized in Table 4.1.

TABLE 4.1

ATTITUDES TOWARD LABOR POLITICAL ACTION
IN THE CAMPAIGN

Was it all right for the unions to work for Stevenson?

	Stevenson Voters	Eisenhower Voters	Did Not Vote	Total Sample
All right	87%	53%	73%	78%
Not all right	6	33	15	14
Can't say; no answer; other	7	14	12	8
	100%	100%	100%	100%
No. of cases	(170)	(116)	(65)	(351)

A parallel question asked:

"As you know, many businessmen and business groups were for Eisenhower. Do you think it was all right for businessmen and business groups to work to get Eisenhower elected, or that it was not all right?"

A tabulation of replies is given in Table 4.2.

TABLE 4.2

ATTITUDES TOWARD POLITICAL ACTION BY BUSINESS
IN THE CAMPAIGN

Was it all right for businessmen and business groups to work for Eisenhower?

	Stevenson Voters	Eisenhower Voters	Did Not Vote	Total Sample
All right	79%	80%	70%	78%
Not all right	12	11	12	12
Can't say; no answer; other	9	9	18	10
	100%	100%	100%	100%
No. of cases	(170)	(116)	(65)	(351)

Reference to the last column in Table 4.1 shows that only one union member in seven said that it was not all right for the union to work for Stevenson's election. Corresponding figures in

Table 4.2 indicate that still fewer believed that it was not all right for business groups to work for Eisenhower. But this trifling difference is much less important than the significant expression of overwhelming sentiment in favor of organized political participation in the presidential campaign *both* by unions and by business. From the standpoint of our primary question concerning members' approval or disapproval of the union's political activity, the answer is clear that a very great majority do approve.

The difference between Stevenson and Eisenhower voters in Table 4.1 is substantial and in the expected direction. Nevertheless it is notable that even among Eisenhower voters in the union a decided majority thought it all right for the union to campaign for Stevenson.

The disappearance of difference between Stevenson and Eisenhower voters in Table 4.2 probably occurred because the question concerning business followed the other; considerations of fairness and consistency impelled many pro-Stevenson members to grant the same right to businessmen that they had just claimed for the union. Despite this tendency, however, it is apparent that some persons responded differently in regard to labor and to business—for example, note the excess of the 80 per cent of Eisenhower voters favoring business participation over the 53 per cent accepting union participation, and the 12 per cent versus 6 per cent of Stevenson voters expressing disapproval of political action by business and labor respectively.

These persons who said it was all right for one group to be in politics but not for the other constitute two extremely partisan minority sections of the union membership, of approximately equal size. The percentages taking these positions are as follows:

All right for unions but not for business	12%
All right for business but not for unions	11%
All other responses	77%

We compared the two extreme groups on a number of characteristics to see how they differ from other union members. The analysis points to these differences:

Among Members Saying All Right for Unions but Not for Business

Especially strongly Democratic (88%); 90% for Stevenson (of the Eisenhower-Stevenson vote)

High proportion of non-voters (22%)

Below average scores on Political Interest

Slightly below average in Union Attachment and Interest

Many women (31%)

More than average number semi-skilled; few skilled and white collar

Less education than average (especially less than 8th grade)

Average age

Decidedly more than average have Authoritarian attitudes and feelings of Social Alienation

Among Members Saying All Right for Business but Not for Unions

Far below average in Democratic strength (52%); 69% for Eisenhower (of the Eisenhower-Stevenson vote)

Below average number of non-voters (9%)

Slightly above average on Political Interest

Decidedly below average in Union Attachment and Interest

Almost no women (5%)

More than average number skilled and white collar

Slightly below average education

More of older (past 45)

Somewhat more than average have Authoritarian attitudes and feelings of Social Alienation

All in all, the pro-labor extreme partisans appear not so much an extremely ardent union group but rather poorly educated and socially alienated individuals; almost one-third are women; more than average numbers are Democratic and opposed to business influence in politics but they are without strong union loyalty, active political interest or readiness to participate. The extreme business-partisan group, on the other hand, is made up of older men, substantial numbers of skilled and white collar workers, many Republicans and members with slight loyalty to the union; they tend to be somewhat inclined toward feelings of personal futility or alienation and toward authoritarian attitudes, but they are above average in political interest and voting participation.

The foregoing conclusions are suggestive only. The groups are small and we have not pushed the analysis far since answers to the question on support of candidates by unions and business comprise part of a more inclusive score on attitudes toward labor's political position which will be described later in this section of our report. More thorough analyses making use of this inclusive score will occupy much of our attention in this and the following chapter.

We return now to some additional replies of the whole sample to the two general questions under discussion. Each person interviewed, after he had answered the main question about unions and the parallel one about business by saying that he thought it "all right" or "not all right," was asked: "Why do you feel that way?" A classification of the reasons given for favoring or opposing political action (see Tables D.1 and D.2 in the Appendix) shows frequent mention of the interests of workingmen, the view that Democrats and Stevenson are for unions and labor, whereas Republicans are for business, and similar reflections of belief in opposed group interests. Approximately half the reasons expressed are of this nature and most of the remaining ones are indefinite or mere reiterations that it is proper for unions and business to support their chosen candidates. Of the reasons for opposing union political activities the only ones that went beyond very general and indefinite comments and that were offered by more than one per cent of the members were these: that political pressure groups are undesirable, that unions are not justified in spending members' money in political campaigns, and that people should be allowed to make up their own minds. Objections to business groups in politics were quite general for the most part (business should not be in politics; business is anti-union, etc.); the only specific feeling voiced by several members was that business put too much money into the campaign, "they went too far."

Still further qualitative opinions were sought by asking those members who approved political action by unions (or business), "Were there any things the unions [businessmen and business groups] did in the election campaign that you didn't like? (If yes) What things?" In answer to these questions, 14 per cent of the members expressed criticisms of union campaign activities and 15 per cent criticized things that business did. These results and the division by Stevenson and Eisenhower voters are shown in Table 4.3. All these figures are over and above the corresponding ones expressing negative reactions ("not all right") in Tables 4.1 and 4.2.

TABLE 4.3

AMOUNT OF DISAPPROVAL OF UNION AND BUSINESS ACTIVITIES IN ELECTION CAMPAIGN*

	Stevenson Voters	Eisenhower Voters	Did Not Vote	Total Sample
Did not like some things unions did	13%	24%	7%	14%
Did not like some things business did	19	11	1	15
No. of cases	(170)	(116)	(65)	(351)

* Asked only of persons approving union or business political activity respectively.

The principal things named as not liked about the union's political activities are:

> They forced leaflets (or buttons) on you.
> Spent union dues and took men out of the shop to work for PAC.
> Over-emphasized depression fears.
> Tried to tell you how to vote.

The main criticisms of campaign activities by business are:

> Too much slander and mudslinging.
> Contributed too much money.
> Criticized the Democrats too much.
> Tied up media of information (radio, TV, newspapers).

2. The second of the three key questions on attitudes about union political activities aimed to learn whether the workers trust or distrust the union's political recommendations and how their willingness to accept the union leadership compares with their feeling about other groups who support candidates. This set of questions came earlier in the interview than the direct questions described above under 1. The questioning took this form:

> a. In election campaigns, different groups work for one candidate or another. Are there any groups on this list [respondent was given card listing the following: business groups, church groups, labor groups, veterans groups,

daily newspapers and fraternal organizations] that you
particularly trust—that is, you'd be more likely to vote
for candidates they recommend? Which group?

b. Why is it that you particularly trust recommendations by
[each group named]?

c. Are there any groups on the list that you don't trust,
that is, you'd be more likely to vote against candidates
they recommend? Which groups?

d. Why don't you trust [each group named]?

Tables 4.4, 4.5 and 4.6 summarize the results obtained from
the trust-distrust questions.

TABLE 4.4

GROUP TRUSTED AS TO THEIR VOTING RECOMMENDATIONS

Groups you *particularly trust* (6 groups presented to respondent)

	Stevenson Voters	Eisenhower Voters	Did Not Vote	Total Sample
Labor groups	62%*	10%*	49%*	49%*
Church groups	41	26	41	38
Veterans groups	36	24	25	32
Fraternal organizations	19	18	19	18
Newspapers	4	22	15	9
Business groups	4	15	14	7
No. of cases	(170)	(116)	(65)	(351)

* Percentages are based on all eligible voters in the post-election sample.
Percentages again total more than 100% since many respondents named
more than one group.

In each table, the final column is most important since it gives
the picture for the union members as a whole. Looking at these
last-column figures in Table 4.4, the outstanding fact is the high
position of Labor groups and the low position of Business and
Newspapers. The percentage differences are large and significant. Very favorable opinions are also expressed regarding recommendations of Church groups and Veterans organizations—
with Stevenson voters reacting more favorably than Eisenhower
voters. It is to be remembered that all the figures represent
answers to the question phrased, "Are there any groups in this
list that you particularly trust?" Respondents were thus free to

name none they particularly trusted (26 per cent were in this category); moreover, failure to name a group does not mean that the respondent was necessarily indicating *distrust* but only that he did not select this group as one "particularly trusted." With these facts in mind, the 49 per cent naming Labor groups can be considered clear positive support of union endorsements, especially by contrast with the decidedly smaller percentages naming other groups as trusted.

TABLE 4.5

GROUPS NOT TRUSTED AS TO THEIR VOTING
RECOMMENDATIONS

Groups you do *not trust* (6 groups presented to respondent)

	Stevenson Voters	Eisenhower Voters	Did Not Vote	Total Sample
Newspapers	57%*	22%*	31%*	46%*
Business groups	43	19	23	35
Labor groups	7	32	8	12
Fraternal organizations	11	7	8	10
Church groups	9	11	7	9
Veterans groups	5	11	5	8
No. of cases	(170)	(116)	(65)	(351)

* See note at Table 4.4.

This interpretation receives further confirmation in Table 4.5. Here Newspapers and Business are seen to be much more frequently distrusted than Labor or any other group in the list. Only 12 per cent express *distrust* of Labor recommendations as against 49 per cent expressing trust; corresponding percentages for Business and Newspapers run strongly in the reverse direction (46 per cent distrust to 9 per cent trust for Newspapers and 35 per cent distrust to 7 per cent trust for Business groups). There is greater willingness (or ability) to express definite attitudes pro or con Labor groups than toward Business: 61 per cent either trust or distrust Labor as against 42 per cent in the case of Business. The difference may reflect a state of ambivalence in respect to Business leadership, a not unnatural condition in view of the cross-pressures and counter-pulls to which working people are exposed in this connection. It is important to note further that among the 12 per cent who distrust Labor, 7 per cent also distrust Business. In addition to all the percentages of distrust of particular groups, another 2 per cent of the sample say that they distrust them all; 41 per cent do not express distrust of any groups.

TABLE 4.6

RELATIVE TRUST-DISTRUST OF GROUPS' VOTING RECOMMENDATIONS

Percentage Index of Trust vs. Distrust*

	Stevenson Voters	Eisenhower Voters	Did Not Vote	Total Sample
Veterans groups	87%	69%	82%	83%
Labor groups	90	24	86	80
Church groups	81	70	86	80
Fraternal organizations	63	72	64	65
Business groups	8	44	37	18
Newspapers	6	50	32	17

* The index is the number trusting a group as a percentage of all who express either trust or distrust of that group. For example, the first index (87%) is arrived at as follows: 127 Stevenson voters (the figures have been weighted to make them representative of our total sample) chose "Veterans'" as a group they "particularly trust"; 19 others said it is a group they "do not trust"; 127 is found to be 87% of (127 + 19).

Comparison of Stevenson and Eisenhower voters in Tables 4.4 and 4.5 calls attention to the wide difference of attitudes between the union majority and the dissenting pro-Eisenhower minority. Labor recommendations are trusted by 62 per cent of Stevenson voters as against a mere 10 per cent of Eisenhower voters. Distrust of Labor recommendations is expressed by only 7 per cent of the pro-Stevenson workers and by 32 per cent of those for Eisenhower. In fact, Eisenhower voters more frequently trust Newspaper and Business recommendations than those of Labor (though these percentages all remain small) and they likewise *distrust* Labor groups more than any other. A striking tendency is evident for the Eisenhower voters to have low percentages trusting *any* of the groups (Table 4.4); they tend to be "men without a country," politically speaking. Thirty-six per cent of them mention *no* group whose recommendations they trust as compared with only 19 per cent of Stevenson voters unwilling to trust any group. The popular image of Eisenhower as a man above party and group interests would naturally have unusually strong appeal to workers characterized by these attitudes.[2]

Table 4.6 combines the data used in Tables 4.4 and 4.5 to bring out contrasts in the relative esteem in which the several endorsing groups are held. The index we have used in Table 4.6 is simply a percentage showing the ratio of those who "particularly trust" a group to the number who name it *either* as trusted or not trusted. That is, we add together the number who "trust" and the number who do "not trust" the group and express the number who trust as a percentage of the sum. (See example under Table 4.6.) If this index is above 50 per cent it means that more people trust than distrust the group; when it is below 50 per cent it means a preponderance of distrust over trust. Inspection of the figures in the last column of Table 4.6 shows Labor, Veterans and Church groups with very high indexes of trust; Business groups and Newspapers have very low indexes. The contrast may also be stated in the form of ratios of trust to distrust:

4 to 1 *trust* Labor recommendation.
4½ to 1 *distrust* Business recommendation.
5 to 1 *distrust* Newspaper recommendations.[3]

These trust-distrust questions also yielded interesting qualitative information in the *reasons* the members gave for trusting or not trusting voting recommendations by the different groups. Data from these answers to the "why" questions are contained in Tables D.3 to D.8 in the Appendix. In respect to Labor and Business groups, which are most directly relevant for our purposes, the principal conclusion from the tables is simply this: that the reasons predominantly express belief in opposed group interests and a sense of belonging to, or being identified with,

---

[2] For data and discussion bearing on this point see Herbert H. Hyman and Paul B. Sheatsley, "The Political Appeal of President Eisenhower," *Public Opinion Quarterly*, Vol. 17, No. 4 (Winter, 1953-54), pp. 443-460.

[3] Newspapers likewise received a definitely unfavorable ratio of trust to distrust responses in the question concerning media. See pp. 89-91.

one side. As to why Labor group recommendations are trusted, for example, far and away the most frequent answers were in these two categories:

> They know who has done most for workers; for the poor man.
> They're my class of people; I'm a labor man; they represent my interests.

Similarly, the leading reasons for distrusting Business groups were:

> They favor anti-labor party; are anti-labor; don't represent workers' interests; they don't have same interests I have.
> Selfish; only want to make money; only for candidates who are just pro-business.

On the other side, but with a relatively small number of such responses, those trusting Business and distrusting Labor, gave such answers as these:

> What's good for business is good for country; country built by business; what they do helps us.

And concerning distrust of Labor, the few reasons are:

> Selfish; try to get candidates who are just pro-union.
> Too much propaganda.
> Should not be in politics.

Opinions regarding Newspaper recommendations are frequently in the same vein. Aside from comments on bias or fairness of news reporting, which are irrelevant to the question asked, the principal ideas expressed on Newspapers are:

> Too pro-Republican; controlled by Republicans; always smearing Democrats; with the wrong party or side.
> Aligned with business group; for the big guys.
> Anti-labor; don't represent labor.
> For themselves only.
> Advertisers control policy.

The findings on this entire question indicate that the most generally accepted position among UAW members is one of trusting union voting recommendations and distrusting those offered by Business and Newspapers. The declarations of trust and distrust, along with the reasons assigned, leave little doubt that a large sector of the membership (approximately one half of all members) feels that they have political interests opposed to those of Business and Newspapers, interests that they can protect and advance by supporting the union's position on the political front. At the same time it is clear that a small but significantly numerous group in the union holds dissenting opinions and does not trust union political recommendations; they include a minimum of one in eight who *express* distrust (and presumably some others who refrain from stating their views). The remaining 30 to 40 per cent of the members are the uncommitted—people who are not prepared to declare themselves as either trusting or distrusting political endorsements by Labor groups. Most of them fall into the 41 per cent of respondents who refrained from naming *any* group they do not trust. They constitute a considerable portion of the union, the politically less aroused and less partisan, who presumably will go along with the union in any particular election or will not, depending upon the social forces and cross-pressures affecting them at the time. We shall have much more to say later about these people who are weakly identified with the union politically; they will be singled out, however, on the basis of their answers to several questions rather than taking their response to the trust-distrust question alone.

Before leaving the present set of results, it is worth pointing out that they call seriously into question the conclusions that have been drawn from research studies of recent years to the effect that workers feel the aims of unions and management to be harmonious and that they feel favorable to the objectives of *both* their company and their union (so-called "dual allegiance").[4] Our findings suggest that it may depend on what

---

[4] See, for example, "Dual Allegiance to Union and Management: A Symposium," *Personnel Psychology*, Vol. 7, No. 1 (March 1954), pp. 41-80; also L. R. Dean, "Union Activity and Dual Loyalty," *Industrial and Labor Relations Review*, Vol. 7 (1954), pp. 526-536.

range of company and union aims one considers. The typical employee attitude survey, on which conclusions of the kind mentioned are based, inquires only into employment relations and organizational goals *within the company-union situation.* Employees may (or may not) approve management purposes and achievements in running the business and yet diverge sharply from their social and political goals. If social scientists are to generalize concerning an absence of felt opposition, it is surely necessary to explore all important areas of possible disagreement. Within our sample and with questions pertaining to political recommendations, no support is found for the view that workers tend to favor *both* sides. Of the 49 per cent who "particularly trust" Labor groups, only a scattered few (less than 4 per cent) indicate that they trust recommendations of *both* Labor and Business groups. These statistics certainly do not support any notion of "dual loyalty" on the political level.

3. The last of the three questions to be examined here, though no less significant than the preceding ones, can be treated more briefly. The two parts of the question follow:

> Would you like to see labor unions have *more* to say or *less* to say about things the government does that are important to working people?

> Would you like to see businessmen and business groups have *more* to say or *less* to say about things the government does that are important to working people?

The replies are summarized in Tables 4.7 and 4.8.

TABLE 4.7

ATTITUDES CONCERNING AMOUNT OF INFLUENCE UNIONS
SHOULD HAVE ON GOVERNMENT

Unions should have:	Stevenson Voters	Eisenhower Voters	Did Not Vote	Total Sample
More to say	68%	27%	41%	55%
Less to say	7	33	16	14
Neither more nor less	16	26	16	18
Can't say; no answer	9	14	27	13
	100%	100%	100%	100%
No. of cases	(170)	(116)	(65)	(351)

TABLE 4.8

ATTITUDES CONCERNING AMOUNT OF INFLUENCE BUSINESS
SHOULD HAVE ON GOVERNMENT

Business should have:	Stevenson Voters	Eisenhower Voters	Did Not Vote	Total Sample
More to say	18%	29%	8%	19%
Less to say	45	31	42	41
Neither more nor less	21	27	24	23
Can't say; no answer	16	13	26	17
	100%	100%	100%	100%
No. of cases	(170)	(116)	(65)	(351)

If we focus first on the columns for the total sample, it is apparent that the findings are consistent with the results from previous questions. The responses predominantly express loyalty to labor's political objective of having greater voice in governmental decisions important to working people. A clear majority declare that unions should have more to say, while only one member in seven says they should have less. Here again, opinions regarding businessmen and business groups are correspondingly unfavorable, though not quite as preponderantly in the negative direction as the union responses are on the positive side. The union members, that is, are more clearly for the union having "more to say" than for business having "less to say." This may reflect a feeling on the part of many that in a democratic society *no* group should have *less* voice but rather that those having excessive power should be balanced by *increasing* the influence of opposed groups. Nevertheless, if we consider only those persons whose opinion definitely favors greater or less influence by labor unions, the vote is 4 to 1 that they should have *more* to say while the corresponding vote in regard to business groups is slightly over 2 to 1 that they should have *less* influence.

Another type of analysis would indicate that the contrast is more extreme than that just presented. The figures in Tables 4.7 and 4.8 include many cases where the respondent advocated either greater or smaller influence for *both* labor and business. While these replies are not necessarily inconsistent or illogical, the answer that applies to labor or to business does assume a different meaning by virtue of an identical response to the parallel question pertaining to the other party. Thus, for example, the 19 per cent who say that business should have more to say turns out to include 13 per cent who are of the opinion that labor unions should also have more to say. If we eliminate all the responses that suggest greater influence for both (13 per cent), since they contain no clue as to whether either is thought to have excessive power relative to the other, it leaves us with the following percentages (in place of the 55 per cent vs. 19 per cent of the tables):

> 42% think that *unions* should have more to say, without also believing that business should.
>
> 6% think that *business* should have more to say, without also believing that unions should.

In the same manner, if we eliminate the 8 per cent who state that both labor unions and business should have *less* to say, the following percentages remain:

> 6% think that *unions* should have less to say, without also believing that business should.
>
> 33% believe that *business* should have less to say, without also believing that unions should.

Neither the position that advocates more influence for both labor and business nor less influence for both can well be interpreted as according with a strong labor political outlook. Consequently, in constructing a score to represent degree of agreement with labor's political position, these answers will be scored in a way that does not increase an individual's total pro-labor rating.

Examination of the columns for Stevenson voters and Eisenhower voters in Tables 4.7 and 4.8 again shows large differences in the expected directions. Perhaps the only source of surprise is that so many Eisenhower voters thought that business should have less to say. This finding is due in great measure to the presence of double-edged replies advocating less influence for *both* business and labor. Half of the 30 per cent of Eisenhower voters answering that business should have less to say were workers who also stated that unions should have less to say. This may make more readily understandable any seeming inconsistency between their vote and their attitude that business should have less influence. As to the remaining half of persons in this category, an inspection of their reasons for voting for Eisenhower reveals no explanation. The reasons they assign for their vote conform closely to the general run of reasons given by other respondents (see Tables 2.24 and 2.26). Apparently these people either did not believe that an Eisenhower victory would run counter to their desire to see business influence reduced or their preference for Eisenhower was strong enough to overcome any such opposing consideration. In any event, it is important to notice that substantial numbers of Eisenhower voters were in full agreement with their Stevenson-supporting fellow members in wanting to see the political influence of unions increase and that of business groups decrease.

Results have been summarized in this section based on answers to three sets of questions about the participation of unions and business groups in politics. The findings as a whole indicate that UAW members predominantly approve and support their union's political viewpoint. A large part of the membership trusts union election recommendations and would like to see labor unions have a larger voice in governmental affairs. Many of these members at the same time express negative attitudes toward business leadership on the political front.

On all these matters, however, there exists a small dissenting group within the union, amounting to some 10 to 20 per cent, and a somewhat larger group (perhaps one-fourth to one-third) of uncommitted and ambivalent members who are neither for nor against the broad political goals of the union but who probably go along for the most part, as they did in the '52 election, with the prevalent union sentiment on candidates and issues. It is probably this unsure group, however, that would include voters most likely to swing to a non-union position in local and national elections where the cross-pressures (in respect to war fears, taxes, Negro residential opportunities, domestic Communism, etc.) become intensified and where the members may be brought to feel that their own security as home owners, as parents, as tax-payers, as white Protestants or Catholics, or as Negroes, are endangered. The importance of the dissenting and uncommitted portions of the union membership is not to be dismissed or played down. The future role of unionism in public affairs may depend in no small measure upon the extent to which the support of these groups is won or lost by labor organizations.

Our results certainly offer no support for statements of a kind not infrequently made to the effect that union members in general do not trust or voluntarily follow their union leadership, particularly in the political arena. While it is true that substantial numbers of members are negative or on the fence, our evidence justifies the conclusion that among UAW members in the Detroit area the prevailing attitudes are decidedly positive in regard to the union's political activities. The preponderance of pro-labor attitudes is especially clear; somewhat fewer members express opinions in opposition to business political influence. This last fact may or may not be due to the strenuous public relations and communications efforts of the business community over recent years. On all these matters, our data furnish useful bench marks against which it will be enlightening to measure unionists' attitudes, say, in 1956, 1960 and later.

A Rating of Pro-Labor Political Orientation

Responses on the three sets of questions examined in the preceding section were combined to yield a score or rating for each individual. This rating is intended to show to what extent the union member is in accord with certain salient features of labor organizations' political outlook. A rating based on several related questions tends to be a more stable and reliable measure than is the response to a single question; it provides a more balanced, composite picture of the person's feelings, in this instance concerning the union's political role. The present rating, along with others to be described, will enable us to make instructive comparisons among the differing opinion groups of which the union is composed.

The rating of attitude toward union political activities gives us a simple numerical score running from 0 to 8. (Detailed description of the scoring procedure is included in Appendix C.) A rating of 0 means that the person does not go along with or endorse labor's political efforts, that he reacts negatively to the union on at least two of the three questions or that he expresses

116   *When Labor Votes*

preference for political leadership by business groups. At the
other extreme, an 8 rating signifies responses fully favorable to
union political action on at least two questions, with no offsetting
anti-union or pro-business response.

A few examples will make the meaning of the ratings more
concrete:

> Member K—Rating 0
>> All right for both unions and business to work for their
>> candidates.
>> Trusts neither.
>> Like to see unions have less to say and business have
>> more to say.
>
> Member L—Rating 2
>> All right for unions to work for Stevenson and qualified
>> approval of business for Eisenhower.
>> Trusts business recommendations but not labor's.
>> Influence of both should remain as it is.
>
> Member M—Rating 4
>> All right for both to back candidates.
>> Trusts recommendations of *both* groups.
>> Thinks *neither* should have more or less to say; stay
>> as they are now.
>
> Member N—Rating 6
>> All right for union, not for business, to back candidate.
>> Trusts recommendations of both groups.
>> Like to see unions have more to say and busines have
>> less to say.
>
> Member P—Rating 8
>> All right for both unions and business to work for their
>> candidates (willingness to let business work for
>> Eisenhower is not scored as pro-business since it
>> seems to be viewed simply as fair play).
>> Trusts labor recommendations; distrusts those of busi-
>> ness.
>> Like to see unions have more to say and business have
>> less to say.

For purposes of this rating, then, we have used three elements
thought to be important characteristics of a pro-labor political
position:

> Approval of the union's working for Stevenson.
> Feeling of trust in union political recommendations (with
> no expression of similar trust in recommendations by
> business groups).

Desire to see labor have *more* to say, and business *less* to say, about governmental actions affecting working people.

Obviously these do not represent the entire political position of organized labor, not even all that is fundamental. Nevertheless, these are three important components, sufficiently indicative for our present exploratory purpose.

The proportion of members receiving each score or rating is as follows:

Rating of Pro-Labor Political Orientation	Per Cent of Union Members
8	26%
7	17
6	12
5	14
4	10
3	6
2	5
1	4
0	6
	100%

Although any particular grouping of these ratings is bound to be somewhat arbitrary, we believe that the answers leading to different scores make the following grouping most reasonable.[5]

Strongly pro-labor (Ratings 6, 7, 8)	55%
Intermediate (Ratings 4, 5)	24%
Not pro-labor—including anti-labor (Ratings 0, 1, 2, 3)	21%

A grouping of this kind again calls attention to the large "on-side" section of the union membership, while at the same time it indicates the sizable "off-side" minority and the equal minority of "in-betweens" who only partially identify with the union politically.

---

[5] "Strongly pro-labor" ratings in this classification typically signify that the worker approves of unions working for their political candidates, that he trusts the political recommendations of labor and not those of business and/or he is in favor of unions having greater influence on government and business *not* having more influence. A person in the low-rating group, the "not pro-labor" group, typically gives answers indicating that he does not think unions should work for the election of a candidate or that he does not trust labor political recommendations (or does trust those of business) and/or that he does not want labor to have more to say in government (or that he does want business to have greater influence).

If we go behind these figures and keep in mind the content of the responses which enter into the ratings, the simple classification above points to conclusions of far-reaching importance. It should be remembered that this is a picture of the political orientation and allegiance not of union leaders and intellectuals but of rank and file UAW members, by the tens of thousands. What it signifies is that somewhat more than half of these union members definitely view the labor union as representing their broad political interests; they trust the leadership's voting recommendations and they want the unions to have greater influence on government. Most of the members of this majority group see business (and newspapers) as offering political leadership that is not to be followed, and they want to see the political influence of business curtailed. The evidence suggests that most of these people see the political world in terms of opposed goals and group interests as between organized labor and business. The findings indicate that the unionism of these UAW members extends a long distance beyond simple job-centered concerns and, as stated before, it is even farther from the currently popular philosophy of emerging unity, basic harmony, and "dual allegiance."

The preceding comments apply to a majority of the union members; the views outlined appear to reflect the main tone of political thought in the union. But there are also the other two categories of members. One member in five is politically opposed to the position sketched; he is either critical of the union's political participation, or at least is disinclined to trust its voting advice and is against any increase of political power of labor in comparison with that of business. An additional one-fourth of the membership is non-committal, ambivalent, or uncertain. Most of these members approve union political action but they have doubts and qualifications about following labor leadership or rejecting business leadership in political affairs. They tend to take a middle position of neither particularly trusting (or distrusting) *both* labor and business; of wishing to see *both* have more influence or less influence. In the main, it appears reasonable to expect that they will go along with prevailing attitudes and that they will exercise relatively slight influence in the union.

Further analysis shows that pro-labor political feelings are by no means distributed at random among the union members. The most pronounced tendencies are for pro-labor orientation to be strong among Negroes, among workers of low socio-economic status,[6] and among younger union members (age under 40). There is some indication, that is, that the less privileged groups and those in relatively unfavorable economic positions are more pro-union politically. The fact that the younger generation of workers is more pro-labor than the older probably reflects the influence of the depression and the New Deal during their formative years. In any event, the data refute the idea that the loyal union members, at least in respect to political action, are to be found mainly among the old-timers who grew up with the organization.

By considering combinations of the aforementioned characteristics (along with religious affiliation and amount of education) we discover groupings of union members who manifest particularly high or low proportions of pro-labor political sentiment. Several of the most pro-labor and least pro-labor categories are the following:

	Per Cent Strongly Pro-Labor
Most Pro-Labor	
Under 40 years of age, relatively low socio-economic level	73%
Under 40 and 8th grade or less	72%
More than 8th grade education; relatively low socio-economic level	69%
All Negroes	81%
Least Pro-Labor	
8th grade or less, relatively high socio-economic level	37%
40 and over, Protestant, relatively high socio-economic level	25%
40 and over, Catholic, 8th grade or less	34%

This last group in the list, the older Catholics, highlights the fact that education has quite different relations to political attitudes, depending upon other characteristics of the group. Among both Catholics and Protestants under 40 years of age, those with eighth grade schooling or less are a little more pro-

---

[6] See footnote 12, p. 44.

labor politically than are the better educated. For workers over 40, education makes little difference if they are Protestants but a very large difference appears among Catholics, with those of limited schooling having only 34 per cent strongly pro-labor, while those of more than eighth grade education have almost double that proportion (63 per cent) who express strongly pro-labor political sentiments. A reasonable explanation may lie in the large number of first generation immigrants among the older, less educated Catholics—and the disinclination of these people to take any strong political stand. In any event, it is notably within this group (and in the high socio-economic category) that the less educated are also the less pro-union politically.

TABLE 4.9

PRESIDENTIAL VOTE IN RELATION TO RATING
OF PRO-LABOR POLITICAL ORIENTATION

Voted for:	Political Orientation		
	Strongly Pro-Labor	Intermediate	Not Pro-Labor
Stevenson	80%	66%	29%
Eisenhower	6	24	61
Did not vote, etc.	14	10	10
	100%	100%	100%
No. of cases	(157)	(83)	(98)

Returning now to the political rating itself, the question may be asked: Does this rating represent something "real," something that affects behavior, that makes a difference? Our assumption is that it does. What we seek is a measure that indicates the general political outlook as this is manifested in varied forms of political behavior and attitudes, most notably in elections. We are trying to look beyond or beneath *particular* voting decisions, like those for Stevenson or Eisenhower. Our hypothesis is that the rating of political orientation provides a relatively stable and generalized measure of certain core elements of union members' political disposition and that as such it should relate rather closely to their voting behavior. The way the people in our sample voted for President in 1952, should, therefore, offer a first rate test of whether their choice of candidate does in fact correspond to their general political outlook as represented in our rating. Table 4.9 contains the results of this test.

The high degree of relationship shown in this table provides considerable support for the use of our political rating. It indicates that this index of general political outlook does correspond to differences in voting behavior. If we take still more extreme scores on the index than those used in the table, the Stevenson-Eisenhower vote goes 95 per cent for Stevenson among the very strongly labor-oriented as against 15 per cent for Stevenson and 85 per cent for Eisenhower in the group having the least pro-labor political orientation. Although the usefulness of the rating lies in its more general character, which transcends any particular vote, the results obtained here add to the confidence with which the rating can be counted on to be indicative of unionists' political behavior in other situations.

It is also interesting to look at the data used in Table 4.9 when the question is asked: How do Stevenson and Eisenhower voters and non-voters differ in their political ratings? This converse relationship is shown in Table 4.10.

TABLE 4.10

RATING OF PRO-LABOR POLITICAL ORIENTATION
IN RELATION TO PRESIDENTIAL VOTE

Political attitude	Stevenson Voters	Eisenhower Voters	Did Not Vote	Total Sample
Strongly pro-labor	67%	16%	62%	55%
Intermediate	24	25	21	24
Not pro-labor	9	59	17	21
	100%	100%	100%	100%
No. of cases	(167)	(114)	(57)	(338)

This table again brings out the striking contrast between Eisenhower and Stevenson voters. It is further to be noted that the eligible non-voters are very nearly as high as the Stevenson voters in their ratings of pro-labor political orientation. The failure of these members to register and vote is evidently not associated with any estrangement from a labor political position.

Actually, as may be seen in Table 4.9, the proportion of non-voters is a trifle higher among the strongly pro-union members than among others (though this is not a statistically reliable difference). Evidently a strongly pro-labor political position is no guarantee of effective political participation as manifested by the act of voting.

The small group of persons who were *undecided* about their vote during the weeks before the election turn out to have ratings of pro-labor political attitudes just about midway between those of Stevenson voters and Eisenhower voters (strongly pro-union, 30 per cent; intermediate, 34 per cent; not pro-union, 36 per cent). Their ratings as a whole thus run considerably lower in pro-labor attitudes than those for the union as a whole. To what extent they were undecided *because* of their partial disagreement with the union we cannot say. But the relationship is interesting in its exposure of these late "undecideds" as union members who are neither as "on-side" as the Stevenson supporters nor as preponderantly "off-side" as the Eisenhower supporters. Their group picture fits the expected pattern of people under cross-pressures, people in conflict.

At this point we can temporarily place this political rating on ice; we shall make extensive use of it later.

Degree of Political Interest by Union Members

In assessing the support for labor political action by union members it is not enough to look only at the extent of their agreement with the action program. Unless they are also aroused and politically active, the program may not get far off the ground. Consequently we concluded that a second crucial variable to be measured in order to judge members' relationship to the union's political efforts is the degree of their concern and participation, their political information and interest, their freedom from indifference and apathy.

Some relevant findings have already been reported in Chapters 2 and 3. The most significant parts of this evidence plus responses to certain other relevant questions are brought together in this section of the report. These data will be combined into a second general rating or index paralleling that of the preceding section. Let us begin by listing the separate questions that contribute to a total rating. They can be grouped as follows:

Indications of active interest during the campaign

1. Doing anything to help (*E or S*) get elected (Pre-election interview).
2. Did anything to help (*E or S*) get elected (Post-election interview).
3. Talked with people about the election (Pre-election interview).
4. Talked with people about the election (Post-election interview).
5. Listened to candidates on radio or TV (Post-election interview).
6. Listened to other election speeches on radio or TV (Post-election interview).
7. Read about candidates and election in newspapers (Post-election interview).
8. Read about candidates and election in magazines, etc. (Post-election interview).

Information that reflects interest in the election

9. Know any of the campaign issues (Pre-election interview).
10. Know names of presidential and state candidates (Pre-election interview).
11. Know anything for and against presidential candidates (Pre-election interview).

Concern regarding the election outcome

12. Care who wins (Pre-election interview).
13. Any favorable or unfavorable feeling over the election results (Post-election interview).
14. Either glad or sorry that Eisenhower won (Post-election interview).

We shall comment on the findings from each of these questions in turn—very briefly for those previously reported and a little more fully for those introduced here for the first time.

Questions 1 and 2 may best be considered together. They are among the questions not previously discussed. The wording of each question is given below, together with a table showing how the question was answered (Tables 4.11 and 4.12).

1. Are you personally doing anything to help (*S or E*) get elected, like talking to people or anything like that? (If yes): What are you doing?
2. Did you personally do anything to help get (*S or E*) elected—like giving money for his campaign, telling people why they should vote for him, handing out leaflets or buttons, or anything like that? (If yes): What did you do?

TABLE 4.11

PRE-ELECTION REPORT OF PERSONAL PARTICIPATION
IN THE CAMPAIGN

	Vote Intention			
	Stevenson	*Eisenhower*	*Undecided; Refused to Say, etc.*	*Total Sample*
Not doing anything	50%	54%	91%	56%
Talk to people	44	41	7	38
Hand out leaflets, buttons, etc.	2	2	—	2
Display posters, wear button, etc.	2	—	1	2
Other answers	2	3	1	2
	100%	100%	100%	100%
No. of cases	(486)	(118)	(86)	(690)

For purposes of computing our political interest rating, the answers "not doing anything" and "did nothing" were scored zero while any other response to each question received a score of one.

The findings in Tables 4.11 and 4.12 reveal a lack of active participation or involvement on the part of most union members. Other studies have obtained similar results for quite different segments of the population. We have no reason to think that auto workers are below par in this regard. Nevertheless, in view of the union's vigorous political efforts, the extent of active participation by members may be considered rather limited. Aside from talking about the election, only 6 per cent before the election and 10 per cent afterward say they did anything to help elect their candidate.[7] Even with allowance for forgetting and non-reporting, it would appear that in 1952 the tie-in between approval of the union's political program and active personal involvement in the campaign was weak indeed.

TABLE 4.12

POST-ELECTION REPORT OF PERSONAL PARTICIPATION
IN THE CAMPAIGN

	Stevenson Voters	Eisenhower Voters	Did Not Vote	Total Sample
Did nothing	70%	70%	86%	73%
Talked to people	17	26	9	17
Handed out leaflets, etc.	6	2	4	5
Displayed posters, wore buttons, etc.	3	1	1	2
Gave money	3	1	—	2
Other answers	1	—	—	1
	100%	100%	100%	100%
No. of cases	(170)	(116)	(65)	(351)

This failure of the political program actively to involve more than a small number of members is also seen in certain of the findings reported in Chapter 3. For example, it may be recalled that only 7 per cent said that they got most of their "information about candidates and what they stand for" from union sources (p. 88). Similarly, only 7 per cent referred to union publications when asked, following a question about daily newspapers, "Did you read about the candidates and the election in any magazines or other papers?", and, "What magazines and other

---

[7] UAW officials estimate that 25 per cent of the members made campaign contributions to PAC (CIO's Political Action Committee). The large discrepancy between this figure, if correct, and the insignificant number of members in our sample who mentioned financial contributions is presumably due to errors of memory, to members thinking of their dollars to PAC as contributions to the *union* for political purposes and not as money for any particular candidate's campaign, and to other such reasons for not reporting their campaign gifts.

papers did you read?" (p. 83). In response to a question, "Were there any particular groups or organizations whose ideas you wanted to get before you decided how you would vote?", only 8 per cent named the union (almost none named any other organization) (p. 92).

Little difference is manifested between Stevenson and Eisenhower supporters in the findings reported in Tables 4.11 and 4.12, though slightly more Eisenhower voters report having talked in favor of their candidate while more Stevenson backers report that they handed out leaflets, displayed posters and buttons, or donated money. The union members who were undecided shortly before the election, or who refused to express a preference, were almost totally non-participants in the campaign. The same tendency is found in the post-election interview among non-voters; very few of them report any activity on behalf of a candidate.

The substantial difference in results between the two tables is to be accounted for partly by the time lapse and partly by the change of question wording. The latter is probably more important since the pre-election question clearly suggested the "talked to people" response. For this reason the results of Table 4.12 give a more realistic report of actual behavior.

Questions 3 to 8: All the remaining questions listed under evidences of interest during the campaign were dealt with in Chapter 3 (pp. 77-84). This earlier analysis brought out a number of facts which have bearing on our present concern with assessing degrees of political interest. Question by question, the relevant results to be utilized here are these:

   3. Within the past few weeks, have you talked politics with anyone? (If yes): Who did you talk with?

65 per cent of registered voters answered in the affirmative; 35 per cent said they had talked with no one.

   4. In the weeks before the election, did you talk with any people about the election and the candidates? (If yes): What people did you talk with?

Since this question included the days just before the election, it is natural that the percentage of affirmative replies increased.

Only 22 per cent now reported not having talked with anyone; 78 per cent had talked with others.

For both questions 3 and 4, a yes answer was scored "1", a negative answer "0", in computing the political interest rating.

5. In the last few weeks before the election, did you listen to radio or TV programs by the candidates? (If yes): How often would you say? (About how many times a week?)

Seventy per cent of the registered voters stated that they listened to candidates once a week or oftener; 14 per cent did not listen at all; most of the remainder were vague about the extent of their listening. For purposes of the general rating, we gave a score of "1" to those listening once a week or oftener and "0" to all others.

6. Did you listen to radio or TV speeches about the election by people who were not candidates?

Fifty-three per cent of the total sample answered "yes". This response is scored "1" and all others "0" in compiling the overall rating of interest.

7. In those last weeks before the election, did you read about the candidates and the election in the daily newspapers?

Eighty-four per cent say they read election news in the papers. Again this positive indication of interest is scored "1", a negative reply "0".

8. Did you read about the candidates and the election in any magazines or other papers?

The percentage of affirmative replies here dropped to 31 per cent. The question was scored in the same way as the preceding ones.

The next group of questions indicative of political interest (Questions 9 to 11 on page 123) are three pre-election items having to do with the respondents' knowledge about issues and candidates. We assume that familiarity with simple facts and points of discussion in the campaign is one sign of political interest. The questions utilized here that deal with issues and candidates' qualifications have been previously considered in connection with voting behavior (Chapter 2). They are briefly brought together now in a different perspective, as they enter into our rating of political interest.

9. a. What would you say are the main issues or things being talked about in the presidential campaign?
   b. What issues or things being talked about are the most important ones to you?

Answers to these questions were summarized in Tables 2.15 to 2.17. The fact on which we now focus attention is that substantial percentages of the union members were classified in the categories "no answer", "don't know", and "indefinite, unclassifiable". Response of this kind we view as indications of low political information and interest. More specifically, we gave a score of "1" if the person interviewed responded with at least one definite idea to each part of the question; it was taken as a sign of low interest and scored "0" if he failed to give an understandable, classifiable response to each part. 73 per cent of registered voters received the positive score; 27 per cent were unable to answer both parts of the question.

10. We are interested in how many people know who the candidates are for president and for governor and senator in Michigan. Would you tell me who the candidates are: For president? For governor of Michigan? For senator here in Michigan?

Since answers to this question have not been included in earlier chapters, the results are summarized here.

Of the 677 registered voters who answered, 8 per cent did not know the names of both presidential candidates. Four per cent simply said they didn't know; 3 per cent named Stevenson but not Eisenhower; 1 per cent named Eisenhower alone.

Forty-six per cent could not name both candidates for the governorship; 8 per cent said "don't know" or gave wrong names; 37 per cent named Williams (Democrat) but not Alger (Republican); 1 per cent named Alger but not Williams.

Sixty-one per cent could not name both candidates for the Senate; 28 per cent said "don't know" or gave wrong names; 32 per cent named Moody (Democrat) but not Potter (Republican); 1 per cent named Potter but not Moody. It is to be noted that within two weeks of the election, 29 per cent of these UAW members did not know Moody's name as a candidate for the Senate, although he was the candidate openly endorsed and recommended by the UAW and the CIO. By contrast, only 8 per cent did not know Williams' name as a candidate for Governor. It should be noted, however, that Williams had twice previously been a successful candidate and had occupied the governor's chair for four years. Moody had served a year and a half in the Senate by appointment but had not previously run for office.

Another count was made to see how many of the people interviewed knew all six names, how many knew five, and so on. The percentage of registered voters in each category follows:

Number of the 6 Candidates Named	Per Cent of Registered Voters
6	35%
5	18
4	20
3	17
2	5
1	1
0	4
	100%

It may come as a surprise that within two weeks of election day only a third of these voters were able to name the two candidates for the three highest offices. More than one-fourth could name only three or fewer of the six candidates. We have no comparable figures for other segments of the voting population but it is our guess that the results for industrial workers as a whole would not differ greatly from these.

In scoring the answers to this question, we decided to give partial credit if a person knew most but not all the names; accordingly he received a score of "2" if he named all six, "1" if he named four or five correctly, and "0" if he knew fewer than four.

11. I'd like to ask you about the good and bad points of the two candidates for president. Is there anything in particular about Eisenhower that might make you want to vote for him? (What is it?)

   Is there anything in particular about Eisenhower that might make you want to vote against him? (What is it?)

   Is there anything in particular about Stevenson that might make you want to vote for him? (What is it?)

   Is there anything in particular about Stevenson that might make you want to vote against him? (What is it?)

Answers to these questions were summarized and discussed in Chapter 2 (pp. 57-65). In the present connection we are interested only in people's ability to mention arguments for and against the presidential candidates since the possession of such knowledge provides one more indication of political interest. If a person offered ideas on any two of the four questions, he was scored 1; failure to answer two or more gave a score of 0. The actual proportions of registered voters who responded to all four parts of the question, to three of the four, etc. are as follows:

Number of the 4 Questions Answered	Per Cent of Registered Voters
4	9%
3	23
2	44
1	17
0	7
	100%

Where only one of the four questions was answered it was typically a reason in favor of the preferred candidate; where two were answered, it ordinarily meant a reason for the preferred man and a reason against the opposition candidate. This tendency to reply in terms of one's partisan position rather than to cite both pros and cons was pointed out in the earlier discussion.

The remaining three questions bearing on political interest all have to do with expressions of concern in regard to the election (items 12, 13, 14 in the list of page 123). They offer particularly direct evidence of each person's degree of interest.

The results for these three questions are described here since they have not been previously introduced.

> 12. Would you say that you personally care very much which party wins the presidential election, or that you don't care very much? Why do you feel that way?

The proportions of people who "care very much" and who "don't care very much" are shown in Table 4.13. The "care" response was scored 1 for purposes of the total political interest rating. It is apparent from the results that Stevenson supporters "cared" in considerably greater numbers than Eisenhower supporters. The "undecided" were much more inclined than others to acknowledge that they did not care very much.

TABLE 4.13

PROPORTIONS OF REGISTERED VOTERS SAYING THAT THEY CARE VERY MUCH WHICH PARTY WINS THE PRESIDENTIAL ELECTIONS (PRE-ELECTION INTERVIEW)

	Vote Intention				
	Steven-son	Eisen-hower	Unde-cided	No Answer; Refused to Say	Total Sample
Care very much	89%	72%	45%	68%	81%
Don't care very much	10	27	49	27	17
No answer; unclassifiable	1	1	6	5	2
	100%	100%	100%	100%	100%
No. of cases	(486)	(118)	(49)	(37)	(690)

The reasons people gave for caring or not caring are summarized in Table 4.14 (pp. 132-133). The tendency is again apparent for many of the Democratic voters to stress the group interests of working people and unions. The largest percentages of reasons reflect the belief that workers' interests will be best served if the Democrats win and will be harmed by a Republican victory.

> 13. How do you feel about the way the election came out? (How do you mean? What other feelings do you have about it?)

TABLE 4.14

REASONS FOR CARING OR NOT CARING WHICH PARTY WINS
(Pre-election Interviews)

Would you say that you personally care very much which party wins the Presidential election, or that you don't care very much? *Why do you feel that way?*

	Vote Intention				
	Steven-son	Eisen-hower	Unde-cided	No Answer; Refused to Say	Total Sample
CARE VERY MUCH					
Pro-Democratic or Anti-Republican					
Democrats good for working people; good for me	27%	—	2%	19%	20%
Democrats are better; I've always been a Democrat	19	—	6	16	14
Democrats should stay in; don't want a change	8	—	2	—	6
Specific benefits from Democrats (employment; security; pensions; pro-union legislation, etc.	6	—	2	3	5
Stevenson better; positive reference to his record	2	—	—	3	2
Specific harm from Republicans (depression; anti-labor; pro-business; war; isolationism, etc.)	11	—	4	8	9
Eisenhower not the right man; military man, etc.	3	—	—	—	2
Don't like Republicans	2	—	2	—	2
Total Pro-Democratic or Anti-Republican	78	—	18	49	59
Pro-Republican or Anti-Democratic					
Time for a change; Democrats in too long	°	37	4	—	7
Republicans (or Eisenhower) better; don't like Democrats; Specific criticisms of Democrats (e.g. corrupt; socialist, etc.)	—	16	2	—	3
Total Pro-Republican or Anti-Democratic	°	53	6	—	10

TABLE 4.14—*Continued*

	Vote Intention				
	Steven-son	Eisen-hower	Unde-cided	No Answer; Refused to Say	Total Sample
CARE VERY MUCH					
Other Reasons					
It's my duty; important; everybody should care	2	2	2	3	2
Get a man who will work for good of country; want a good man to win	2	3	2	3	2
Means peace; end of war	°	5	—	3	1
Miscellaneous, indefinite and unclassifiable	6	8	16	10	7
Total number who "care very much"	89	72	45	68	81
DON'T CARE VERY MUCH					
The two parties are about the same	5	10	14	10	7
Not interested in politics	1	3	6	3	2
Miscellaneous, indefinite and unclassifiable	4	14	29	14	8
Total number who "don't care very much"	10	27	49	27	17
No answer; unclassifiable as to "care" or not	1	1	6	5	2
	100%	100%	100%	100%	100%
No. of cases	(486)	(118)	(49)	(37)	(690)

° Less than 1%.

Answers to this question were first classified into simple favorable and unfavorable categories. The results are shown in Table 4.15. A person who gave any favorable or unfavorable comment received a score of 1 on the political interest rating; any other answer scored 0.

The final question that entered into our political interest score is closely related to the preceding one and can well be considered along with it. It was worded as follows:

14. Are you glad or sorry that Eisenhower won? Would you tell me why you are glad (sorry)?

TABLE 4.15

FEELINGS REGARDING THE ELECTION OUTCOME

	Stevenson Voters	*Eisenhower Voters*	*Did Not Vote*	*Total Sample*
Favorable comments	13%	87%	50%	34%
Unfavorable comments	63	2	22	44
Neutral and ambiguous comments	11	3	9	9
Don't know; can't say, etc.	13	8	19	13
	100%	100%	100%	100%
No. of cases	(170)	(116)	(65)	(351)

The percentages answering in each way are reported in Table 4.16. A response of either glad or sorry was taken as indicative of political interest and was scored "1"; other replies were scored "0".

TABLE 4.16

PROPORTIONS SAYING THEY ARE GLAD OR SORRY THAT EISENHOWER WON

	Stevenson Voters	*Eisenhower Voters*	*Did Not Vote*	*Total Sample*
Glad	19%	90%	39%	37%
Sorry	43	1	24	31
Neither	37	7	35	30
Don't know; can't say, etc.	1	2	2	2
	100%	100%	100%	100%
No. of cases	(170)	(116)	(65)	(351)

The data reported in Tables 4.15 and 4.16 were also classified in greater detail according to the content of the favorable and unfavorable ideas expressed. These more detailed results are shown in Tables D.9 and D.10 in the Appendix.

In Tables 4.15 and 4.16 it is seen that the number of persons who expressed negative feelings about the election results is very much smaller than might have been expected in view of the predominantly Democratic sentiment and Democratic voting intentions of these union members.

Before the election, nine out of ten Stevenson-supporters declared that they "cared very much" which party wins (Table 4.13); but after the election fewer than one-half said they were sorry that Eisenhower won. It is evident that many voters who had hoped for a Democratic victory nevertheless welcomed Eisenhower's election while still more accepted it with no expression of sorrow. Undoubtedly this is partly due to the sportsmanship spirit carried over from athletic competition to election contests. Partly, too, it is the attitude that dictates cheerful acceptance of whatever comes—as several expressed it, "nothing is gained by feeling sorry." But whatever the particular tone of the feelings, the fact is important that even among Stevenson voters less than half felt greatly enough disturbed to say they were sorry that Eisenhower won. Although a substantially larger number did express unfavorable opinions when they were asked to tell in their own words how they felt about the way the election came out, even then 37 per cent of the Stevenson voters responded either with positive or neutral comments.

Results like these give rise to a question whether, for large numbers of the union members (as well as for other sections of the population), elections remain at a rather superficial level, akin to a baseball game in which one tries to win but the results of which are accepted with a sportsmanlike smile if one is on the losing side. Perhaps this is the nature of American politics. Psychologically considered, however, it is difficult to think that a person who holds well grounded political convictions, who believes that important group interests and national welfare are at stake, can so readily shed his concern and express no lasting regret over a lost election. In other words, our results suggest that a good many of the pro-Stevenson union members were merely going along with the prevailing group opinion without themselves having any deep personal convictions in regard to the election pros and cons or that a good many of these members do not feel that the outcome of the election affects them directly. This question is not unrelated to the evidence showing a relatively small amount of active individual participation in the election campaign (see p. 124). We shall have another look at these matters in the light of additional data when we deal in a later section with political apathy and feelings of political futility.

A Rating of Political Interest

This completes the description of the fourteen questions that enter into the general rating of political interest. The total possible raw score for an individual ranges from 0 to 15 (one question allowed a score of "2", all others a score of "1"). Since such fine divisions of score were unnecessary, and in order to simplify the tabulations, this range was reduced to a final set of ratings running from 0 to 8 (for details, see Appendix C).

The distribution of the total political interest scores for registered voters in our sample of UAW members follows:

Political Interest Rating	Per Cent of Union Members (Registered Voters Only)
8	21%
7	13
6	11
5	11
4	13
3	11
2	6
1	6
0	8
	100%

As was previously pointed out in respect to the ratings of agreement with the union's political position, a grouping and interpretation of such scores, although necessarily somewhat subjective, nevertheless is meaningful and useful. We shall employ two different groupings of the above scores as our analysis proceeds, each proving appropriate for certain types of comparisons. Where we wish a broad division into those having somewhat greater and somewhat less political interest, we shall combine the scores as follows:

Considerable political interest (Ratings 5 to 8)	56%
Little political interest (Ratings 0 to 4)	44%
	100%

At other times we shall want to look at those members who manifest especially strong interest in contrast to those at the other extreme—and both of these as distinguished from a large middle group. Using this type of division, our cases fall into these categories:

High political interest (Rating 8)	21%
Medium political interest (Ratings 3 to 7)	59%
Low political interest (Ratings 0 to 2)	20%
	100%

Consideration of the answers that yield scores of different size justifies the statement, we believe, that the rating of "high political interest," achieved by one-fifth of the registered voters, does really mean that these people are politically aroused and function at a rather high level of political awareness. Likewise the 20 per cent rated "low" are people who apparently concern themselves relatively little with political affairs.

The next step is to examine these political interest ratings in relation to social characteristics of the workers, in relation to voting behavior, and also in relation to the rating derived earlier as a measure of members' pro-labor political orientation.

When we examine the data to learn what subgroups within the union manifest greater or less amounts of political interest, it becomes apparent that education is decidedly the most significant factor. Among workers who went beyond the eighth grade 65 per cent are above average in political interest as compared with 40 per cent of those with less education. Political interest is also somewhat greater among men than women; a little higher among workers at better economic levels; and slightly higher among Protestants than Catholics (presumably due to the larger number of Catholics who are first generation Americans). Closer relationships to political interest are found when we consider differences of schooling along with other characteristics. For example, the differences between workers who went beyond the eighth grade and those who did not is especially great among Negroes (74 per cent to 33 per cent above average political interest), among people under 40 (63 per cent to 28 per cent), and among people of either high or low economic status (74 per cent to 33 per cent and 67 per cent to 30 per cent respectively). Even more extremely, if we take only persons under 40 who are at the high economic level and with more than eighth grade education, 83 per cent are above average in political interest while those at the low economic level with only eight grades of school or less have only 21 per cent above average.

The foregoing relationships and several others are shown in the following tabulation:

Most Political Interest	*Per Cent Above Average*
More than 8th grade education, relatively high socio-economic level	74%
More than 8th grade, relatively high socio-economic, under 40 years of age	83%
More than 8th grade, 40 and over, Protestant	77%
More than 8th grade, 40 and over, relatively low socio-economic level	79%
More than 8th grade, relatively low socio-economic, Protestant	75%
More than 8th grade, Negro	74%
Least Political Interest	
8th grade or less, under 40 years of age	28%
8th grade or less, relatively high socio-economic	33%
8th grade or less, relatively low socio-economic	30%
8th grade or less, relatively low socio-economic, under 40	21%
8th grade or less, under 40, Protestant	16%
8th grade or less, over 40, Catholic	35%
8th grade or less, Negro	33%

Turning now to the question of political interest in relation to voting, comparison of Eisenhower and Stevenson voters shows that their *average* political interest scores are nearly the same, with the Eisenhower supporters a little higher. This hides the interesting fact, however, that the Stevenson voters tend to fall at *both* the high and low ends of the scale more frequently than do the Eisenhower voters. This is shown by the figures in Table 4.18. The Eisenhower supporters in the union, that is to say, tend to be people of moderately high political interest but, compared to Stevenson voters, fewer of them show very great or very slight political interest.

It is time now to consider the non-voters. Indeed, it may be questioned why we did not include information on whether an individual voted or not as part of the political interest rating, since this is so obviously one indication of interest. The fact is that we decided to treat voting versus non-voting separately because of the interest in seeing to what extent non-voters really are persons low in political interest as judged by such items as entered into our rating. We also wish to make other comparisons independently in order to find whether non-voting and low political interest do show identical relationships to other variables.

TABLE 4.18

DEGREE OF POLITICAL INTEREST IN RELATION
TO PRESIDENTIAL VOTE

Political Interest	Stevenson Voters	Eisenhower Voters	All Registered Voters
High	24%	13%	21%
Medium	55	74	59
Low	21	13	20
	100%	100%	100%
No. of cases	(162)	(107)	(279)

It is impossible to compare non-voters with others on our total political interest score since the people who were not registered to vote were not asked the pre-election questions about candidates and issues. However, we are able here and in many later tabulations to surmount this obstacle by utilizing a political interest score based on answers to the post-election interview alone. We find that a score derived from the eight questions of Interview II (see the items so designated on page 123) agrees closely with the rating from all fourteen questions. The correlation coefficient between the two is .82 and this would undoubtedly be increased if it were possible to include the non-voters since they would tend to stand low in both scores. The ratings based on Interview II range from 0 to 8 (a score of "1" for each of the eight questions). These ratings can be grouped in a way that makes the three divisions roughly parallel to those for the total ratings. The percentages of registered voters (the same cases as for the total ratings) are as follows:

High political interest (Ratings 7 and 8)   18%
Medium political interest (Ratings 4 to 6)   61%
Low political interest (Ratings 0 to 3)   21%
                                                     ————
                                                     100%

Using these Interview II ratings of political interest, non-voters may be compared with Stevenson and Eisenhower voters. The comparisons are shown in Table 4.19. According to this set of ratings, the Eisenhower voters again show slightly greater political interest than do the Stevenson voters. The tendency observed in Table 4.18, for Stevenson supporters to be more numerous at the high interest level as well as at the low, disappears here. This is accounted for by the fact that on two of the items comprising the Interview II score Eisenhower supporters were particularly more likely to reply in a manner that added to their rating—namely the questions asking whether they read about the candidates in magazines and whether they were glad or sorry at the election results. Both these questions tend to

TABLE 4.19

POLITICAL INTEREST IN RELATION TO PRESIDENTIAL VOTE AND NON-VOTING

Political Interest	Stevenson Voters	Eisenhower Voters	Did Not Vote	Total Sample
High	19%	20%	4%	18%
Medium	59	70	56	61
Low	22	10	40	21
	100%	100%	100%	100%
No. of cases	(169)	(116)	(60)	(345)

give Eisenhower supporters undue credit as compared with Democratic voters since the predominantly pro-Republican magazines appealed most to Republican voters[8] and the glad-sorry question tended to evoke neutral and evasive replies from many Stevenson voters in contrast to the almost unanimous "glad"

————

[8] This was probably true even though we intentionally phrased the question to include not only the usual magazines but also "other papers" to cover labor union publications, etc.

response from Eisenhower voters. Consequently, the relationship shown in Table 4.18 at the *high* political interest level is not invalidated by the results of Table 4.19. At the *low* extreme, the tables are in agreement.

Our chief interest in Table 4.19 is the comparison of non-voters with voters. Only those non-voters who are legally eligible to vote are included. It is seen that a negligible number of non-voters rate high in political interest and that low ratings occur twice as frequently as among voters. Nevertheless, it is noteworthy that the majority of these non-voters fall in the middle range of political interest scores, *not* at the extremely low points. Failure to vote by this largest group cannot be ascribed simply to lack of interest, since their degree of political awareness and concern is equal to that of most voters. This can be taken to mean that, while low interest is clearly one factor for some UAW members, other special causes account for many of the individual cases of non-voting. We shall need to look for additional explanatory clues as we examine other indexes and personal data in relation to voting.

Before we leave the political interest ratings it is important to see how they relate to our other main index, the measure of pro-labor political orientation. These two together represent major objectives of the union so far as the political involvement of its members is concerned. We shall use both these measures, singly and in combination, through most of the remaining analysis. The question arises, however, whether these two ratings are merely duplicating each other or whether they are getting at different sets of attitudes. In the main we find that they do measure independent dimensions of political disposition. Neither of them alone yields nearly as much information as the two together. At the same time, it is most interesting to inquire into their relationship to each other; to learn, for example, whether the strongly pro-union members are also politically aroused and whether the individuals having slight political interest tend to be the dissenters from labor's political aims.

The percentage tabulations in Tables 4.20 and 4.21 enable us to look at these relationships. The two tables are based on the same data; they merely interchange the position of the variables so that we can conveniently make percentage comparisons either among the degrees of pro-labor political attitude or among the different degrees of political interest.

TABLE 4.20

POLITICAL INTEREST IN RELATION TO PRO-LABOR POLITICAL ORIENTATION

Rating of Political Interest	Rating of Pro-Labor Political Orientation				Total Sample
	0-3	4-5	6-7	8	
7-8	21%	25%	28%	44%	30%
5-6	32	18	16	33	24
3-4	31	36	25	18	27
0-2	16	21	31	5	19
	100%	100%	100%	100%	100%
No. of cases	(98)	(83)	(88)	(69)	(338)

TABLE 4.21

PRO-LABOR POLITICAL ORIENTATION IN RELATION TO POLITICAL INTEREST

Rating of Pro-Labor Political Orientation	Rating of Political Interest				Total Sample
	0-2	3-4	5-6	7-8	
8	7%	17%	35%	38%	26%
6-7	48	27	20	27	29
4-5	27	32	17	20	24
0-3	18	24	28	15	21
	100%	100%	100%	100%	100%
No. of cases	(61)	(95)	(99)	(83)	(338)

The following conclusions may be drawn from these tables:

1. In the first place, it is clear that the correspondence between the two ratings is not close. Although some relationship is shown, it is apparent that high or low degrees of each attitude may be present in association with various degrees of the other. This finding supports our working assumption that the two measures are largely independent of each other and that both must be used in order to portray union members' political interest as well as their political orientation.

2. The most significant relation in the tables is the contrast of political interest between the extremely pro-labor members and all others. Among these strongest pro-labor people, shown in the fourth column of percentages in Table 4.20, 77 per cent have an interest rating of 5 or higher, while ratings of this size are obtained by only 46 per cent of all others in the sample. Only a few of these members who, from a union standpoint, are fully "on side" (5 per cent) turn up in the lowest political interest category. As seen in Table 4.21, it is also true that members with high political interest tend to agree most with the union politically; very few of those lowest in interest are intensely pro-labor (7 per cent).

3. This tendency exhibited in the extreme pro-labor group does not hold for the moderately high pro-labor people (third column of percentages, Table 4.20). On the contrary, the latter are especially numerous at the *lowest* interest level (31 per cent of them contrasted with 14 per cent of all others). Correspondingly, in Table 4.21, the lowest interest category contains a surprisingly great number who are *moderately high* in the pro-labor direction (48 per cent in column 1 of Table 4.21). Our interpretation is that these are people of slight political interest who are loyal to the union and who go along with it politically, thus scoring fairly high in union agreement, though not feeling any active involvement and without taking an extreme partisan position. Those who agree more strongly with the union in political matters no longer remain at the low interest level; hence the sudden drop from 48 per cent to 7 per cent between the fairly pro-union and the extremely pro-union.

4. One or two other relationships in these tables, though less definite, are rather suggestive. The people low in their agreement with the union (first column, Table 4.20) are found a little more at the moderately high level of political interest and less at the extremely high than would most likely occur by chance. This group is mainly composed of Republicans and others who dissent from the union's position. These members might be expected to tend, as they do here, toward moderate political interest rather than being very high or low, since they would find it difficult to maintain high interest in the hostile climate of opinion surrounding them; on the other hand, they are unlikely to be people of

extremely low interest, since in that case they would hardly have remained "off-side" as far as labor is concerned, but would have been prevailed upon to accept the views of their co-workers. A parallel interpretation would apply to the tendency observable for moderately high interest to be associated with either very strong or very weak pro-labor political attitudes, but not with intermediate degrees (third column of percentages, Table 4.21). This column is likely to include two different groups: those somewhat politically aroused in support of their strongly pro-labor sentiments, and others opposed to labor's political participation, for whom relatively strong political interest is required to motivate them to maintain their dissent against the counter-pressures exerted by their associates. At the same time, they are unlikely to develop *very* strong political interests, since they lack group support and encouragement for their type of political expression.

In closing this chapter, we may again take our bearings by referring to the road map provided by Chart 1 (page 97). This chapter has been concerned with Level 3 of the chart. Earlier chapters dealt with major aspects of Levels 1 and 2. The five clusters of attitudes shown at Levels 4 and 5 will be described in the next chapter, where we shall also see how they are related to one another and to the other variables represented in the chart.

Throughout these further analyses and interpretations, the key nature of the two variables considered in the present chapter will be apparent. Labor political orientation and degree of political interest lie at the very center of our inquiry. The directions which union political action is likely to take, its possibilites and its limitations, are intimately bound to these two sets of attitudes. For only as members are in agreement with basic union political thinking and goals, and only as they are sufficiently aroused to participate and support political action, can the union operate effectively in the political field. If political interest and agreement with the union's position both are high, the political behavior in line with union objectives is likely to follow. So long as either is lacking or seriously deficient, political endeavors of the union can amount to little.

On the whole, the evidence reported here indicates that among auto workers in the Detroit areas there is fairly strong backing of union political activities and a moderate amount of political interest, though active personal involvement remains at a rather low level. The predominant political outlook or "philosophy" is clearly one that conceives of workers' and union's goals as opposed at many points to those of business and wealthy groups. This is not to be translated as "class consciousness," belief in "class struggle," or a desire to overthrow the "capitalist system." We shall return to this important distinction in the final chapter. Contrary to common assertions, moreover, a majority of these unionists trust union organizations and leadership on the political as well as on the economic front. At the same time, our findings point to the conclusion that large numbers of those who go along with the union on political matters do so in a relatively passive and unaroused spirit.

Since much additional evidence relevant to these issues remains to be examined in the following chapters, we shall postpone more detailed interpretations and statement of conclusions at this time. The ratings and questions thus far considered will take on further meaning as we view them in the light of other attitudes and personal data.

CHAPTER 5

Attitudes Related to Political Behavior

In the preceding chapter we developed the view that the voting behavior of union members can be interpreted as an expression of their political agreement or disagreement with the union and of their political interest or arousal. The next question, to be considered now, is whether other, more general personal attitudes help us to understand the differences in members' political orientation, interest, and voting. Our interviews with auto workers provided several measures of such underlying dispositions which we thought might have significant bearing on their political views. These expectations were based both on results of previous studies and on psychological analysis of probable motivations involved in political behavior. We shall describe the interview responses and ratings used and shall consider their relations to the measures previously discussed— political interest, pro-labor political orientation, and 1952 voting behavior.

Individuals' Attachment to the Union

A rating of attachment to the union—members' active interest in the union—was derived from replies to a series of questions pertaining to membership in organizations (Interview II, Ques. 31). The respondent was asked to name the organizations he belongs to, to indicate the amount of interest he feels in each organization, how often he attends meetings, and whether he has held any office or committee post. The replies naming the organizations belonged to were summarized in Chapter 1 (page 28). We are concerned here only with the evidence on the individual's interest and activity in his labor union. The question was asked principally to obtain this information without singling out union organizations and calling special attention to them.

A score or rating was obtained which runs from 0 to 6. The zero rating means that the person did not even mention that he belonged to a union—although he was shown a list of organizations as a reminder, including labor unions as one item. A rating of 6 signifies that the member expresses "a great deal of interest" in the union, reports frequent attendance at meetings, and has held some union office or served on a committee. Typical responses for the different ratings are the following[1]:

0 Does not mention belonging to a union.

1 Says he belongs but has "little or no interest" in it, never or hardly ever attends a meeting, has never held office or been on a committee.

2 Same as "1" except that he has "some interest" in the union; *or* attends meetings "sometimes," "once every few months," etc.; *or* has been an officer or committee member.

3 Belongs and has "some interest," attends meetings "often," "most of the time," "once a month," etc.; *or* has "a great deal of interest" but does not attend meetings and has not held office.

4 Has "a great deal of interest" and attends one to six times a year; *or* "some interest" and attends oftener; *or* "some interest," attends once in 2 or 3 months and has been an officer or committee member.

5 Same as "6" but has not held office; *or* attends meetings every 2 or 3 months instead of every month; *or* expresses "some interest" instead of great interest.

6 "A great deal of interest," attends once a month or more often, has held office or been on committee.[2]

---

[1] The scoring procedure is more fully described in Appendix C.

[2] A "6" rating extends a little beyond the meaning of union "interest" or "attachment" since it requires the holding of union office; a member may be extremely attached to the union and yet not hold office. It may be, too, that some local unions meet less frequently than once a month, in which case even the highly interested member could not score 6.

The proportions showing these different degrees of involvement or attachment are as follows:

Union Attachment Rating	Per Cent of Union Members
6	7%
5	11
4	17
3	20
2	21
1	15
0	9*
	100%

* The best information we have indicates that this figure includes 2 per cent who are really not members of the union but were on the mailing list by reason of having been members at one time or through error. Omitting them would reduce the percentage of zero scores among actual members to 7 per cent.

Most of the membership falls into the middle range of scores, with roughly one-fifth showing very strong interest and active involvement in the union and a slightly larger number revealing extremely weak union attachment. Since a rating of 4 or above signifies a rather high degree of interest and participation and ratings of 0 and 1 indicate decidedly weak relations to the union, for most of our later comparisons we shall classify the members into the following three groups:

Strong attachment to the union (Ratings 4 to 6)	35%
Intermediate (Ratings 2 and 3)	41%
Weak attachment (Ratings 0 and 1)	24%

The question concerning the amount of interest the member had in the union asked: "How do you feel about belonging to this group (organization that respondent has named)? Do you have: (1) a *great deal* of interest in it, (2) *some* interest, or (3) *little or no* interest?"

Responses to this question in reference to union membership are:

Great deal of interest	31%
Some interest	34
Little or no interest	21
No answer or other answer re interest	5
No mention of belonging to a union	9*
	100%

* This percentage also becomes 7 per cent if we omit the persons from our sample who are probably now not members of the union.

The question, "About how often do you go to its meetings?" gave these results (omitting those not answering):

Once a month or more often	23%
Once in 2 or 3 months	5
1 to 3 times a year	26
Often, most of the time, etc.	4
Sometimes; fairly often	4
Never; hardly ever; once in 2 years, etc.	38
	100%

This may be simplified into the following form to yield a clearer picture:

Once a month; "often," "most of the time," etc.	27%
1 to 6 times a year; "fairly often," "sometimes"	35
Never, hardly ever, once in 2 years, etc.	38
	100%

It may be assumed that the reports of attendance err on the side of exaggeration. Since this is true and since some 12 per cent either did not say they belong to a union or did not tell how often they go to meetings, the figures mean that approximately half of all members never or hardly ever attend meetings.

The only other question used in this connection inquired: "Were you ever an officer or on any Committee?" 17 per cent of those answering stated that they had held union office or served on committees.

We return now to the overall rating based on these questions. Does this index of attachment to the union relate to the way the members vote and to their political interest and agreement with the union? The answer in respect to voting is contained in Table 5.1.

Attachment to the union apparently has little effect on whether a member votes or not; those having low ratings of attachment are no more likely to be non-voters than are others and those strongly attached likewise show extremely slight difference in this respect. However, answers to the specific question regarding interest in the union do show a slight (though not statistically reliable) relation to non-voting: those explicitly saying "little or no interest" have 17 per cent non-voters, the "some interest" have 14 per cent, and those with "a great deal of interest" drop to 10 per cent. No such differences appear between members who attend meetings and those who do not; the proportion of non-voters remains constant regardless of frequency of attendance. People who have held union office, however, have only 7 per cent of non-voting compared to 14 per cent for non-office holders.

TABLE 5.1

PRESIDENTIAL VOTE IN RELATION TO INDIVIDUALS'
ATTACHMENT TO THE UNION

Voted for:	Attachment to Union			Total Sample
	Strong	Intermediate	Weak	
Stevenson	72%	66%	54%	65%
Eisenhower	17	20	33	22
Did not vote, etc.	11	14	13	13
	100%	100%	100%	100%
No. of Cases	(104)	(146)	(95)	(345)

Attachment to the union is significantly related to the way members vote: the ratio of Stevenson to Eisenhower votes is roughly 4 to 1 among members with strong union attachment, 3 to 1 for the middle group, and less than 2 to 1 among those weakly identified with the union. This means that the members who are more closely tied to the union tend also to go along with it politically. It is to be noted, nevertheless, that even among members strongly attached to the union 17 per cent voted for Eisenhower and among those who report holding union offices 23 per cent voted for him, which is just about the same as among persons who never held office. We conclude, then, that the influences causing members who feel identified with the union to vote according to union recommendations are by no means rigid and compelling; however, these members clearly have a greater tendency to vote "right" from a union standpoint than do members who identify less closely with the union.

The next question is whether this is a generalized difference, whether degree of union attachment is associated not only with the 1952 presidential vote but also with differences in political orientation as measured, for example, by our rating of pro-labor political attitudes. Table 5.2 returns an unmistakably affirmative answer. The greater the union attachment of members, the more likely they are to have a strongly pro-labor political orientation. Among those with strong union attachment, three and a half times as many are politically in the strongly pro-labor group as are in the not pro-labor group; this ratio drops to two to one among members with intermediate attachment and in the weak attachment group there are more who are politically *not* pro-labor than there are strongly pro-labor. At the same time it is to be observed that considerable numbers deviate from the main direction of the relationship. Notably there are those weakly attached to the union or intermediate (i.e., members who express little interest in the union and infrequent attendance), who nevertheless are strongly pro-labor in political orientation. These would appear to be people high in their potential identification with the union but ones the union has failed to involve in its activities.

TABLE 5.2

RATING OF PRO-LABOR POLITICAL ORIENTATION IN RELATION TO INDIVIDUALS' ATTACHMENT TO THE UNION

Political Orientation:	Attachment to Union			Total Sample
	Strong	Intermediate	Weak	
Strongly pro-labor*	53%	42%	28%	42%
Intermediate	32	38	37	36
Not pro-labor	15	20	35	22
	100%	100%	100%	100%
No. of cases	(102)	(146)	(90)	(338)

* The line dividing "strongly pro-labor" from "intermediate" has been changed here from that used in Chapter 4 to avoid having such a large proportion of cases in the top category for purposes of statistical comparison.

Taken altogether, however, the figures of Table 5.2 show a clear tendency for people actively interested in the union to be also the ones who are most on side politically. Although causal interpretations cannot be established from our data, it seems plausible to assume that the causation operates in both directions here—that closer general ties to the union bring increased political agreement and support while at the same time arousal

over political aims produces greater union attachment and involvement on the part of members. The causal relation may, of
course, also be due to certain common social background factors
that predispose some members toward both union attachment
and pro-labor political orientation. It is found, for example,
that both occur in above average degree among younger workers
at lower socio-economic levels and among Negroes.

Comparison of union attachment with degree of political
interest reveals a similar positive relationship though the linkage
is not quite as close. As may be seen in Table 5.3 stronger ties
to the union are associated with higher levels of political interest
—the interest being measured by our previously described rating
of members' attitudes and participation in connection with the
1952 election. Especially striking is the preponderantly high
political interest among the members who identify most closely
with the union (those in column one). If we take an even more
extreme group of members in terms of high attachment or involvement, the percentages become 65 per cent and 7 per cent
in the high and the low political interest categories respectively.

TABLE 5.3

RATING OF POLITICAL INTEREST IN RELATION TO
INDIVIDUALS' ATTACHMENT TO THE UNION

Political Interest (II)	Attachment to Union			*Total Sample*
	Strong	*Intermediate*	*Weak*	
High	55%	39%	24%	41%
Medium*	33	37	47	38
Low	12	24	29	21
	100%	100%	100%	100%
No. of cases	(104)	(146)	(94)	(344)

* The lines dividing this category have been changed here from those
used in Chapter 4 to reduce the large proportion of cases in any one category.

One other type of analysis should be reported before we
turn to the next of our underlying attitude clusters. We compared
the ratings of union attachment for men and women, white and
Negro members, age and educational groupings, and for several

other personal and social variables. In general, the separate objective factors which we sampled show only moderate relations to union attachment scores. The only large difference is that by sex: women members are less closely attached to the union than are men (only 14 per cent of women members in the "strong attachment" category as against 37 per cent of the men; 40 per cent of the women versus 22 per cent of the men receive a "weak attachment" rating).

For the union membership as a whole, no differences of equal size occur by race, age, education, or other social characteristics. However, some tendencies manifest themselves for union attachment to be greater among those educated beyond the eighth grade (except at the higher socio-economic level where those with *less* schooling identify more with the union), among workers of either upper or lower socio-economic status in contrast to the middle bracket,[3] and among Negroes. Certain of these variables in combination mark off subgroupings that are well above or below average in their degree of active attachment to the union. Examples are the following:

	Per Cent Above Average
Strongest Union Attachment	
Relatively high socio-economic level, eighth grade or less	79%
Relatively low socio-economic, under forty years of age	70%
Relatively low socio-economic, Catholic	69%
Negro, more than eighth grade education	72%
Weakest Union Attachment	
Middle socio-economic level, eighth grade or less, under forty years of age	32%
Middle socio-economic, eighth grade or less, Catholic	30%
Relatively low socio-economic, forty and over, Protestant	40%

We also compared larger and smaller local unions to see whether there is evidence that smaller locals encourage and afford opportunity for individual participation in a manner impossible for the massive units having many thousands of members. No consistent relationship at all is found between local size and ratings of individuals' attachment to the union. In this connection we also asked several staff officials of the union's international headquarters to furnish us with their estimates of

[3] See footnote 12, p. 44 for explanation of the socio-economic ratings.

the comparative *espirit de corps,* or levels of interest and participation, in the different local unions. These ratings likewise
yield no consistent relationship to individuals' union identification or attachment scores. The individual scores do average
higher in the locals judged to be best; however, members of the
locals ranked poorest come next, ahead of those in the middle
ranking locals. These results by size and *esprit* of locals suggest
that any effects such organizational conditions may have are
hidden by the many other individual and group influences at
work.

To summarize, the evidence considered in this section indicates that those union members who are most interested and
active in union affairs as a whole tend also to be most on side
and most interested politically as well. The rating that we have
labeled "individuals' attachment to the union" crudely represents
a basic set of attitudes—the members' closeness of identification
with their organization—which appears to underlie both their
approval and support of the union's political action and also
their own active interest and participation in a presidential
election. A more cautious statement would be not that certain
of these attitudes underlie others but that there is marked
interdependence among them all, each affecting the others and
in turn being affected by them, in a dynamic pattern of motivational interaction.

Again it is necessary to remind ourselves, however, that the
positive interrelations are of quite moderate magnitude. Although they deserve emphasis in our search for connections
among the complex attitudes that bear on political behavior,
they also leave a large place for deviant cases that fail to
conform to the main tendency. Fairly safe meanings can be
ascribed to certain of these deviant portions of the correlation
tables; others present challenging questions for further research
—challenging both for scientific and practical purposes. Tempting and worth while as it is to seek explanations for these "off-
cases," we must refrain from that pursuit of additional determinants in order to continue our exploration of relationships
among the variables already outlined in the design of this study.

Among those sets of attitudes bearing on political behavior,
as sketched in Chart 1 (page 97), we are now ready to con-

sider the second of the variables at the level of "general attitudes toward union and politics," namely feelings of political effectiveness or futility.

Attitudes of Political Futility

It is reasonable to suppose that one important factor in people's political behavior is the degree to which they believe that they can be personally effective in and through political action, or negatively, the extent to which they feel impotent in regard to politics. Accordingly, we included in the interview a few simple questions that might serve as indicators of such attitudes.

Four items in the interview schedule were used for the purpose of securing a single index or rating of the respondents' sense of political effectiveness or futility. The items were part of a larger list of statements on which the individual was asked to express his agreement or disagreement.[4] The actual form of the question is as follows, together with the four specific parts of particular interest here and the answers given by our UAW sample:

Now I'd like to ask you another kind of question. Here are things that some people say and we want to find out how other people feel on these things. I'll read them one at a time and you just tell me offhand whether you *agree* or *disagree*.

	Agree	Disagree	Qualified or No Answer
The way people vote is the main thing that decides how things are run in this country.	73%	22%	5%
People like me don't have any say about what the government does.	33%	60%	7%
All candidates sound good in their speeches, but you never can tell what they will do after they are elected.	82%	13%	5%
Politics and government are so complicated that the average person can't really understand what's going on.	73%	24%	3%

[4] The items employed here are taken with minor changes from ones used by the Survey Research Center in its 1952 election study. As explained

The percentages responding in each way to these questions give evidence that feelings of political ineffectiveness or impotence are frequent enough among union members to create a serious obstacle to active political participation. Probably the same is true of most other parts of the population. This problem, which has received a good deal of attention both by practitioners and social theorists, still stands in need of thorough and detailed study by researches specially aimed at exploring the reasons for political indifference, the grounds for such attitudes as those reflected here. We can report only the limited but suggestive findings from the few questions quoted above.

For present purposes we combined each person's answers to these four questions to obtain a rating of his feelings. A score of 1 was assigned for each response indicating doubts or disbelief concerning the power of the ordinary citizen (the "disagree" response to the first question and, the "agree" response to the others). Thus a 0-score means that none of the person's answers indicate feelings of political futility or ineffectiveness; a score of 4 means that all the items were answered in accord with such feelings. The actual futility scores run as follows:

Rating of Political Futility Feelings	Per Cent of Union Members
4	5%
3	34
2	36
1	19
0	6
	100%

The fact that 39 per cent of the union's members answer either three or four of the questions in a way that indicates feelings of political futility suggests a very large amount of skepticism or negativism concerning their role in political affairs. These attitudes represent a condition which merits serious attention, for feelings of political impotence surely run counter to a vigorous democratic process. Whether from the standpoint of healthy

in the preface, the Survey Research Center generously placed their entire interview schedule at our disposal. The published report of their study utilizes a scale measuring "sense of political efficacy" that is closely similar to that described in this section (though statistically more refined). See Angus Cambell et al, *op. cit.*, Appendix A.

democratic government as a whole, or from that of organized labor's advancement of its group interests, the fact that one-third of the union members agree that "people like me don't have any say about what the government does" is a danger signal that can not well be ignored. Corrective efforts, moreover, if they are to be valuable, must be guided by greatly increased knowledge of what lies back of the attitudes under discussion and what precise meanings these attitudes have for the people who hold them. A little relevant evidence can be presented here—but it is only a beginning.

First of all, we may inquire in what ways the union members who feel politically ineffective differ from their fellows who lack this sense of futility. We shall do this by comparing members who agree with those who disagree that "people like me don't have any say about what the government does." This is the most discriminating question entering into the futility rating. It offers an even more direct and extreme declaration of impotence than is represented by the general political futility score. We shall use it here in place of the total rating. One-third of the members subscribed to the statement that they "don't have any say." Who are these people? What personal and social characteristics distinguish them from others?

Education is the most important factor: the "don't have any say" response is accepted by 55 per cent of those with eighth grade schooling or less and by only 22 per cent of those who went beyond the eighth grade. Older persons answer in this way more often than younger (43 per cent to 27 per cent) and women are more inclined to agree than men (45 per cent versus 32 per cent).

Smaller and more doubtful differences occur on other characteristics. Negroes give the futility-type reply slightly *less* than whites (24 per cent to 35 per cent). No consistent relations appear by religion or nationality, though there is a hint that the foreign-born feel impotent more than the native-born (43 per cent versus 35 per cent) and that the country of father's birth has an influence (52 per cent of respondents having German fathers as against only 17 per cent with British fathers agree that they "don't have any say"). These last groups are too small, however, to make the findings other than suggestive. There is also a slight indication that union members of lowest socio-economic status express feelings of political futility less than do those in the average socio-economic range (30 per cent versus 40 per cent—with those in the above average bracket at 33 per cent). Size of the local union to which members belong, contrary to our expectation, bears no relation to feelings of political effectiveness. However, the locals judged by international staff officials to have superior spirit and involvement of members do show somewhat greater feelings of effectiveness (25 per cent gave the futility-type response as against 39 per cent in other locals).

Certain of the above factors in combination produce more striking contrasts. Examples of percentages answering in the politically impotent direction for a few extreme groupings are the following:

Low Futility

Beyond 8 grades; age under 40	18%
Beyond 8 grades; low socio-economic group; White	11%
Beyond 8 grades; Negro	14%

High Futility

8 grades or less; age 40 or over; Catholic	65%
8 grades or less; Negro	72%

In all these comparisons, decidedly the most important component is education. It is clear that in respect to the attitude tapped by this question amount of formal schooling matters tremendously. This is a hopeful finding suggesting that as the educational level of the population continues to rise there is the prospect that attitudes of political futility will diminish and consequently that active interest and participation can be expected to increase.

We shall now consider the ratings of political futility in relation to other attitude measures. As might have been expected, feelings of political impotence or futility are associated, inversely, with degree of political interest evidenced in the election campaign. But contrary to expectation, ratings of futility do not differ between voters and non-voters. The fact that non-voters express no greater feeling of futility than voters rules out the assumption, as far as our data are concerned, that non-voting is due to the feeling that voting is not worth while, that it accomplishes nothing. Non-voters in our sample are characterized by such attitudes not a whit more than are voters. Apparently the causes for non-voting must be sought elsewhere. Neither is there any relationship of futility ratings to members' voting for Eisenhower or Stevenson, to whether or not they decided late in the campaign, to their degree of pro-labor political orientation, or to their attachment to the union.

Among the attitude ratings thus far described, only that for political interest is related to the effectiveness-futility score. Other attitudes still to be described, however, also show interesting correlations with futility feelings. All the interrelations will later be brought together.

The table for political interest in relation to attitudes of futility (Table 5.4) shows the tendency for high interest and low futility feelings to be associated and correspondingly for low interest and high futility to go together.

TABLE 5.4

RATINGS OF POLITICAL INTEREST IN RELATION
TO ATTITUDES OF POLITICAL FUTILITY

Political Interest (II)	*Political Futility*			*Total Sample*
	High	*Medium*	*Low*	
High	33%	41%	55%	41%
Medium	41	39	30	38
Low	26	20	15	21
	100%	100%	100%	100%
No. of cases	(132)	(124)	(87)	(343)

Thus among the people who feel politically effective (low futility), almost four times as many rate "high" in interest as rate "low" (55 per cent versus 15 per cent), while by contrast in the high futility group the proportions having high and low interest are nearly equal (33 per cent versus 26 per cent). The relation is in part a reflection of educational differences since workers with more schooling are higher than average in political interest and also have lower feelings of political futility. However, the association between political interest and feelings of effectiveness persists, though in reduced degree, when people at each educational level are taken separately.

This inverse correlation between political interest and futility is probably to be understood in terms of several types of interdependence. The simplest causal interpretation would be that a sense of impotence naturally deters a person from participation since he believes his efforts are useless, while feelings of effectiveness will stimulate and inspire active interest toward goals that he is sure he can help to attain. Less obvious motivations undoubtedly also play a part, however. For many persons, political interest and involvement are bound to bring feelings of accomplishment and effectiveness simply because one is "doing things"; even in the absence of actual evidence of effectiveness, the interest tends to sustain itself by discovering or assuming such evidence. Likewise political indifference, whatever its source, may produce a belief in individual ineffectiveness rather than the other way round—for example, through the not unusual tendency of justifying one's inertness (to himself as well as to others) by insisting that political participation is futile.

Other Questions Pertaining to Attitudes of Political Futility

In addition to the four interview items that were included in the rating of political futility, several other questions throw light on the same cluster of attitudes. These questions deal with the respondent's feelings in regard to the Democratic and Republican parties, whether they are believed to differ significantly, whether they offer a genuine choice that makes voting meaningful, whether it makes any difference which one wins. Along this line, the pre-election interview asked:

> Now, as one of the last questions, would you tell me: Do you think it will make a great deal of difference to the country whether the Democrats or the Republicans win the election, or won't it make much difference which side wins? (In what way would it make a difference? or: Why do you feel that it won't make much difference?)

Results from this question are summarized in Table 5.5. Approximately two-thirds of the registered voters thought that it would make a great deal of difference which party won. This opinion was more generally held among Stevenson than among

Eisenhower supporters or among the undecided and non-committal voters. As in the political futility score, here again about one-third of the respondents answer in a way that is indicative of indifference or doubts about the effectiveness of their votes. When people who actually voted for Stevenson or Eisenhower are compared, the percentages closely parallel those of Table 5.5. The reasons members gave for their opinions (Table D. 11 in the Appendix) reflect the same considerations as those mentioned in explaining what issues they felt were important and why they intended voting one way or the other (see pp. 344-345).

TABLE 5.5

PRE-ELECTION OPINIONS OF REGISTERED VOTERS AS TO WHETHER REPUBLICAN OR DEMOCRATIC VICTORY WOULD MAKE MUCH DIFFERENCE

	Vote Intention			
	Stevenson	*Eisenhower*	*Undecided, Refuse to Say, etc.*	*Total Sample*
Great deal of difference	73%	57%	43%	67%
Not much difference	21	38	36	26
Can't say; no answer, etc.	6	5	21	7
	100%	100%	100%	100%
No. of cases	(488)	(117)	(85)	(690)

A closely similar question was asked after the election was over. It was phrased:

> Now that the Republicans won the election, do you think it will make a great deal of difference to the country, or won't it make much difference? (In what ways will it make a difference? or: Why do you feel that it won't make much difference?).

Table 5.6 give the results on this post-election question. Most notable is the sharp drop from the pre-election interview in the proportion believing that the election outcome makes a great deal of difference. Instead of two-thirds it is now less than half the members—and the change occurs almost entirely among the Stevenson voters. Before the election, three-fourths of these

Democratic voters said it would make a great deal of difference; after the election fewer than half held to this opinion. These post-election responses are probably no longer so much an expression of belief that the parties do not differ as it is a combination of sportsmanship spirit (being a good loser, etc.) and whistling in the dark, looking on the bright side, or accenting the positive. Although this attitude presumably signifies no permanent increase of futility feelings about politics but only a temporary attempt to minimize the disappointment of defeat, nevertheless, it carries some implication that the election really doesn't matter much. To the extent that this inference is valid it means that the post-election figures must be taken along with those from before the election as a basis for estimating the amount of effectiveness or ineffectiveness felt. The answers to the later question suggest that more than half the union members are at best only partly and weakly convinced that their voting behavior is truly important.

TABLE 5.6

POST-ELECTION OPINIONS ON WHETHER THE REPUBLICAN
VICTORY WOULD MAKE MUCH DIFFERENCE

	Stevenson Voters	*Eisenhower Voters*	*Did Not Vote*	*Total Sample*
Great deal of difference	46%	50%	43%	46%
Not much difference	41	43	35	41
Can't say; no answer; ambiguous	13	7	22	13
	100%	100%	100%	100%
No. of cases	(170)	(116)	(65)	(351)

Tabulations of members' post-election explanations of their opinions (see Appendix, Table D.12) show that among those saying "a great deal of difference" there is a marked increase in the proportion of pro-Republican reasons and a corresponding decrease in the variety as well as in the number of anti-Republican and pro-Democratic comments. The diminished variety is more notable than it otherwise would be, inasmuch as *two* ideas were coded for the post-election question and only one for the pre-

election question. These qualitative differences tend to support
the interpretation offered above that, once the votes are counted,
many persons on the losing side quickly convince themselves that
all is for the best. The arguments which they stressed a few days
earlier against the winning party and for the unsuccessful one
are now forgotten or suppressed. This familiar phenomenon of
American political life can be construed as evidence that the
individuals who thus change have no deep feeling that the election has serious consequences, favorable or unfavorable. To that
extent they are viewing political action as more or less perfunc-
tory and the voter as more or less ineffective.

One other question in the post-election interview inquired
more directly: "Do you think there is any important difference
between what the Democratic and Republican parties stand for,
or do you think they are about the same?" Replies to this question
are shown in Table 5.7. Only slightly over half the members
believe that there is "any important difference "between the
parties.

TABLE 5.7

OPINIONS ON WHETHER THE DEMOCRATIC AND REPUBLICAN PARTIES ARE THE SAME OR DIFFERENT

	Stevenson Voters	Eisenhower Voters	Did Not Vote	Total Sample
Different	64%	39%	25%	53%
Same	26	50	53	35
Don't know; no answer	10	11	22	12
	100%	100%	100%	100%
No. of cases	(170)	(116)	(65)	(351)

Eisenhower voters are much less inclined than Stevenson voters to see the parties as different, an attitude which may serve
both as real reason and as self-justification for the Democrats
who voted for Eisenhower. Among Stevenson voters who stated
that the parties do differ, 69 per cent volunteered a pro-Democratic remark (57 per cent consisted of comments that the
Democrats are for labor and working people or that Republicans
are for the few, the wealthy, etc. and bad for labor). Only 36

per cent of the Eisenhower voters who thought the parties different volunteered pro-Republican remarks (most frequent were references to governmental efficiency and balanced budget). Belief that the parties do not differ significantly is especially common among non-voters and here too it is probably in part explanatory and in part an excuse.

Taking the results on this question as a whole, the outstanding finding is that only 53 per cent of the members see any important difference between the parties. This attitude in itself may go far to undermine feelings of political effectiveness since one is pushed toward a position of utter futility if he believes that the choice presented to him in elections is essentially no choice at all.

Two other interview questions have some bearing on feelings of political futility, though along a somewhat different dimension that refers to belief in *governmental* impotence. The questions inquired about the respondent's expectations of war and of depression and then continued with queries as to whether he thought the government could do anything to prevent war or depression (Post-election interview, Ques. 27 and 28). Although it is the last portion of the questions that is especially relevant here, replies to the first part are equally worth noting.

In regard to "a bad business depression and unemployment in the next few years," the responses were:

A very great chance	14%
Some chance	49%
No chance at all	37%

A similar tabulation with respect to "danger of another world war in the next few years" shows these responses:

A very great chance	20%
Some chance	67%
No chance at all	13%

Differences between Eisenhower and Stevenson supporters are not large on these questions, but their direction is decidedly suggestive. Workers who believed there was a "great chance" of depression were somewhat more heavily for Stevenson, while those who thought there was great likelihood of war had a larger proportion than average for Eisenhower. The findings offer some support, that is, for the contention that concern over economic depression predisposed voters toward Stevenson and concern over war dangers predisposed toward Eisenhower. Among those who saw a great chance of business depression, 86 per cent intended to vote for Stevenson as against 78 per cent of those not having this expectation. Correspondingly, in respect to war fears, the Eisenhower-intent figures were 29 per cent versus 19 per cent. Stating the relationship another way, among Eisenhower supporters the ratio of those saying "no chance" of depression to those saying "great chance" is 4 to 1, as against 2 to 1 among Stevenson supporters. Regarding war, the ratios were 1 to 3 in the Eisenhower group and 1 to 1 among Stevenson advocates.

Differences in respect to governmental action to prevent depression are likewise suggestive. In the total sample, 85 per cent said "the government can do things to keep the country from having a depression"; 15 per cent said it cannot. The view on war was a little less optimistic, 25 per cent saying that the government "can't do anything to stop it." Workers who thought that government can do something about preventing depression were slightly more for Stevenson than were those saying the government could do nothing (80 per cent to 70 per cent). Among Eisenhower supporters, 21 per cent declared that the government cannot do anything; this figure drops to 14 per cent in the pro-Stevenson group. Belief in the government's ability or impotence in respect to preventing war showed no relation to Democratic versus Republican dispositions.

Workers who have high political futility ratings tend a little more than others to hold the view of government ineffectualness in these matters (regarding depressions, 18 per cent of people with high futility scores versus 11 per cent of those with low futility scores; in regard to war, 27 per cent versus 19 per cent).

Authoritarian Attitudes

The remaining three sets of attitudes to be analyzed lie at the most general level of motivational factors affecting political behavior (Level 5 of Chart 1, page 97). They are among the personality components or dispositions that pervasively enter into social behavior. The three dispositions we shall deal with can be labeled "authoritarian attitudes," "life satisfactions," and "feelings of social alienation." These are, of course, only a few of the many attitude-clusters that might have been included— for example, individuals' aspiration levels and achievement needs, their attitudes of hostility or of helpfulness and concern for the welfare of others, their desires for independence and self-expression, for status and power, for personal security, and similar motivational traits and tendencies. The attitude patterns dealt with here, while not at all exhaustive, permit us to explore the connections that these variables may have with political behavior and political attitudes. Since these dispositions are ones that appear important in the light of previous research and theory, their relationships may be expected to add to our understanding of the variations of political feeling among organized workers.

In this section we deal with an index of authoritarian or anti-democratic attitudes. The concept of authoritarianism has proved valuable in a number of research studies concerned with interpretations of complex social behavior like that exhibited in prejudice and other aspects of intergroup relations, in leader-follower interaction, and in political affiliations and attitudes.[5] Following the lead of the California psychologists, authoritarianism is now usually conceived as referring to a personality type, "syndrome," or pattern of interrelated predispositions including tendencies toward conformity, rigidity, conventionality and submissiveness to in-group authority; aggressiveness toward people who violate conventional values; emphasis on power and tough-

---

[5] The most comprehensive, intensive, and influential studies are those reported in detail by the California group in T. W. Adorno, Else Frenkel-Brunswik, Daniel J. Levinson, R. Nevitt Sanford, *The Authoritarian Personality*, New York, Harper, 1950. The most notable earlier contributions were those of Erich Fromm, *Escape From Freedom*, New York, Farrar and Rinehart, 1941. Research on authoritarianism in relation to political behavior, more closely related to the present inquiry, is reported by Fillmore Sanford, *Authoritarianism and Leadership*, Philadelphia, Institute for Research on Human Relations, 1950; and by Morris Janowitz and Dwaine Marvick, "Authoritarianism and Political Behavior," *Public Opinion Quarterly*, vol. 17, no. 2 (Sept. 1953), pp. 185-201. For penetrating criticisms of research on authoritarianism, particularly of the California studies, see Richard Christie and Marie Jahoda (ed.), *"The Authoritarian Personality,"* Glencoe, Free Press, 1954.

ness, strong leadership, assertion of strength; generalized hostility and a variety of other symptoms. The measure of authoritarian attitudes employed for our purposes is a greatly simplified version of the scales that attempt to tap all facets of the syndrome. We have utilized a few simple questions pertaining to the perception of people as strong or weak, to the need for powerful and strict leaders, to training for obedience, and to aggressive reactions against non-conformists (sex criminals). The resulting rating is admittedly only a rough indication of anti-democratic, authoritarian tendencies. Even in this crude form, however, it enables us to observe a number of meaningful and interesting relationships.

As explained in the section on political futility feelings, a list of statements was read to the person interviewed, with the request that he tell whether he agreed or disagreed with each statement. Five items of the list were used as a basis for estimating the respondent's authoritarian attitudes. The statements are as follows:[6]

	Agree	Disagree	Qualified or No Answer
The most important thing to teach children is absolute obedience to their parents.	62%	30%	8%
Any good leader should be strict with people under him in order to gain their respect.	58%	35%	7%
There are two kinds of people in the world, the weak and the strong.	70%	25%	5%
Prison is too good for sex criminals; they should be publicly whipped or worse.	43%	40%	17%
A few strong leaders could do more for this country than all the laws and talk.	40%	55%	5%

In each instance agreement with the view expressed is scored as an indicator of authoritarian attitude. The total individual scores, from 0 to 5, occur with the following frequencies:

---

[6] The statements are adapted from ones developed by Fillmore Sanford (*op. cit.*) and used in similar form by the Survey Research Center and Morris Janowitz (*op. cit.*).

Authoritarian Attitude Score	*Per Cent of Union Members*	
5	12%	} —High
4	23	
3	21	} —Medium
2	21	
1	16	} —Low
0	7	
	100%	

More than one-third of the people interviewed subscribe to either all or all but one of the statements. Conversely, only one in four rejects all or all but one. The responses as a whole indicate disturbingly weak adherence to the democratic and humanitarian ideals contradicted by the statements. Back of this might be inferred the personal insecurities and confusion of values that tend to make present-day political allegiances unsteady and potentially dangerous. In down-to-earth terms, findings such as these underscore the tremendous educational job that confronts democratic leadership in labor unions and in the community generally. The results tend to confirm the views of thoughtful observers who believe that vast number of citizens, auto workers included, look eagerly for strong men to save them. The temper of the times offers little support for a doctrine of free, independent self-determination by the common people themselves—the non-obedient, the non-conformists, citizens devoted to "laws and talk" rather than to "a few strong leaders." Perhaps the greatest significance of the authoritarian attitude scores lies in their highlighting of this challenge.

At the same time, it is important to see how the more authoritarian individuals differ from those who maintain a more democratic stand—how they differ both in respect to their personal and social characteristics (who they are) and in respect to their political outlook and actions. We find that their most distinguishing characteristic is limited education. Persons who did not go beyond the eighth grade receive high authoritarian scores twice as often as do those having more schooling (46 per cent versus 24 per cent). Age also has some bearing, though differences by age are confined to persons of more than eighth grade schooling. Among persons under 40 years of age who attended high school, only 18 per cent have high authoritarian ratings—in contrast to

35 per cent of those 40 and over. For white workers alone the 18 per cent shrinks further, to 13 per cent. Complete tabulations by education and age are given in Table 5.8. The differences in authoritarian attitudes by education are found to hold not only for both young and old but also for workers at relatively high, medium, and low socio-economic levels and for both Catholics and Protestants. The differences are not found among Negroes in our sample.

TABLE 5.8

AUTHORITARIAN ATTITUDES IN RELATION TO AGE AND EDUCATION

	8th Grade or Less		Above 8th Grade	
Authoritarian rating:	*Under 40*	*40 and over*	*Under 40*	*40 and over*
High (Score 4-5)	42%	47%	18%	35%
Medium (2-3)	43	36	58	34
Low (0-1)	15	17	24	31
	100%	100%	100%	100%
No. of cases	(32)	(87)	(103)	(66)

The pronounced effect of education affords encouragement for believing that as the educational level continues to improve, authoritarian attitudes will diminish. The fact that younger workers express more non-authoritarian views reinforces this optimistic outlook as to trend.[7] However, it must be noted that in no group of the table do even one-third fall in the safely pro-democratic category which rejects all the five statements or all but one. Clearly a big job remains to be done if non-authoritarian sentiments are to become the prevalent dispositions among working people.

Other findings in regard to social and personal characteristics associated with authoritarian attitudes are the following:

---

[7] Alternative, less optimistic interpretations are possible, of course, according to which it is not the absolute amount of education that is significant but the individual's education relative to that of others and that consequently those having less education and correspondingly more restricted opportunities will continue to develop more authoritarian attitudes. Likewise, the relation to age could mean that in each generation the younger are less authoritarian but that the younger people become more authoritarian as they grow older. We know of no evidence that would establish the truth or falsity of these alternative interpretations.

Women score a little higher in the authoritarian direction than do men; 48 per cent versus 33 per cent have rating of 4 and 5. Women in our sample agree more than men that children should be taught absolute obedience, that people divide into the weak and the strong, and that sex criminals should be "publicly whipped or worse."

Negroes answer the questions in a slightly more authoritarian way than do white respondents (43 per cent versus 33 percent have high scores and, if we compare those of more than eighth grade schooling, the percentages are 41 per cent versus 22 per cent). Negroes agree more than others that there are two kinds of people, the weak and the strong, and that the country needs a few strong leaders; but they agree much *less* than whites that sex criminals should be violently dealt with.

There are slight but suggestive differences by socio-economic status, authoritarian attitudes occurring most often at the middle level. In the upper and lower economic groupings of workers, as many have low as high authoritarian scores while in the middle economic group there are more than twice as many high as low.

Although no overall differences occur by religion (the extremely slight difference present—taking white workers alone —shows Protestants more authoritarian than Catholics), there is an interesting tendency for the *least* authoritarian attitudes to be found among Protestants at the *upper* socio-economic level and among Catholics at the *lower* level.

The percentages with high, medium, and low authoritarian ratings in these two groups, contrasted with all other workers interviewed, are as follows:

	Protestants, upper economic	Catholics, lower economic	All Others
High Authoritarian	25%	19%	36%
Medium	40	48	45
Low	35	33	19

White auto workers born in the south express authoritarian attitudes somewhat more than do those from the north. This is particularly true if we consider those extremely low on authoritarian scores—ratings of 0 to 1 on the index. While 31 per cent of northerners have these low authoritarian scores, only 4 per cent of southerners do.

Although our sample contains too few foreign-born persons to provide reliable figures by separate countries, it is noteworthy that all those of foreign birth taken together show decidedly greater authoritarianism in their responses than do the native-born Americans, 58 per cent of the foreign versus 28 per cent of the American-born scoring 4 and 5. When respondents are classified by their *fathers'* country of birth, sizable differences appear for two nationality groups, though here, too, the samples are small and the figures correspondingly subject to error. Authoritarian responses are given most by workers of Italian and Canadian parentage; little difference is shown from one to another of the remaining nationalities. This last-stated absence of differences is itself a fact worth underscoring since widespread opinions exist to the contrary. No greater authoritarianism than average occurs in groups whose fathers were East European (Poland, Russia, Roumania, Hungary, etc.) and German.

If, now, we select from all our tabulations those groupings of auto workers who are most and least authoritarian, the following are illustrative of the results (with the repeated warning that the percentages are based on small numbers and hence are suggestive only):

	Authoritarian Attitudes		
Least Authoritarian	High	Medium	Low
More than 8th grade education, under 40 years of age, relatively high socio-economic level	7%	63%	30%
More than 8th grade, 40 and over, relatively low socio-economic	10%	25%	65%
More than 8th grade, Catholic, relatively low socio-economic	12%	44%	44%
More than 8th grade, Protestant, relatively high socio-economic	20%	40%	40%
Most Authoritarian			
8th grade or less, relatively high socio-economic	53%	25%	22%
8th grade or less, relatively high socio-economic, Catholics only	70%	12%	18%
8th grade or less, 40 and over, Protestant, relatively low socio-economic	57%	38%	5%
40 and over, Protestant, medium socio-economic	53%	36%	11%

Important as it is to know the social characteristics of authoritarian workers—important partly in dispelling fallacious opinions
as to the groups that are anti-democratic but important also for
better understanding the influences that produce this personal
orientation, for predicting trends and planning measures to
modify the attitudes—these are not, in the context of the present
study, the major reasons for giving attention to authoritarian
dispositions. For purposes of this research, the principal question
is how authoritarian attitudes relate to other political attitudes
and behavior. The following paragraphs summarize our findings
on these relationships.

Within our population of auto workers, authoritarian attitude
scores are unrelated to differences in voting behavior but they
are linked in significant ways with other politically relevant
indexes. In respect to vote, Stevenson and Eisenhower voters
have almost identical authoritarian scores—this in contradiction
to the popular assertion that Eisenhower as a military man and
supposedly strong leader had special appeal for persons of authoritarian tendencies. The same absence of difference in authoritarianism is found when respondents are compared by their
declared partly affiliation; Republicans among these auto workers
are not a whit more authoritarian in their responses than are the
Democrats. Nor are there differences worth speaking of between
voters and non-voters or between undecided voters—those who
still had not made up their minds by late October—and others
who had made firm decisions.

Consistent with the foregoing results is the additional fact
that authoritarian ratings bear almost no relationship to the
index of pro-labor political attitudes or to members' closeness
of attachment to the union. However, a very slight tendency is
observable for those lowest in authoritarianism to be weak in
their union interest or attachment. Further analysis indicates an
explanation for this unexpected finding in that the small category
of low authoritarianism and low union attachment includes more
than a proportionate number of workers who are better educated,
Protestant, of American-born parentage, and in white collar jobs.
This combination of biographic characteristics was associated
with a trifle less authoritarianism than that for the sample as a
whole and also with a trifle less active interest in the union.

This association constitutes a very minor exception, however; the overall generalization remains that, among the auto workers studied, authoritarian attitudes bear almost no relationship to voting activities and preferences or to other indicators of the *direction* of political sentiments and attachments.

The foregoing is far from meaning that authoritarian attitudes have no important bearing on other phases of political behavior. Authoritarian ratings do show clear linkage with political interest and feelings of political effectiveness. Workers who are least authoritarian exhibit greatest political interest (56 per cent of those with low authoritarian scores rate high in political interest as compared with 37 per cent of all others). Conversely, people high in political interest tend to be low in authoritarianism (31 per cent of those with high political interest versus 17 per cent of those not high in political interest). The principal differences are between the least authoritarian and others; those with highly authoritarian attitudes differ very little in political interest from the middle or average authoritarian group. These results are compatible with the view that authoritarian attitudes imply personal frustration and resulting hostility and impatience with democratic efforts—that absence of authoritarian tendencies correspondingly predisposes people toward more vigorous expression of political interest.

Supporting this interpretation is the further finding that highly authoritarian persons in our sample likewise tended to express feelings of political futility while those low in authoritarianism felt more politically effective. This very marked relationship reveals itself in the figures of Table 5.9. Among those high in authoritarianism four times as many have high as have low ratings on political futility while for all remaining individuals there are actually more low than high in futility. It would appear that the presence or absence of authoritarian attitudes goes far to explain feelings of political futility or effectiveness—and indirectly the degree of political interest and participation. But it is safer to interpret these sets of attitudes not as if one accounts for the others but as all parts of a basic personal orientation. The pieces belong together as portions of a total constellation of motivations characteristic of large numbers of people in our present-day world of insecurity and frustration. Feelings of ineffectualness combine with aggressive impulses and devotion to a system of authority, power, convention and conformity in an effort to achieve security, to protect the self from intolerable acknowledgement of inadequacy, defeat and guilt, to "escape from freedom" and personal responsibility.[8] These motivations do not necessarily bring about any particular political affiliation or direction of voting. These actions, and even voting as against not voting, are apparently determined by a variety of circumstances; they have become the thing to do within given social environments and are performed more or less perfunctorily. At least these are suggested explanations for the fact that our data show authoritarian attitudes to be intimately tied to feelings of political interest and effectiveness but not to voting behavior or political preferences.

TABLE 5.9

FEELINGS OF POLITICAL FUTILITY IN RELATION
TO AUTHORITARIAN ATTITUDES

	Authoritarian Rating		
Political Futility Ratings:	*High*	*Medium*	*Low*
High	54%	31%	26%
Medium	33	42	32
Low	13	27	42
	100%	100%	100%
No. of cases	(123)	(135)	(80)

Additional light is cast on authoritarian attitudes and the part they play in political behavior by another comparison provided by our data. We reported above that workers who are strongly pro-union on political matters differ very little in authoritarianism from those who are not pro-union. But when we now compare the *extreme* partisans—both those for and those against union political activity—it is found that these extreme positions are adopted much more by the "authoritarians." The extreme partisans are here defined as the workers earlier de-

---

[8] For elaborations of such interpretations, see Erich Fromm, *op. cit.*; T. W. Adorno et al, *op. cit.*; A. H. Maslow, *Motivation and Personality*, New York, Harper, 1954.

scribed who said that it was all right for unions to support
Stevenson but not all right for business groups to support Eisenhower, or, on the other side, ones who approved such action
by business but not by unions. These two groups are compared
with the remainder of the sample in Table 5.10. It is seen that
among the highly authoritarian, 30 per cent belong to one or the
other of the extremist groups, while among those with low
authoritarian ratings only 12 per cent are in these groups.

TABLE 5.10

EXTREME PRO-UNION AND PRO-BUSINESS PARTISANSHIP IN RELATION TO AUTHORITARIAN ATTITUDES

Partisanship:	Authoritarian Rating		
	High	*Medium*	*Low*
Extreme pro-union	18%	11%	5%
Extreme pro-business	12	12	7
All others	70	77	88
	100%	100%	100%
No. of cases	(123)	(135)	(80)

Looking at the relationship the other way round, we find that in
these two extreme partisan groups combined, the ratio of high
authoritarianism to low is approximately 4 to 1 while for all
other more moderate workers the ratio is only a trifle over 1 to 1
(the percentages in the three authoritarianism categories, high
to low, for the partisans are 46%, 42%, and 12%; for all others
32%, 42%, 26%).[9]

This evidence accords well with the interpretation that
workers with more authoritarian attitudes may line up on the
union side or against it, but that in either case they tend to be
the absolutists, taking extreme stands. At the same time, it should
be recalled, they tend to display less political interest and to
entertain a greater sense of political futility than is characteristic
for the general run of their less authoritarian fellow workers.

---

[9] Any apparent inconsistency between the proportion mentioned here
and the figures of Table 5.10 is due to the fact that all percentages are
computed from *weighted* figures as explained in the note to Table 2.1
(p. 29).

Altogether, our results suggest that these people present a special challenge to political leadership, both in the union and in the general society. Although they voted about the same as others in 1952, their faith in powerful leaders, absolute obedience, violence against deviates and similar attitudes points to the danger of their being potential adherents of anti-democratic movements. From the standpoint of the labor organization, even when the authoritarian-inclined are on side, their lack of balance and democratic footing justifies skepticism regarding their value to the organization. Evidence that these patterns of motivation exist, together with growing knowledge of their political implications and of the social backgrounds that produce the dispositions, it is hoped, may spur intensified efforts to strengthen educational influences and to achieve social conditions that will create healthier, more democratic personal and political attitudes.

Attitudes Regarding Equality for Negro Workers

A question on the treatment of Negro workers, though not included in the authoritarian ratings, is of special interest in this connection, since the assumption based on other studies is frequently made that prejudice is associated with authoritarianism. The question, asked of white respondents only, reads as follows:

> Do you think Negro and white workers should be treated equally in hiring, promotions, and lay-offs or not? Could you tell me more on how you personally feel about that?

Replies to this question were classified into three categories, with the number of answers falling into each category shown by the percentages:

For equal treatment, without qualification	55%
Mainly for equal treatment but with qualifications or reservations about living in the same neighborhood, mixing socially, etc.	30%
Against equal treatment, either flatly or in a qualified way	15%

Many workers did not limit themselves to the specific question of equal treatment on the job but asserted their more general views concerning Negroes. Typical comments were:

I believe in equality
They are human as well as white people are
What difference does skin color make?
They are equal under the law

On the less favorable side:

I don't want to live near them
No social mixing
Should keep away from colored race
I don't want to work with them
I don't like them
Etc.

Our classification took the entire answer into account. If the replies are considered only in reference specifically to job treatment, almost everyone in the second category and a few in the last group, along with all those in the first category, gave or implied affirmative answers. In other words, more than 85 per cent of these white auto workers believe in equal job treatment, whatever reservations they may have about complete racial equality in community relations as a whole.

This is a much more favorable picture from a democratic viewpoint than were the answers to the more general questions used as a basis for the authoritarian scores. To some extent this may reflect the effects of educational and propaganda efforts on this particular theme within the union and it likewise may result from actual experience in working with Negroes. In any event the high proportion favorable to equal employment treatment is important and particularly significant in view of the extent of authoritarian attitudes among these same working people.

When responses to this race equality question were compared with authoritarian ratings, there proved to be only a slight tendency for the strongly authoritarian to express more anti-Negro feeling than do others (19 per cent against equal job treatment as against 11 per cent among all others). This difference, while in the expected direction, is so small that it can hardly be considered in close agreement with earlier research findings and theory which tie ethnocentric attitudes to the "authoritarian personality."[10] Our evidence would dictate caution against any too general conclusions that advance authoritarianism as a main explanation for prejudice. The limited association in our data may signify that full acceptance of Negroes in employment relations has become the social norm among Detroit auto workers and that consequently individuals do not deviate greatly by reason of personal dispositions.

But additional analysis points to a striking fact about the preceding relationship. The figures cited turn out to be a net balance between relationships that run in opposite directions within higher and lower socio-economic groupings of auto workers (see Table 5.11). At upper and middle levels, people with authoritarian attitudes are more anti-Negro, more opposed to full equality. But among workers economically less favored the reverse is true—the most authoritarian are *less* anti-Negro, more for equal treatment.

TABLE 5.11

PROPORTIONS OPPOSED TO EQUAL EMPLOYMENT TREATMENT
OF NEGROES—BY DEGREE OF AUTHORITARIANISM
AT THREE SOCIO-ECONOMIC LEVELS

	Socio-economic Status			Total
Authoritarian Rating	*High*	*Middle*	*Low*	*Sample*
High	28%*	19%	7%	19%
Medium and Low	8	9	17	11

* Each percentage figure represents the proportion of persons expressing prejudice among all those of that socio-economic status and that degree of of authoritarianism. Percentages are based on 21 to 98 cases.

Thus in the upper economic group, the highly authoritarian have three and a half times as many prejudiced, proportionately, as do the less authoritarian (28 per cent versus 8 per cent); at the low economic level the ratio is sharply opposite (7 per cent to 17 per cent). If we include along with the definitely anti-equalitarian group those who expressed only qualified approval of equal treatment, the same reversal effect persists (upper economic, 59 per cent among highly authoritarian versus 37 per

_____
[10] Adorno et al, *op. cit.*

cent among others; lower economic, 24 per cent among highly authoritarian versus 47 per cent among others).

In general, speaking of the population of auto workers here studied, we conclude that a *combination* of high authoritarianism with average or better socio-economic status predisposes to anti-Negro orientation but that similar authoritarian attitudes among the economically disadvantaged (low socio-economic status) lead to the opposite orientation. This makes sense if we assume that the upper level authoritarians, in terms of their perceived or imagined self-interests as home owners and favorably situated workers, would tend more to direct their hostilities against Negroes as a threat, whereas the lower level authoritarians would incline rather to sympathize with Negro workers as fellow underdogs and to turn their aggressive impulses against the upper groups.

Regardless of whether this or other interpretations prove correct, however, the important point stands that personality differences like those represented by an authoritarian rating may have dissimilar, even opposite, consequences depending upon the social context in which people are acting. Authoritarians may be vigorous battlers on the side of the angels as well as on the side of the devil. This is not to overlook the dangers inherent in their emotionalism and extremism. It is necessary, however, to guard against any easy assumption that these dispositions operate only in a reactionary or fascist direction. That depends on the accepted values and orientations within the groups to which the particular authoritarians are attached.[11]

Attitudes on race relations had no observable effect on the way Detroit auto workers voted in the national election. Stevenson voters and those for Eisenhower were indistinguishable in their answers to the question on whether Negroes should be accorded equal treatment. Unexpectedly, however, non-voters (eligible to vote) did differ from voters. A greater proportion of them were for full equality—71 per cent of non-voters versus 52 per cent of voters—and only 10 per cent of them definitely disapproved equal treatment as against 16 per cent of voters.

---

[11] For elaboration of this critical view in regard to the social orientation of the "authoritarian personality" see E. A. Shils, "Authoritarianism: 'Right' and 'Left'" in Richard Christie and Marie Jahoda, *op. cit.*

This is an additional bit of evidence suggesting that many non-voting workers may be not the unaroused or unconcerned but rather the alienated—the tired, disillusioned, cynical. Earlier we saw that they are no less pro-union and no less politically interested than the voters; now it appears that they are even freer of racial intolerance.

Replies to the question on equal treatment for Negroes were also compared for groups differing in age, education, religion and other social variables in order to see what parts of the union membership feel each way. In summary, here is what we find (again with the reminder that the numbers become very small in these subdivisions of our sample and hence that the conclusions are very tentative):

> Union members born in the South approve equal treatment of Negroes fully as much as do Northerners (we refer here to white workers only, of course). In fact, the difference that occurs shows the Southerners *more* generally for *employment equality* (66 per cent of Southern born versus 51 per cent of Northern).

> Workers of foreign born parents do not differ on the whole from those of American parentage. However, this overall comparison hides a sharp contrast of attitudes between different nationality groups. The Polish and German ethnic groups express most frequent anti-equalitarian views; workers of all other national backgrounds support Negro equality more staunchly than do Americans of native-born parents (25 per cent of the Polish and German gave answers against equal treatment as against only 3 per cent of all others having foreign parents—and 17 per cent of those of American parentage).

> Education, age, religion and socio-economic status join together as an additional network of influence. Thus, though education and socio-economic status considered separately do not correlate with responses to the question on race, we find that poorly educated workers at upper and middle economic levels are more anti-Negro than average while at the lower level they are the least prejudiced. For example,

among those who have eighth grade schooling or less and who are above average economically, 23 per cent are opposed to equal treatment; with similar education but below average economically, only 8 per cent have the negative attitude. Corresponding percentages for full equality in these two groups are 40 per cent and 69 per cent.

The influence of age likewise differs depending on amount of education: the most democratic expressions come from those past 40 who went beyond eighth grade and from those under 40 who did not go beyond eighth grade. Religious affiliation similarly shows markedly different associations with race feelings for groups differing in age, education and economic standing. A few examples of these complex linkages follow:

Especially Favorable to Equal Treatment of Negroes

	Fully for Equality	Qualifiedly for Equality	Against Equality
Catholic, low ec. status	69%	25%	6%
Catholic, over 40, beyond 8th grade	80	20	—
Protestant, over 40, upper and middle ec. status	66	30	4

Especially Unfavorable to Equal Treatment

	Fully for Equality	Qualifiedly for Equality	Against Equality
Catholic, 8th grade or less, upper and middle ec. status	43%	30%	27%
Catholic, 8th grade or less, under 40	56	9	35
Protestant, over 40, beyond 8th grade	48	25	27
Protestant, beyond 8th grade, low ec. status	22	52	26

If we hypothesize that race prejudice to some extent reflects feelings of frustration and that such frustration may be occasioned in part by a socio-economic position below that which one's education would imply, then we would expect a tendency for better educated workers at the low economic level to be more anti-Negro than either the better educated at higher levels or the poorly educated at low levels. We might also expect a disparity in the opposite direction—the poorly educated who are

When Labor Votes

high socio-economically—to result in uneasy tensions concerning status and consequently to predispose also toward race prejudice. Our findings are in accord with these hypotheses, as may be seen in Table 5.12, though the magnitude of the differences is not great. The two groups in which education and socio-economic status agree (columns 1 and 4) have higher proportions for full equality and lower proportions against equality than do the two groups in which a discrepancy exists (columns 2 and 3).

TABLE 5.12

ATTITUDES TOWARD EQUALITY FOR NEGRO WORKERS IN
RELATION TO DISCREPANCY BETWEEN EDUCATION
AND SOCIO-ECONOMIC STATUS

	High ed., high ec. status	*High ed., low ec. status*	*Low ed., high ec. status*	*Low ed., low ec. status*
Fully for equality	62%	54%	40%	69%
Qualifiedly for equality	27	29	37	23
Against equality	11	17	23	8
	100%	100%	100%	100%
No. of cases	(43)	(29)	(22)	(31)

One further finding—a negative one—is that feelings on treatment of Negroes show no relationship to the size of local unions nor to the ratings of *esprit de corps* in the locals.

Satisfaction With Life

The two remaining measures of underlying attitudes have to do with feelings of personal adjustment, first in the form of contentment or acceptance of life conditions and second in respect to attitudes of personal futility and social alienation. The first, which we are calling "satisfaction with life," was derived from responses to the seven questions reproduced below. Under each question the distribution of answers is shown and an asterisk marks those responses that were scored positively in compiling the life satisfaction rating.

Q.26a. On the whole, how satisfied would you say you are with the life you have? Which one of these answers here (respondent is shown a card) comes nearest to telling how you feel about your life?

*Completely satisfied	16%
*Well satisfied	47
Neither satisfied nor dissatisfied	23
A little dissatisfied	10
Very dissatisfied	2
No answer or not classifiable	2
	100%

Q.26b. Do you worry a lot about the future?

Yes	30%
Yes and no; sometimes	3
*No	64
No answer or not classifiable	3
	100%

Q.26c. Do you often feel restless, wanting to be on the move doing something, but not knowing what?

Yes	37%
Yes and no; sometimes	4
*No	57
No answer or not classifiable	2
	100%

Q.26d. Taking your life as it is now, do you feel that you have as much chance to enjoy life as you should have?

*Yes	76%
Yes and no; sometimes	4
No	18
No answer or not classifiable	2
	100%

Q.26e. Do you feel that you are accomplishing the sorts of things you would like to in your life?

*Yes	59%
Yes and no; somewhat	5
No	34
No answer or not classifiable	2
	100%

Q.26f. How do you feel about your chances for getting ahead?

*Good chances	40%
Some chance; as good as most workers, etc.	13
Poor chance; dim, etc.	35
No answer or not classifiable	12
	100%

Q.27e. Would you tell me which of these answers (respondent is shown a
card) comes nearest to the way you feel about your job? Would
you say you are:

°Completely satisfied	16%
°Well satisfied	51
Neither satisfied nor dissatisfied	13
A little dissatisfied	13
Very dissatisfied	4
No answer or not classifiable	3
	———
	100%

Allowing one point for each response that indicated personal
adjustment or satisfaction, we obtained a score for each person,
a total of 7 signifying greatest satisfaction with life and 0 least
satisfaction. The scores are distributed as follows:

Satisfaction Rating	Per Cent of Union Members
7	10%
6	18
5	22
4	19
3	14
2	10
1	6
0	1
	———
	100%

For convenience in later comparisons we shall combine these
ratings into the three categories—

High satisfaction (Ratings 6 and 7)	28%
Medium satisfaction (Ratings 4 and 5)	41%
Low satisfaction (Ratings 0 to 3)	31%

On the average, four of the seven questions were answered
in the satisfied direction while three were not. More than one-
fourth of the workers declared themselves content on all seven
points or on all but one. These results, both the total scores and
the percentages shown on separate questions, surely convey no
picture of widespread unhappiness or disaffection; most auto
workers feel at least moderately comfortable concerning their
life conditions. This is not so true, however, of a sizable group

who rate toward the lower end of the scale. One-third declared that they "worry a lot about the future" and a somewhat larger number feel that they "are not accomplishing the sorts of things [they] would like to in life." The same proportion "often feel restless, wanting to be on the move doing something but not knowing what." Approximately one-fifth feel that they do not "have as much chance to enjoy life as [they] should have"; one in six states that he is either a little dissatisfied or very dissatisfied about his job and one in eight expresses similar dissatisfaction about his life as a whole. Who these less satisfied people are and how they differ socially and politically from persons better satisfied is a first question for attention.

The small number of women workers in our sample do not differ to a reliable extent from the men on this measure but the data suggest that slightly fewer of them are highly satisfied (19 per cent in the high category compared with 28 per cent of the men). The difference is most marked in answer to the question "Do you worry a lot. . . ." (62 per cent of women as against 26 per cent of men responded with a flat "yes"). On one other question—feelings about your "chance to enjoy life"—women are also distinctly less satisfied (40 per cent say "no" or are doubtful compared to 20 per cent of the men).

Negro workers tend to have lower than average life satisfaction ratings (41 per cent in the "low" category versus 30 per cent of white workers;[12] 14 per cent "high" versus 30 per cent of whites). The separate responses that most definitely reflect less satisfaction on the part of Negroes are those on the general question of "how satisfied would you say you are with the life you have" (27 per cent of Negroes versus 63 per cent of whites say "well satisfied" or "completely satisfied"; 20 per cent versus 12 per cent say they are dissatisfied) and the question on "the way you feel about your job (31 per cent of Negroes versus 66 per cent of whites say they are completely or well satisfied; 23 per cent versus 18 per cent say they are dissatisfied).

Comparisons by socio-economic status reveal substantial differences. As might be expected, workers of relatively high status

---

[12] This contrast increases at the extremely low ratings, 30 per cent of Negroes as against 15 per cent of whites having scores of 0, 1 or 2.

are decidedly better satisfied; however, lowest life-satisfaction
ratings occur not in the group least well off but in the middle
economic range. In terms of people's aspirations and expectations
—intensified ambitions and upward strivings of the middle group,
greater spirit of "keeping up with the Joneses"—this result is quite
meaningful. Dissatisfaction at the middle level is especially
pronounced among persons past 40 years of age. The three
socio-economic categories show the following percentages above
and below a midpoint on the life-satisfaction scale (Table 5.13).
The contrast between the middle socio-economic group and
others is still greater if Negroes are omitted. The percentages
above the midpoint (top row of the table) then become 70, 41,
and 65.

TABLE 5.13

LIFE-SATISFACTION RATINGS IN RELATION TO SOCIO-ECONOMIC STATUS

Life-Satisfaction Ratings:	Socio-Economic Level			Total Sample
	High	Middle	Low	
Above midpoint (Ratings 5 to 7)				
Below midpoint (Ratings 0 to 4)	70%	42%	56%	52%
	30	58	44	48
	100%	100%	100%	100%
No. of cases	(65)	(145)	(81)	(291)

Life-satisfaction ratings are less clearly and consistently associated with age, education, and religion. For the sample as a
whole, none of these is closely linked to satisfactions. However,
slight tendencies are present for older persons (past 40) to be
less satisfied (especially at upper and middle economic levels)
and for Catholics to be more satisfied than Protestants. Schooling
makes very little difference, whether in the total sample or by
separate age groups or socio-economic levels save that in the
low economic range those with only eighth grade schooling or
less are better satisfied than those who went beyond the eighth
grade.

The character of these interrelations can best be illustrated by listing a few of the groupings that show particularly large or small percentages of high satisfaction ratings.

Greatest Satisfaction	*Percentage of Satisfaction Ratings above Midpoint*
High socio-economic, Catholics	77%
High socio-economic, age under 40	81%
Low socio-economic, white, eighth grade or less	72%
Least Satisfaction	
Low socio-economic, Negroes	35%
Middle socio-economic, age over 40	34%
Middle socio-economic, age over 40, more than eighth grade	30%

The central question for present purposes is how life-satisfaction ratings are linked to political behavior and attitudes among these auto workers. The findings are as follows.

Voting behavior is not related in significant degree to individuals' feelings of general satisfaction or dissatisfaction. Neither on the overall rating nor on the separate satisfaction questions do Eisenhower and Stevenson voters differ beyond variations that may occur by chance. Generalized discontent was apparently not a significant determinant of presidential vote among these workers. Nor is degree of satisfaction associated with non-voting; the eligible non-voters are neither disproportionately the smugly satisfied nor the personally disaffected. Likewise the "undecided" voters, those who had not made up their minds shortly before election day, are by and large no different from other voters.

Agreement or disagreement with labor's political position also has little if any linkage with members' overall life satisfactions. However, the data do suggest a slight tendency for the people who are neither markedly satisfied nor markedly dissatisfied, those who are just a little unhappy about their life situation, to be most pro-labor politically. Certainly there is nothing in the findings to indicate that the deeply dissatisfied or disgruntled are particularly strong supporters of labor political activities.

A somewhat closer connection is found between life satisfactions and degree of political interest. The least satisfied are not as politically aroused as are those better satisfied. This seeming paradox, that dissatisfied people often are apathetic about changing things, has been repeatedly commented on by students of society. Many of the dissatisfied are passively resigned to their lot, disillusioned in regard to political remedies, or overwhelmed by feelings of impotence. According to this interpretation we should find that the least satisfied also have greater feelings of political futility. The data bear out this expectation. Attitudes of political effectiveness tend to accompany feelings of life satisfaction—a result that in part reflects the effects of higher socio-economic status on both satisfaction and political involvement.

Percentage comparisons bearing on the above relationships are these: Among low-satisfaction workers, 33 per cent manifested strong political interest (30 per cent among *extremely* low-satisfaction) as compared with 46 per cent of high-satisfaction workers. On the dimension of political futility, 21 per cent of the low-satisfaction people felt politically effective compared with 31 per cent of the high-satisfaction workers. Feelings of political futility or impotence occur in 46 per cent of the low-satisfaction category and in 36 per cent of the high-satisfaction. Taking more extreme groups in respect to satisfaction sharpens the contrast—52 per cent futility at the low-satisfaction end as against 28 per cent among the highly satisfied.

Individuals' attachment to the union also shows some association with life-satisfaction ratings. The dissatisfied are least identified with the union (31 per cent of them are in the group lowest in union interest and participation while only 17 per cent of all others are in this lowest category; 27 per cent of the dissatisfied as compared with 41 per cent of others rate high in union attachment). The fairly satisfied and well satisfied do not differ in their attachment to the union. Here again, then, the evidence points to inertia among the dissatisfied; they participate less actively in the union on the average than do the better satisfied workers just as they show less political interest and feeling of effectiveness.

The dissatisfied people tend also to be ones who have authoritarian attitudes. This accords with a frustration interpretation of authoritarianism; the expressed dissatisfactions rather directly bespeak thwarting of felt needs and desires. Among the dissatisfied in our sample, three times as many have high as have low authoritarian attitudes (44 per cent to 15 per cent) while for all others high and low authoritarian attitudes are almost equal (32 per cent to 27 per cent). This same comparison, using the extremely satisfied and dissatisfied, yields the following more striking results: among the extremely dissatisfied, 47 per cent have highly authoritarian attitudes and only 12 per cent are low; among the extremely satisfied, there are more low authoritarian scores than high (25 per cent high to 38 per cent low).

All these results pertaining to life-satisfaction ratings can be seen in better perspective after we report the last of the attitude measures, those having to do with feelings of social alienation.

Attitude of Social Alienation ("Anomie")

This last of our measures of underlying attitudes is derived from answers to five remaining items of the list in which respondents expressed their agreement or disagreement with selected value statements. These items pertain to feelings of personal morale (or demoralization), social alienation and lack of trust, insecurity or "lostness," Durkheim's "anomie." Dr. Leo Srole, who used these five items in a study of prejudice,[13] describes them as covering the following components of the anomic pattern, in the order named—"the individual's sense of the unresponsiveness to his lot and to his needs shown by community leadership"; "perception of the social order as essentially fickle, unpredictable and orderless"; "sense that the framework of immediate personal relationships . . . was no longer predictive or supportive"; "loss of faith in the doctrine of progress as applied to the self"; "deflation or loss of meaning of internalized group norms, values, goals, . . . meaninglessness and futility of life itself."

---

[13] Leo Srole, "Social Dysfunction, Personality and Social Distance Attitudes," mimeographed paper read before the American Sociological Society, 1951 annual meeting, Chicago.

The five items, with percentages responding each way, follow:

	Agree	Disagree	Qualified or No Answer
There's little use in writing to public officials because often they aren't really interested in the problems of the average man.	40%	53%	7%
Nowadays a person has to live pretty much for today and let tomorrow take care of itself.	32	63	5
These days a person doesn't really know who he can count on.	61	34	5
In spite of what some people say, the lot of the average man is getting worse, not better.	27	67	6
It's hardly fair to bring children into the world with the way things look for the future.	22	73	5

An individual's total score is simply the number of the above statements with which he agrees. The individual scores or ratings occur with the following frequencies:

Social Alienation Rating	Per Cent of Union Members
5	3%
4	10
3	19
2	19
1	26
0	23
	————
	100%

Since the five statements are all rather strongly pessimistic and indicative of a seriously distrustful outlook on life, the large number of 0 and 1 ratings was to be expected. Indeed one may be inclined to ponder the fact that *only* one-fourth of these working people felt like rejecting all five statements. But more definite basis for concern is contained in the finding that one-third of the sample agree with three or more of the five items. Considering the content of the statements, such responses, to say the least, reflect a lack of assurance about life, a questionable enough state of personal morale to undermine any smug complacency regarding the "psychology" of the present-day American worker.

In line with the foregoing thinking about the five statements it appears reasonable to group the ratings, for convenience in later analysis, as follows:

High degree of social alienation (Ratings 3 to 5)   32%
Intermediate degree of social alienation (Ratings 1 and 2)   45%
Low degree of social alienation (Rating 0)   23%

Here, as in the case of our other general attitudes, we are interested in two types of analysis—first, to identify and characterize the people who possess the feelings of alienation, distrust and hopelessness in greater or in less degree; and second, to discover whether these feelings are related to political behavior and associated attitudes.

Comparisons of individuals who manifest above average degrees of social alienation with those below average yield these conclusions:

Though women have high alienation ratings in just about the same proportion as men, there are fewer of them who are not at all alienated or distrustful on these questions (only 12 per cent have 0 ratings compared to 24 per cent of men). It happens that almost exactly the same quantitative relationship holds true of Negroes compared with whites. There are few persons in either of these subgroups (women workers or Negroes) who are not moved to endorse at least one of the pessimistic statements.

Age, education, socio-economic status, and religion show only moderate relationship to alienation ratings when each is considered alone. However, the connections turn out to be much closer when combinations of these characteristics are considered. This is well illustrated by the case of religion and socio-economic status. Protestants as a whole average a little higher in the "anomie" direction than do Catholics; and the people of higher and middle economic status are a trifle more alienated than those of lower status. However, these differences are found to be resultants of much larger but partly offsetting relationships. Among Protestants, the high and low status groups express greatest alienation, the middle group least; among Catholics the reverse is true, the highest degree of alienation occurring at the middle economic level with decidedly less in the lower status group. These interrelations are brought out by the following figures (tabulation is for whites alone) showing the percentage having ratings above average on social alienation:

Protestants Socio-Economic Rating			Catholics Socio-Economic Rating		
High	*Medium*	*Low*	*High*	*Medium*	*Low*
59%	45%	64%	40%	51%	24%

Similar cross-relationships occur in respect to age and education. Workers with limited education (eighth grade schooling or less) have greater numbers who are socially alienated. This holds true at all socio-economic levels but it is especially pronounced among those lowest in economic status (for the total sample, 58 per cent of those with eighth grade or less had alienation ratings above average compared with 41 per cent of the better educated; at the low economic level the corresponding percentages are 62 and 33). The age comparison shows that persons 40 and over are slightly more alienated, but there is a significantly large difference only in the high economic grouping. Combining age and education, we find that younger, better educated workers express much less spirit of social alienation than the average (36 per cent are above average while 55 per cent of all others are above average).

Groupings of personal characteristics in relation to the alienation ratings are further illustrated in combinations such as those listed below. These include the subgroups manifesting the attitudes in highest and lowest degree.

	Percentage of Alienation Ratings Above Average
Greatest Social Alienation	
Protestant, 8th grade or less, age under 40	87%
Relatively high socio-economic, Protestant, age over 40	78%
Middle socio-economic, Catholic, age over 40	67%
Relatively low socio-economic, Protestant, 8th grade or less	78%
Least Social Alienation	
Catholic, more than 8th grade, age under 40	25%
Relatively high socio-economic, more than 8th grade, age under 40	30%
Middle socio-economic, Protestant, 8th grade or less, age over 40	28%
Relatively low socio-economic, Catholic	24%
Relatively low socio-economic, Catholic, more than 8th grade	18%

Our analysis now turns to the question of how the feelings of alienation relate to political behavior and attitudes. We look first at the way individuals voted in 1952. Eisenhower and Stevenson voters are found to differ slightly in the number who are extremely high in "anomic" feelings; 17 per cent of Eisenhower supporters as against 9 per cent of those for Stevenson received ratings of 4 and 5 (high anomie). Non-voters likewise differ from voters only at the upper extreme of ratings, 25 per cent of non-voters to 11 per cent of voters having ratings of 4 and 5. Looking at the figures the other way round, of all the workers showing extreme alienation, only 46 per cent voted for Stevenson (25 per cent did not vote and 29 per cent were for Eisenhower); for all others in the sample, 68 per cent voted for Stevenson (11 per cent did not vote and 21 per cent voted for Eisenhower). These results indicate that the most hopeless and cynical workers tend not to vote at all or to vote contrary to the prevailing sentiment among their fellow workers. The non-voters answered every one of the five questions in this index a little more in the distrustful direction than did the voters. Undecided voters, those who had not made up their minds shortly before election day, did not have particularly high feelings of alienation; if anything, a few more of them than average were free of such attitudes on all five questions.

Ratings of alienation show no correlation with degree of pro-labor political orientation nor with attachment to the union. However, the ratings are definitely associated with political interest and feelings of political effectiveness or futility. The relationship to political interest is summarized in Table 5.14. Workers relatively free of feelings of social alienation have decidedly higher interest in political activities (61 per cent are in the high interest category compared to only 30 per cent in the case of persons strongly alienated). Among the more extremely alienated (rating 4 and 5, not shown separately in the table) 25 per cent are high in political interest and the same number are low. This sharply contrasts with the "low alienation" group in which there are five times as many high as low (61 per cent to 12 per cent). The personal orientations toward life clearly do have important bearing on political attitudes and behavior.

TABLE 5.14
POLITICAL INTEREST IN RELATION TO ATTITUDE
OF SOCIAL ALIENATION

Ratings of Political Interest (II):	Ratings of Social Alienation			Total Sample
	High	Intermediate	Low	
High	30%	42%	61%	43%
Medium	49	34	27	37
Low	21	24	12	20
	100%	100%	100%	100%
No. of cases	(114)	(143)	(77)	(334)

Along with the foregoing goes the even closer relationship of political effectiveness-futility feelings to the attitudes of social alienation. As would be expected, there is a marked tendency for political futility to be associated with the feelings of personal futility reflected in our rating of "anomie" or alienation. In some degree feelings of political futility are merely an extension or special application of the general pessimistic and despairing outlook. The linkage between these two attitude measures is shown in Table 5.15. It is apparent that very great differences are present in the political futility ratings of people high and low in social alienation. Persons whose general outlook is one of hopelessness and alienation express marked feelings of political futility five times as often proportionately as do those who have little feeling of alienation (60 per cent versus 12 per cent). Conversely, these non-alienated workers express a sense of political effectiveness (low futility six times as frequently as do the highly alienated (56 per cent to 9 per cent).

TABLE 5.15
FEELINGS OF POLITICAL FUTILITY IN RELATION TO ATTITUDES
OF SOCIAL ALIENATION

Ratings of Political Futility:	Ratings of Social Alienation			Total Sample
	High	Intermediate	Low	
High	60%	35%	12%	38%
Medium	31	44	32	37
Low	9	21	56	25
	100%	100%	100%	100%
No. of cases	(115)	(146)	(78)	(339)

There is also a strong tendency for expressions of social alienation to be accompanied by authoritarian attitudes and for persons relatively free of alienated feelings to be non-authoritarian. This is shown in the figures of Table 5.16. With equal justification, the relationship can be described in the reverse direction; that is, authoritarian persons have much more pronounced attitudes of alienation, distrust and pessimism than do those who are less authoritarian.

TABLE 5.16

AUTHORITARIAN ATTITUDE IN RELATION TO FEELINGS OF SOCIAL ALIENATION

Authoritarian Attitudes:	Ratings of Social Alienation			Total Sample
	High	Intermediate	Low	
High	59%	30%	13%	35%
Medium	36	44	43	42
Low	5	26	44	23
	100%	100%	100%	100%
No. of cases	(113)	(145)	(77)	(335)

Neither can be said to cause the other; rather both are manifestations of continued emotional tensions arising from disturbed interpersonal relations and inner conflicts of earlier life. For present purposes the important thing is that different aspects of the "syndrome" indicated by our attitude scores are associated in varying degrees with politically relevant interests, feelings, and behavior.

The attitude rating given by our index of life-satisfaction belongs with the grouping just mentioned. It was seen earlier to be linked to authoritarian attitudes; it is likewise tied to feelings of social alienation. The greater people's feelings of life-satisfaction, the less they give hopeless, distrustful or despairing responses to the questions here under consideration. Those with low life-satisfaction ratings are in the strongly alienated category four times as often as they are in the group relatively free of such feelings (45 per cent to 12 per cent); among high-satisfaction workers the corresponding ratio is in the reverse direction (27 per cent to 37 per cent).

Summary of Chapters 4 and 5

Some of the high points of the foregoing interrelations will be re-stated here before we proceed in Chapter 6 to view the total picture from another angle. Then, in the final chapter, we shall look at all the results in perspective to ascertain what general conclusions can be drawn.

In Chapters 4 and 5 we have analyzed data that might add to our understanding of the political attitudes and voting behavior of Detroit auto workers. To this end, we set up and examined seven indexes of broad political attitudes or dispositions. Two of these are conceived as "dependent variables"; they represent goals that union political efforts seek to achieve in respect to the attitudes of their members. These desired political dispositions which we have labeled "pro-labor political orientation" and "political interest" together constitute the subjective conditions for voting behavior and support of political activities in line with union aims. Taken along with data on members' voting (Chapter 2), they serve to define "good citizenship" from the standpoint of union political programs. The other five attitude-clusters were examined both in terms of their direct significance as indicators of politically relevant dispositions and in terms of their relationships to voting behavior and the two broad indexes of political interest and pro-labor political orientation.

Briefly reviewing the analysis of these two chapters, we note the following main points:

1. UAW members in the Detroit area predominantly approve and support labor's political program. A major part of the membership trusts union election recommendations and would like to see labor unions have a larger voice in governmental affairs. At the same time, a great many more members express negative attitudes than positive ones toward business leadership and newspaper influence on the political front. On the other hand, some 15 to 20 per cent of the members are politically off-side from a labor standpoint and another 25 per cent of the membership is non-committal, ambivalent, or uncertain.

Strongly pro-labor political attitudes are most prevalent among workers at relatively low socio-economic levels, among Negroes, and among younger union members (under 40), particularly the younger workers having only eighth grade education or less.

Pro-labor political attitudes are closely linked with votes for Stevenson as against Eisenhower. But strongly pro-labor sentiment is no guarantee that members will vote; they have fully as high a rate of non-voting as do those who are not labor oriented.

2. Only a moderate degree of political interest and personal involvement was shown by auto workers—as evidenced by their campaign activities, information about the election, and concern regarding the outcome. Active forms of participation were infrequent and information was rather limited. This is not to contrast auto workers with other groups; such lack of active participation is characteristic of most parts of the population. It is called "moderate" here in the sense that it reveals no strong and enthusiastic response to the union's efforts to stimulate greater interest. Expressions of political concern before the election were fairly general but very much smaller numbers said, after the election, that they were "sorry" or had other negative feelings about the results. This ready acceptance of election defeat without words of regret would scarcely indicate intense political arousal.

The general political interest index shows one-fifth having "high" interest ratings and one-fifth "low." Most of the auto workers do not manifest either strong interest or notable lack of interest. This is especially true in the case of Eisenhower voters. Surprisingly perhaps, a majority of non-voters do not fall in the low range of political interest but in the middle bracket.

Degree of political interest and involvement is fairly closely related to amount of education. Workers who went to high school manifest much more interest than those with less schooling, especially among those under 40 years of age and in the group at a relatively high socio-economic level.

3. The indexes of pro-labor political attitudes and of political interest are found to measure relatively independent tendencies or dispositions. Extremely pro-labor unionists manifest well above average political interest; otherwise the relationship is not at all close. A combination of the two measures will clearly yield

information beyond that provided by either alone as to the political effectiveness of workers from a union point of view. A classification of UAW members based on the two ratings together will be explored in Chapter 6.

4. The other five attitudes, which have been dealt with in Chapter 5, pertain less directly to voting activities but represent personal dispositions that bear significantly on political behavior as a whole. The first of the attitudes has to do with members' feelings of attachment to the union, their interest and participation in the organization, apart from any special reference to *political* action. About one-third of the members can be considered strongly attached to the union—that is, they express active interest and a considerable amount of participation. About one-fourth appear to have very weak ties to the union; they manifest little interest in it or feelings of identification with it. Most members are in the middle range. Those unionists who are most closely attached to the union tend also to be in accord with it politically and to have somewhat greater political interest than the less attached. However, union attachment has little to do with whether members voted or not and there was a sizable minority with strong union identification who nevertheless voted for Eisenhower. Attachment to the union was considerably greater among men than women and somewhat above average for members who had more than eighth grade schooling and for those at either upper or lower rather than middle socio-economic levels.

5. Feelings of political impotence, futility and skepticism occur frequently enough to suggest that they may seriously interfere with political participation. For example, one-third of the UAW members agree that "people like me don't have any say about what the government does." This attitude is decidedly more common among workers who did not go beyond eight grades of school, among those past 40, and among women. The association of these feelings with relatively low degrees of political interest indicates that they may constitute one factor in political indifference.

Light is also thrown on political futility feelings by the fact that, after Eisenhower had been elected, fewer than one-half the auto workers felt that the election would make a great deal of difference. Even before the election, more than one-fourth said that it would not make much difference which side wins (one-fifth of Stevenson backers said this). Only about half the union members thought that "there is any important difference between what the Democratic and Republican parties stand for."

6. Our "authoritarian attitude" scores indicate a disturbing amount of undemocratic spirit and authoritarian-type thinking among the workers interviewed. These attitudes, like those of political futility, are notably more frequent in the poorly educated sections of the membership and among workers past 40. Authoritarian tendencies in our sample bear almost no relationship to voting, to active identification with the union, or to pro-labor political orientation (e.g., Eisenhower supporters were no more authoritarian than Stevenson advocates). However, those low in authoritarian attitude show much greater political interest and feeling of political effectiveness. The highly authoritarian are more given to feelings of political futility; they tend also to take extremist partisan positions in respect to unions and business engaging in political action.

A question concerning equal job treatment for Negroes yielded a more favorable picture from a democratic viewpoint. Only 15 per cent were against equality in employment relations, though an additional 30 per cent volunteered reservations about residential and social equality. The results do point to important gains on the specific matter of fostering democratic race relations in the economic sphere. Workers having more authoritarian attitudes who were also at upper and middle socio-economic levels (relative to other auto workers) were more opposed than others to equal job treatment for Negroes; this was not at all true of those above average in authoritarianism if they were of relatively low socio-economic status.

7. Questions tapping individuals' feelings of contentment with their life and work indicated that the great majority of auto workers had no strong sense of dissatisfaction or unhappiness; most of them answer in a manner signifying that they are at least moderately content and at peace concerning their lives. Approximately one-third, however, acknowledge feelings of worry, restiveness, non-accomplishment, and dissatisfaction. Greater than average numbers of the dissatisfied are women, Negroes, and workers of middle socio-economic status (espe-

cially ones over 40). There are no clear relations of life-satisfaction ratings to voting behavior or pro-labor political attitudes. The least satisfied do tend to be less politically interested and active, less closely attached to the union, to have less feeling of political effectiveness, and to have more authoritarian attitudes.

8. A last set of attitudes has to do with feelings of alienation or estrangement from society, feelings of personal futility, social distrust, pessimism or despair (the sociologists' concept of "anomie"). The results on our index of "social alienation" reflect a none too healthy state of social morale characterizing perhaps one-third or more of the auto workers studied. Especially large proportions of the alienated occur among those with eighth grade education or less, Protestants of low economic status, and workers over 40 at a relatively high socio-economic level. The most alienated tend to have a disproportionate number of non-voters and Eisenhower voters. Social alienation ratings have no relation to pro-labor political attitudes but they are associated, inversely, with political interest and feelings of political effectiveness. The more alienated tend likewise to be more authoritarian and more dissatisfied with life.

Altogether, the findings combine to create a suggestive sketch of politically relevant attitudes in an urban industrial working population. Though the picture remains fragmentary, it presents both disturbing questions and challenging opportunities for persons concerned with the role of industrial workers and their organizations in the contemporary American political arena.

We shall attempt further to interrelate and interpret these results in the final chapter. First, however, in the immediately following chapter, we shall re-examine our major findings in another perspective, by dividing UAW members into four groupings or political "types" in terms of their political orientation and degree of political interest. We will then be in a better position to suggest our tentative overall conclusions, drawing on the entire analysis.

CHAPTER 6

Four Types of UAW Members

It is apparent that considerable variety of political outlook and behavior exists among UAW members. In order to picture the variations more adequately it will be useful to describe and compare diverse groups within the total membership. One way in which this grouping could have been done is by reference to voting behavior itself—the voters and non-voters, Eisenhower and Stevenson voters, those having clear voting intentions and those undecided, etc. Comparisons of this kind have in fact been described in previous chapters and these differences will be accorded additional treatment in the present chapter.

However, we decided in favor of a different classification or "typology" of union members as our major descriptive framework for this overall analysis. The types we shall use are derived from the ratings of Labor Political Orientation and Political Interest.[1] A classification utilizing these ratings yields the following four types:

---

[1] For details concerning the two indexes and the questions on which they are based, see Chapter 4. The types based on these ratings are arrived at *empirically*, and hence should not be thought of as "ideal types," each possessing its own set of logically related characteristics mutually exclusive of one another. The fact that they are empirical means that we had to "draw a line," thus breaking what is actually a continuum into two separate categories. The fact that each type is not *completely* different from the other three does not negate the fruitfulness of asking, "In what ways *are* they different?" For a detailed discussion of the merits and demerits of the typological approach in the behavioral sciences, cf. T. W. Adorno, in *The Authoritarian Personality*, by Adorno and others, pp. 744-52.

1. *Prolabor-Politicals.* Members who are above average both in pro-labor political orientation and in political interest; that is, the politically aroused and on-side.

2. *Prolabor-Apoliticals.* Members who are above average in labor political orientation but below average in political interest.

3. *Nonlabor-Politicals.* Members who are below average in labor political orientation but above average in political interest.

4. *Nonlabor-Apoliticals.* Members who are below average on both dimensions.

The reason for employing this typology rather than one based directly on voting behavior goes back to the fact that our primary interest is not in the 1952 election but in the continuing, more stable and basic ways in which union members relate themselves to political activity. We wish to avoid too close a tie to the specific influences, personalities, and issues of a particular campaign in order to reach for conclusions pertaining to auto workers' feelings and attitudes that are likely to be more inclusive with respect to the totality of their political behavior. To this end, it appears promising to compare the four groupings of members listed above. From the standpoint of union political effectiveness, type 1 (Prolabor-Political) represents the desired condition while type 2 (Prolabor-Apolitical) is only partially satisfactory from the union's viewpoint, and the last two (Nonlabor-Political and Nonlabor-Apolitical) are least satisfactory.

Examination of differences among these types will indicate the personal characteristics and the associated behavior and attitudes of these broad subdivisions of the union membership. In doing so, it should help to define the union's sources of political strength and accomplishment while at the same time clarifying the union's problem in respect to members who are not politically active and on side. An insight into the nature of the types of members in unions in these terms also is significant as regards the other basic question involved, namely, the emergence of labor as a decisive force in American politics.

The number of members falling into the four types are as follows:

Types	Unweighted Numbers	Weighted Numbers	% of Weighted Total
1. Prolabor-Political	90	173	33%
2. Prolabor-Apolitical	67	117	22
3. Nonlabor-Political	92	113	21
4. Nonlabor-Apolitical	89	125	24
	338	528	100%

No special significance is to be attached to the number in each of the four types since this is determined by the arbitrarily chosen cutting points on the two rating indexes (Labor Political Orientation and Political Interest).

In addition to comparisons among the four broad groupings that have been described, we wished also to compare smaller, more extreme types selected in a parallel manner. It seemed likely that the members who are *extremely* high or low in labor political orientation and political interest might differ in ways that would yield insights beyond those provided by the general types as to the characteristics that make for strong or weak involvement in union political action. To select the extreme types, ratings on Labor Political Orientation and Political Interest were again utilized but the cutting scores were chosen to bring only from 4 to 8 per cent of the sample into each of the four types. Here again the number in each type is of no significance since it is arbitrarily set by the procedure of selection. The figures involved are these:

Extreme Types	Unweighted Numbers	Weighted Numbers	% of Each General Type	% of Total Sample
1. Prolabor-Political	19	43	25%	8%
2. Prolabor-Apolitical	20	36	31%	7%
3. Nonlabor-Political	21	23	20%	4%
4. Nonlabor-Apolitical	22	27	22%	5%
	82	129		

The Four Types as Differentiated by Their Answers
to Questions Used in Selecting Them

The four categories of union members are defined by the questions that entered into the indexes of Labor Political Orientation and Political Interest. A portrait of the types can be sketched by taking each of these questions in turn and noting ways in which the types differ in their replies. We shall do this first for the questions used to define Labor Political Orientation and then for those on which the Political Interest rating was based. It is to be understood that inasmuch as the types are directly based on answers to these questions the positive relationships reported in this section are bound to occur; they are in a sense artifacts. The figures are nevertheless valuable since they picture the specific beliefs and attitudes characteristic of each type. Starting with these descriptions of the types as given by the type-definitions, we shall then fill in and extend the picture by seeing what additional facts are found to be true of workers in each type. The entire chapter, then, will build, piece by piece, toward a somewhat fuller delineation of the four categories of "UAW citizens."

Questions indicative of pro-labor political orientation

First of the three questions having to do with attitude toward union political action is one that asked about the worker's approval or disapproval of labor and business groups working in behalf of candidates. The extent to which replies differ among the types is shown in Tables 6.1 and 6.2.

TABLE 6.1

APPROVAL OF UNION POLITICAL ACTION
IN BEHALF OF STEVENSON[*]

	Prolabor-Political	Prolabor-Apolitical	Nonlabor-Political	Nonlabor-Apolitical
All right	98%	100%	55%	68%
Not all right	2	—	45	32
	100%	100%	100%	100%

[*] Figures exclude respondents giving no answer.

TABLE 6.2

PERCENTAGES OF EACH TYPE APPROVING OF UNION POLITICAL
ACTION WHILE AT THE SAME TIME DISAPPROVING OF
BUSINESS POLITICAL ACTION, AND VICE VERSA

	Prolabor-Political	Prolabor-Apolitical	Nonlabor-Political	Nonlabor-Apolitical
All right for unions, but not for business	9%	23%	7%	10%
All right for business, but not for unions	—	—	29	21
All other combinations of responses*	91	77	64	69
	100%	100%	100%	100%

* The great majority of these combinations fall into the "all right for both" category.

Clearly our scoring procedure resulted, as intended, in iso-lating two pro-labor political types that are practically unani-mous in favoring union support of preferred candidates. Only a little more than one-half to two-thirds of the members in the other two types express such approval. On a parallel question asking about support of candidates by *business groups,* the amount of approval does not differ greatly by types since this response did not help define the types unless it was accompanied by a response *disapproving* similar participation by unions. Actually, from four-fifths to nine-tenths of all four types say it was all right for business to work for its favored candidate. As may be seen in Table 6.2, *all* persons who said it was all right for business but not for labor fall into the two non-labor oriented types.

The next question to be considered deals with groups whose political recommendations are trusted. The two politically pro-labor types differ by even larger percentages from the other two types in their replies to this question than to the preceding one (Table 6.3). Only answers referring to either labor or busi-ness groups were used in selecting the types. It is apparent that nearly all the "best" union citizens. (Prolabor-Politicals) trust labor recommendations and almost none trust business groups. The other politically pro-labor type (Prolabor-Apolitical) leans heavily in the same direction, though with considerably less unanimity. Sharply contrasting percentages occur for the other two types. Less than one-fifth of these members who are not strongly labor-oriented say that they trust union recommendations and almost as many, particularly among the politically interested (Nonlabor-Politicals), trust business.

TABLE 6.3

TRUST IN POLITICAL RECOMMENDATIONS OF LABOR AND BUSINESS

Trust recommendations by:	Prolabor-Political	Prolabor-Apolitical	Nonlabor-Political	Nonlabor-Apolitical
Labor groups	86%	66%	19%	16%
Business groups	1%	5%	18%	10%

Replies regarding groups whose recommendations are *not* trusted yield results fully consistent with the foregoing (Table 6.4). Union members in the first two types express no distrust of labor recommendations while nearly half of the Prolabor-Politicals and about two-fifths of the Prolabor-Apoliticals volunteer that they distrust recommendations from business groups. On

TABLE 6.4

DISTRUST OF POLITICAL RECOMMENDATIONS OF LABOR AND BUSINESS

Do not trust recommendation by:	Prolabor-Political	Prolabor-Apolitical	Nonlabor-Political	Nonlabor-Apolitical
Labor groups	—	—	31%	26%
Business groups	47%	38%	22%	30%

the other hand, the two types that are weakly labor-oriented include many who distrust union endorsements—in fact, a greater number, among the Nonlabor-Politicals, than distrust business. This again points to the Nonlabor-Politicals as containing many workers favorably oriented toward business views and more or less alienated from labor's values. To be sure, as the following discussion points out, the percentage of Nonlabor-Politicals *distrusting* business is greater than the percentage of the same type *trusting* business.

The contrasts are clearly evident in Table 6.5 which utilizes the method of combining trust-distrust responses that was described in Chapter 4 (p. 108). These ratios of trust responses

TABLE 6.5

RELATIVE TRUST-DISTRUST OF POLITICAL RECOMMENDATIONS
OF LABOR AND BUSINESS

Trust vs. distrust of:	Prolabor-Political	Prolabor-Apolitical	Nonlabor-Political	Nonlabor-Apolitical
Labor groups	100%	100%	38%	37%
Business groups	2%	12%	44%	26%

to the total of trust plus distrust not only show the large differences between the first two types and the second two, but they also bring out the way the politically interested and the less interested differ from each other in their attitudes toward business recommendations. The types with high political interest tend to be more extreme, that is, they are less trustful of business in the case of the union-oriented (Prolabor-Political versus Prolabor-Apolitical) and more trustful of business in the case of the nonunion-oriented (Nonlabor-Political versus Nonlabor-Apolitical).

In concluding, it is to be noted that even for the types not strongly aligned with labor, the recommendations of business groups are *distrusted* more often than they are *trusted* (i.e., the ratios of trust in respect to business groups are all less than 50 per cent). This is equally true for the extreme types. It should also be noted that a comparison of the findings of the previous question with those of the present one suggests that approval of political action by business does not necessarily mean that the recommendations of business groups will be trusted. The case in point is the Prolabor-Politicals, who, as suggested by the figures in Table 6.2 (on approval of political action by unions and business groups) display the highest sense of "fair play" or recognition of pressure group activity. On the other hand, this same type has the lowest ratio (2 per cent) of trust-distrust responses. In other words, the Prolabor-Politicals distinguish between granting to business groups the right to engage in political action and trusting their recommendations in this area.

TABLE 6.6
ATTITUDES TOWARD INFLUENCE OF UNIONS ON GOVERNMENT

Unions should have:	Prolabor-Political	Prolabor-Apolitical	Nonlabor-Political	Nonlabor-Apolitical
More to say	86%	75%	22%	38%
Less to say	3	8	33	21
Neither more nor less; no group should have too much, etc.	9	13	32	37
Can't say; indifferent	2	4	13	4
	100%	100%	100%	100%

The remaining question that helped define the pro-labor political types had to do with the respondents' feeling about unions and business respectively having more voice in government. Summary comparisons of the types are given in Tables 6.6 and 6.7. The two labor-oriented types have much higher proportions inclined to think that unions should have more to say and that business should have less to say "about the things the government does that are important to working people." Extremely few in these two groups think unions should have *less* to say or that business should have *more* to say. On the other hand, sizable majorities in the two non-union oriented types answer either that labor should have less voice or that it should remain as it is and, similarly, that business should have greater voice or remain as it is, with neither more nor less influence.

While the first two types are much more favorable to increased union influence than the other two, as a result of the procedure used in classifying members into the types, there is also a marked difference between the more and the less *politically interested* types, even though this difference is not at all due to the way the types were selected. As is evident in Table 6.6, among the nonlabor oriented, many more of the politically concerned (Nonlabor-Politicals) hold that unions should have less to say than think that they should have *more* to say, while the proportions shift strongly in the opposite direction among the non-political (Nonlabor-Apoliticals). A parallel though weaker tendency appears among the labor-oriented, where the politically interested (Prolabor-Politicals) are more nearly unanimous in favoring greater union influence than are the non-political (Prolabor-Apoliticals). The tentative generalization would be (and this is backed by examination of the extreme types) that union members who are active politically, as contrasted with those less politically interested, tend to be especially strongly pro-labor if they are labor-oriented, and especially inclined away from labor's views if they are not labor-oriented. This would accord with the conception that these people in the Prolabor-Political and Nonlabor-Political types are opinion leaders, having views a little more definite and coherent than those held by the non-political types. It will be important to see whether other evidence supports this interpretation and, if so, to examine the distinguishing features of these two types.

TABLE 6.7

ATTITUDES TOWARD INFLUENCE OF BUSINESS ON GOVERNMENT

Business should have:	Prolabor-Political	Prolabor-Apolitical	Nonlabor-Political	Nonlabor-Apolitical
More to say	10%	12%	30%	35%
Less to say	64	58	25	21
Neither more nor less; no group should have too much, etc.	19	14	35	27
Can't say; indifferent	7	16	10	17
	100%	100%	100%	100%

One other fact needs to be underscored in respect to all the comparisons reported in this section. The results indicate that the types labeled non-labor oriented (Nonlabor-Political and Nonlabor-Apolitical) are by no means predominantly *anti*-labor. The people we are considering in this study are all union members. When we subdivide them in terms of adherence to labor's political views, it is natural that we find *clearly pro-union* types and others (the *non-labor* types) which include many who are more or less neutral, ambivalent or confused, along with a smaller number who are anti-labor. The figures of the preceding tables indicate that many members of the "non-labor oriented" types are in accord with the union on a number of the "test" questions. Most of them are *somewhat* pro-labor politically but not strongly and consistently. They give evidence of being people with inner doubts or conflicts on these matters, people subjected to cross-pressures from their social environments. It seems highly probable that this is the case since their working life as auto workers pulls them in a pro-labor direction while various other interpersonal relationships and community influences (newspapers, for example), as well as personal interests (as property owners, etc.) push at times in opposed directions. As we weigh further evidence regarding these people, we shall keep this question before us.

Questions indicative of political interest

Three general sets of questions were asked in both phases of the study (pre- and post-election) which have been used to define and measure political interest here: a) behavior, b) knowledge, and c) evaluations, concerning the campaign and the election. In all, fourteen such questions were used (see page 123 for the list), of which a selected few will be discussed in this section. Again, we want to remind the reader that the two categories of political interest were built on the basis of the answers to these questions.

a) *Behavioral items.* One item used in determining political interest was the respondent's answer to whether or not he personally was doing anything to get his candidate elected. Fully three-fourths of the Prolabor-Politicals and nearly three-fifths of the Nonlabor-Politicals, replied that they were, in marked contrast to the two types with little interest in politics; a little more than one-fourth of the Prolabor-Apoliticals and only one-fifth of the Nonlabor-Apoliticals indicated that they were doing anything. None of the Prolabor-Apoliticals and only about one per cent of the Nonlabor-Apoliticals, did any more than talk to their co-workers and others, while about 10 per cent of each of the two types with high political interest told us that they were doing such things as handing out literature, displaying signs, engaging in PAC, Democratic, or Republican activities, and the like. The same kind of question was asked in the post-election interview, and yielded the same general differences among the four types.

Again, the differences in political interest among the UAW members are reflected in their responses to the pre-election question which asked if the respondent talked politics with anyone. The two politically interested groups are considerably above the other two in this respect. The percentages of each type replying "Yes" were as follows:

	Prolabor-Political	*Prolabor-Apolitical*	*Nonlabor-Political*	*Nonlabor-Apolitical*
Talked politics	91%	29%	79%	50%

Ninety-six per cent of the Prolabor-Politicals and 89 per cent of the Nonlabor-Politicals said they listened to radio or TV programs by the candidates in the last few weeks before the election, as over against 74 per cent and 76 per cent of the Prolabor-Apoliticals and Nonlabor-Apoliticals, respectively. The difference between the politically interested and the less politically interested is accentuated when we consider the matter of frequency of listening, even though it was not included in our definition of the types. The percentage of each type listening to candidates on radio or TV at least three times per week was as follows:

	Prolabor-Political	*Prolabor-Apolitical*	*Nonlabor-Political*	*Nonlabor-Apolitical*
Listened at least 3 times per week	62%	27%	54%	31%

The two types with high political interest had very large percentages indicating that they had read about the campaign in the daily newspapers: 94 per cent of the Prolabor-Politicals and 96 per cent of the Nonlabor-Politicals. But only 69 per cent of the Prolabor-Apoliticals and 83 per cent of the Nonlabor-Apoliticals said that they had done likewise. Moreover, although it was not taken into consideration when constructing the types, the number of papers read differed substantially between the politically interested and the less interested. The percentages reading two or three papers were:[2]

	Prolabor-Political	Prolabor-Apolitical	Nonlabor-Political	Nonlabor-Apolitical
2 or 3 papers read:	49%	17%	55%	35%

The data on the extreme types concerning these behavioral items as indicative of political interest are merely greater accentuations of the differences among the four types. On the post-election question asking if they personally did anything to get their candidate elected, for example, *none* of the two extreme types with low political interest said they had done anything, in sharp contrast to 80 per cent of the Prolabor-Politicals and 57 per cent of the Nonlabor-Politicals. It should be noted that only the Prolabor-Politicals in this case were above the total sample average. As for talking politics, all members of the two politically interested extreme types, but only 60 per cent of the apolitical, indicated that they talked about the campaign and the candidates. The radio and TV listening habits, as well as those of newspaper reading, of the extreme types also reveal the tremendous difference between the two politically interested types and the other two with less interest.

b) *Information items.* As stated in Chapter 4, familiarity with the campaign's content (issues, names of candidates, etc.) is one indication of political interest. The following figures reveal the extent of the differences between the Political and the Apolitical types as measured by the ability to name at least one definite campaign issue:

	Prolabor-Political	Prolabor-Apolitical	Nonlabor-Political	Nonlabor-Apolitical
At least one definite main issue named	76%	36%	73%	43%
At least one definite *personally important* issue named	79%	49%	89%	67%

Ability to name both the Democratic and Republican candidates for the offices of President, Governor, and Senator, in the

---

[2] An interesting sidelight is the fact that the Hearst publication, the *Detroit Times,* was by far the most frequently mentioned paper among the Prolabor-Apoliticals. This is partly to be explained by the fact that this paper is quite popular among Negroes (who are highly represented in this type), and also by the fact that the *Times* makes its appeal to lower socio-economic levels of the population, generally.

1952 election forms another information item used in constructing our types in terms of political interest. As Table 6.8 shows,
the magnitude of the contrasts between the two types with high
political interest, on the one hand, and the two types with less
political interest, on the other, is quite large, especially with
respect to the candidates for Governor and Senator. The figures
indicate the wide range in "political sophistication" among UAW
members. Generally, when a UAW member knew only one of
the candidates for each office, that candidate was the Democrat.

TABLE 6.8

PERCENTAGE OF EACH TYPE KNOWING BOTH DEMOCRATIC
AND REPUBLICAN CANDIDATES FOR PRESIDENT,
GOVERNOR, AND SENATOR

	Prolabor-Political	Prolabor-Apolitical	Nonlabor-Political	Nonlabor-Apolitical
President	99%	80%	97%	88%
Governor	82%	27%	67%	49%
Senator	70%	21%	61%	24%
Average %	84%	43%	75%	54%

The marked difference between the Prolabor-Politicals and
the Prolabor-Apoliticals on this question is indicative of many
others that will be presented in this chapter. In this case, the
Prolabor-Politicals have the *highest* percentage knowing the
names of both Senatorial candidates, for example, while the
Prolabor-Apoliticals have the *lowest* percentage. The information items as an index of political interest among the *extreme*
types are even more sharply differentiating. The extreme Politicals, for example, differ more from the extreme Apoliticals than
is the case for the corresponding general types in their knowledge of the names of candidates in the 1952 election. This holds
true also for the citing of campaign issues.

c) *Evaluational items.* Three questions were asked to get at
the feelings of concern about the election among the UAW
members, as a means of determining degree of political interest.
The first question (asked in the pre-election interview) was
worded, "Would you say that you personally care very much
which party wins the presidential election, or that you don't
care very much?" The answers to this question contribute to

the differentiation of the union's members into greater and less political interest, as Table 6.9 indicates. Our focus of interest here is on the proportions saying "Don't care."

TABLE 6.9

PROPORTIONS OF REGISTERED VOTERS IN THE FOUR TYPES
SAYING THEY CARE VERY MUCH WHICH PARTY
WINS THE ELECTION

	Prolabor-Political	Prolabor-Apolitical	Nonlabor-Political	Nonlabor-Apolitical
Care very much	93%	81%	85%	69%
Don't care	5	19	12	29
Can't say; don't know	2	—	3	2
	100%	100%	100%	100%

The two types with little political interest have a substantial proportion volunteering neutral or ambiguous comments in response to the second question in the evaluation category of political interest indices, which asked simply, "How do you feel about the way the election came out?" These proportions are at least twice those of the two types with high political interest, as shown in Table 6.10.

TABLE 6.10

FEELINGS REGARDING ELECTION OUTCOME
AMONG THE FOUR TYPES

	Prolabor-Political	Prolabor-Apolitical	Nonlabor-Political	Nonlabor-Apolitical
Favorable comments	18%	23%	65%	39%
Unfavorable comments	70	49	24	26
Neutral or ambiguous	12	28	11	35
	100%	100%	100%	100%

Of course, the two types with high political interest differ considerably from each other in the distribution of favorable and unfavorable comments, because of their wide differences in voting behavior, reported on below. The same is true for the two types with less political interest. Here again, though, the high labor political orientation of the Prolabor-Apoliticals probably accounts, in part, for their having a lower proportion (compared to the Nonlabor-Apoliticals) of neutral and ambiguous replies.

Generally, the same relationships as revealed in the above two tables prevail with respect to the third question in the evaluation category used to measure political interest. This question was much more direct than the previous one, and asked, "Are you glad or sorry that Eisenhower won the election?" A "glad" or "sorry" answer was taken as an indication of political interest. The extent to which the replies differ among the types can be seen in Table 6.11. The fact that such a high percentage of Prolabor-Politicals, 28 per cent, said neither "glad" nor "sorry" is probably related to their belief that it was too early to make any evaluation of Eisenhower as a President.

TABLE 6.11

PROPORTIONS OF EACH TYPE SAYING THEY ARE GLAD
OR SORRY THAT EISENHOWER WON

	Prolabor-Political	Prolabor-Apolitical	Nonlabor-Political	Nonlabor-Apolitical
Glad	13%	30%	69%	49%
Sorry	59	27	17	16
Neither	28	42	12	34
Don't know; can't say, etc.	—	1	2	1
	100%	100%	100%	100%

The responses of the extreme types to these three questions tend to be strongly related to the category of political interest in which the members are placed, as expected. In addition, labor political orientation does have some effect on the responses, as indicated, for example, by the fact that the extreme Prolabor-Apoliticals have a higher percentage of unfavorable reactions and a smaller percentage of neutral or ambiguous reactions to the election outcome than their corresponding general type.

The previous pages have dealt with those items that were used to construct the four types of UAW members. To repeat our cautions previously stated, the differences we have been describing among the types are largely an "artifact" of our procedure; they were to be expected. But what about those features and tendencies which were not used to isolate such types—what are the *other* social and psychological characteristics of each type, characteristics that tend to distinguish one type from the others and that can contribute to our further understanding of the four kinds of union members? The remainder of this chapter is devoted to this inquiry.

Social Characteristics of the Types

Let us consider first the distinguishing characteristics of the types as regards factors like age, race, education, income, and other such features. Table 6.12 (pp. 217-219) gives a detailed account of these items. We shall refer only briefly to some of the principal differentiating characteristics of each type.

Prolabor-Politicals. Along with the other type with a high labor political orientation, the Prolabor-Politicals have the most Negroes proportionately. Furthermore, this type is the best educated of all four types. Three-fourths of them went to high school, while only half of all the others in the sample did so (75 per cent versus 49 per cent). This type has the smallest proportion of persons 55 years of age and over and, along with the Prolabor-Apoliticals, the largest proportion of persons under 35. The fact that the two types with a high labor political orientation (and particularly the Prolabor-Politicals) are younger than the other types has an important bearing upon the future trends regarding union loyalty, and it calls into question the notion that such sentiments are strongest among the older workers, the ones who helped establish the union in the early organizing period. More on this below.

The Prolabor-Politicals also enjoy, along with the Nonlabor-Politicals, a higher individual income than do the other types, and to some extent, this is true of their total family income as well. About three out of every ten of them are skilled workers, the highest for any of the types. They are second only to the

TABLE 6.12

CHARACTERISTICS OF THE FOUR GENERAL TYPES

	Prolabor-Political	Prolabor-Apolitical	Nonlabor-Political	Nonlabor-Apolitical
Sex				
Male	90%	80%	94%	92%
Female	10	20	6	8
Race				
White	82	83	95	94
Negro	18	17	5	6
Religion*				
Catholic	47	50	44	54
Protestant	53	50	56	46
(Whites only)				
Catholic	57	62	47	55
Protestant	43	38	53	45
Education				
8 years and under	25	63	41	51
9 years and over	75	37	59	49
Age				
Under 35	36	36	19	24
35-54	46	42	57	48
55 and over	18	22	24	28
Occupation				
White collar	1	2	14	6
Skilled	29	6	21	23
Semi-skilled and unskilled	70	92	65	71
Individual Income				
Under $3000	9	26	7	9
3000-4000	24	38	26	41
4000-5000	41	21	38	27
5000-6000	12	9	12	12
6000 and over	14	6	17	11
Family Income				
Less than $4000	18	45	22	31
4000-5000	32	20	23	26
5000-6000	26	18	19	15
6000 and over	24	17	36	28
Own or Rent				
Home owners	62	50	77	68
Rent	38	50	23	32

TABLE 6.12 (Continued)

	Prolabor-Political	Prolabor-Apolitical	Nonlabor-Political	Nonlabor-Apolitical
Birthplace (whites only)				
United States	79%	74%	81%	83%
North	63	52	73	68
South	16	22	8	15
Europe and Canada	21	26	19	17
Size of Birthplace				
Farm	17	24	12	27
Small town	25	35	24	21
Medium-size town	11	7	15	7
Big city	47	34	49	45
Years in Detroit				
1-11 years	18	23	10	14
12-22 years	18	17	16	11
23 or more years	47	42	54	52
All life	17	18	20	23
Years at Present Job				
Less than 2 years	18	28	13	10
2-10 years	44	38	46	49
Over 10 years	38	34	41	41
Years at Present Home				
Less than 2 years	29	32	22	24
2-5 years	39	37	33	26
Over 5 years	32	31	45	50
Marital Status				
Single	12	14	17	13
Married	88	86	83	87
Father's Political Affiliation				
Democrat	54	49	38	40
Republican	12	10	19	22
Other	12	11	16	10
Don't know; no answer	22	30	27	28
Father's Occupation				
White collar	12	7	12	18
Skilled	19	18	19	16
Semi-skilled	43	33	35	32
Farmer	16	29	23	26
Unskilled	10	13	11	8

TABLE 6.12 (Continued)

Ethnic and Nationality Background (*whites only*)**	Prolabor-Political	Prolabor-Apolitical	Nonlabor-Political	Nonlabor-Apolitical
British Isles and Canada	19%	6%	14%	9%
Germany and Austria	2	6	11	13
Italy	4	10	7	8
Poland and Russia	19	25	20	23
Rumania, Hungary, Yugoslavia, and Czechoslovakia	7	5	7	8
Other European	2	8	5	1
Total Foreign	53	60	64	62
Southern white†	16	22	8	15
Northern white	31	18	28	23

* Excludes the small number of replies other than Catholic or Protestant.
** Based on birthplace of fathers.
† Based on birthplace of respondents.

Prolabor-Apoliticals in having the smallest proportion living in Detroit 23 or more years, or all their life. This feature is related also to the fact that, along with the latter type, the Prolabor-Politicals have the smallest proportion living in their place of residence more than five years (at the time of the interview).

Based on the distribution of Democrats and Republicans only, the fathers of this type, as well as those of the Prolabor-Apoliticals, were far more Democratic in party preference than the other two types. Moreover, the Prolabor-Politicals have the smallest proportion of fathers who were farmers and the highest percentage of fathers who were semi-skilled workers.

The Prolabor-Politicals also have the greatest percentage of native-born fathers, with most of these being born in the northern section of the United States. When nationality background of whites is considered (based on birthplace of fathers), this type has the highest proportion of all the types from the British Isles and Canada, and the smallest proportion from Germany and Austria, Italy, and certain other European countries.

The relatively younger age and higher educational achievement of the Prolabor-Politicals, as well as their high proportion of well-paid skilled workers, warrant some comment. It is a common belief that it is on the older men in the shops that the labor movement can depend for loyalty and support, because they are the ones who still bear the scars of the past when belonging to a union and striking for it bespoke a spirit which could not be expected from the younger generation of men and women entering the factories today and who have their union dues automatically deducted through union-management agreements. As part of this common belief, it is further held that unions in the future will find it increasingly difficult to maintain their hold over the membership because of the passage of years since the era of conflict (which can be counted on to provoke and sustain "in-group" feelings), and because of the increase among workers in years of schooling and their improved economic position, which make for an increasing "middle-class" mentality and higher levels of aspiration than those typically associated with trade union identification.

Thus it is often asserted that improved social status associated with increased education will result in a situation in which unions will increasingly be left with only the less educated, lower-paid workers as loyal members. Our findings at the very least throw doubt upon this kind of supposition. Instead, we have found that the workers in the UAW who are the most active in the union, who are committed to the union politically, and who at the same time are especially concerned with political matters, are not the older, less educated, and lower-paid workers. To be sure, many of the latter continue to be loyal and dependable union members, but in a much more passive, *dependent* fashion than the group of younger, better educated and higher skilled auto workers. Our other data, in the following sections, are in line with the essential findings stated here.

Prolabor-Apoliticals. As the preceding paragraphs indicate, this type is in many ways similar to the Prolabor-Politicals. However, on several key items, they are quite different. They have the greatest proportion of women, in fact, twice that of the total sample. When only whites are taken into consideration, this type has the highest percentage of Catholics, which is partly accounted for by the fact that about one-fourth of the type are of Polish origin. They have the highest percentage of persons who were born in Poland or whose fathers were born in that country.

Southern whites make up a greater proportion of this type than of any of the other three types. Thus, the Prolabor-Apoliticals have the greatest proportion of the combined three distinct ethnic groups in the factories of Detroit's automobile industry, the Negroes, Poles, and southern whites. Indeed, more than half of this type is made up of these three groups.

This type is by far the least educated. Their low educational standing is accompanied by the lowest individual and family incomes, and the fewest in skilled and white collar jobs, of all the four types. Furthermore, they have the highest proportion at the time of the interview who had been at their present jobs two years or less, and the highest proportion of persons born on farms or in small towns, with nearly three-fifths of them of such origins. Correspondingly, their average number of years in Detroit is the lowest of the four types. In the light of their recency in Detroit, and their low income, it is not surprising that they have the smallest proportion of home-owners. They also have the largest proportion of the types whose fathers were farmers or unskilled workers.

Nonlabor-Politicals. In terms of many of the social characteristics under consideration here, this type is quite different from the others. It has the smallest proportion of women and Negroes, and of southern whites. Furthermore, it has the smallest percentage of Catholics. Its proportion of persons under 35 years of age is the lowest of the types. These union members have by far the greatest number of white-collar workers, which explains in part their location in the non-union oriented, but politically interested, category of UAW members. Income-wise, they are in the most favorable position. The Nonlabor-Politicals, also, have the smallest proportion born on farms. Along with this, they have the largest proportion living in the Detroit area more than 11 years, and by far the greatest percentage of home-owners. Thus the image suggested by these facts is that of a group of workers who are older, more settled, and enjoying higher incomes than most auto workers in the Detroit area. Add to this the fact that they have the fewest Democratic fathers.

Nonlabor-Apoliticals. This type is somewhat similar to the Nonlabor-Politicals with respect to their proportion of Negroes, which is low. Furthermore, they are second only to this latter type in having the smallest proportion of persons under 35 years of age, and in fact, have the highest proportion of persons 55 and over. A high proportion of the Nonlabor-Apoliticals, as in the case of the other Nonlabor type, has lived in Detroit more than 23 years, or all their life. Correspondingly, they have the highest proportion having lived in their present residence more than five years, and the lowest proportion who have worked at their present job less than two years. Their fathers have the highest proportion who were white-collar workers, and along with this, the greatest proportion among the types whose fathers were Republicans.

When it comes to religion, however, they are more like the two Prolabor types in their preferences. And they are second only to the Prolabor-Apoliticals in having the largest percentage of persons with individual incomes under $4000.

What light do the findings concerning the *extreme* types (see Table 6.13) throw on the features presented in regard to the general types? Type by type, we have the following picture:

Extreme Prolabor-Politicals: This extreme type is almost completely white in racial compostion, marking a drop from the general type in proportion of Negroes. The religious breakdown is perhaps the most unusual aspect of this type: about eight out of every ten are Catholics, the highest proportion of all the types. It remains decidedly the best educated of the four types, and is in fact better educated than the general Prolabor-Political type. While its age distribution is no different from that of the corresponding general type, it is the youngest of all the four extreme types, thus confirming the findings for the general Prolabor-Politicals. This extreme type is further characterized by a high proportion of well-paid skilled workers. The data also support those on the general Prolabor-Politicals concerning the relatively low proportion of persons born on farms. The same is true with respect to the low proportion of members living in Detroit twenty-three years or more. As in the case of the general types, the extreme Prolabor-Politicals have the highest proportion

TABLE 6.13

CHARACTERISTICS OF THE FOUR EXTREME TYPES

	Prolabor-Political	Prolabor-Apolitical	Nonlabor-Political	Nonlabor-Apolitical
Sex				
Male	98%	73%	87%	88%
Female	2	27	13	12
Race				
White	98	76	96	81
Negro	2	24	4	19
Religion*				
Catholic	78	54	29	36
Protestant	22	46	71	64
(Whites only)				
Catholic	80	71	30	45
Protestant	20	29	70	55
Education				
8 years and under	14	80	35	55
9 years and over	86	20	65	45
Age				
Under 35	37	13	7	22
35-54	45	65	66	60
55 and over	18	22	27	18
Occupation				
White collar	—	—	13	4
Skilled	54	7	44	17
Semi-skilled and unskilled	46	93	43	79
Individual Income				
Under $3000	—	37	—	16
3000-3999	23	44	18	30
4000-4999	27	13	30	32
5000-5999	26	6	14	4
6000 and over	24	—	38	18
Birthplace (whites only)				
United States	73	62	79	87
North	67	53	65	62
South	6	9	14	25
Europe and Canada	27	38	21	13

TABLE 6.13 (Continued)

	Prolabor-Political	Prolabor-Apolitical	Nonlabor-Political	Nonlabor-Apolitical
Size of Birthplace				
Farm	8%	27%	17%	38%
Small town	33	23	33	25
Medium-sized town	11	—	14	4
Big city	48	50	37	33
Years in Detroit				
1-11 years	11	19	18	25
12-22 years	36	—	22	15
23 or more years	45	44	51	49
All life	8	37	9	11
*Ethnic and Nationality Background (whites only)**				
British Isles and Canada	37	7	15	25
Germany and Austria	2	9	5	14
Italy	—	10	13	4
Poland and Russia	13	47	15	18
Other European	6	9	5	4
Total Foreign	58	81	52	66
Southern white†	6	9	14	25
Northern white	36	10	34	9

* See note on religion, Table 6.12.
** Based on birthplace of fathers.
† Based on birthplace of respondents.

of fathers from the British Isles and Canada. Southern whites and persons from other than British and Canadian origins are least represented among them.

Extreme Prolabor-Apoliticals: The features that distinguish this extreme type include its high proportions of women, Poles, and Negroes, and of persons with no more than eight years of schooling—all of these being increases over the general Prolabor-Apoliticals. Accompanying these proportions is the distinction of having by far the highest proportion of individual incomes of less than $4000. They also have the highest proportion of persons having lived in Detroit all their lives. Naturally, nearly all of them are in semi-skilled or unskilled jobs, a fact which sets them apart from the other three types. And their percentage of foreign-born fathers is the highest among the four extreme types.

Extreme Nonlabor-Politicals: This extreme type has the highest percentage of Protestants, which confirms the finding concerning the corresponding general type. Along with the other type with high political interest, its proportion of Negroes is the lowest. Its individual income is the highest of the types, as is its occupational level. In terms of age, it is the oldest of the types. The proportion of fathers born outside the United States is the lowest of the extreme types.

Extreme Nonlabor-Apoliticals: This fourth extreme type is characterized by a high percentage of persons born on farms and it has the highest percentage of persons having lived in Detroit less than 12 years. And it has by far the greatest percentage of southern whites. It is also characterized by a high percentage of Protestants (second only to the preceding type); and also the second highest percentage of a) Negroes, b) persons with no high school education, and c) workers with poorly paid, low-skill occupations.

TABLE 6.14

EDUCATION AND AGE TOGETHER IN RELATION
TO THE FOUR TYPES

	Prolabor-Political	Prolabor-Apolitical	Nonlabor-Political	Nonlabor-Apolitical	Total Sample
8th grade or less					
Under 40	5%	32%	7%	7%	12%
40 or over	19	29	34	43	30
Beyond 8th grade					
Under 40	47	25	29	32	35
40 or over	29	14	30	18	23
	100%	100%	100%	100%	100%
No. of cases	(76)	(58)	(77)	(80)	(291)

Returning to the general types, certain supplementary analyses may usefully be reported that deal with a few of the differentiating personal variables considered jointly or in combination. First, we take age and education together to see how they are associated with the four types. The relationship is reported in Table 6.14. This tabulation brings out more clearly than the figures of Table 6.12 that Type 1 (the Prolabor-Politicals) is made up disproportionately of better educated younger workers and Type 2 (Prolabor-Apoliticals) of the less educated younger workers—and that Type 1 is above average in its proportion of the older workers who are better educated but below average of those poorly educated; while Type 2 is below average in numbers of better educated, both older and younger. It is also seen that Type 3 (Nonlabor-Politicals) has slightly more older workers than average and slightly fewer younger, both among the better educated and the less educated. Type 4 (Nonlabor-Apoliticals) has an especially large percentage of poorly educated older workers.

TABLE 6.15

RELIGION AND EDUCATION TOGETHER IN RELATION
TO THE FOUR TYPES (WHITES ONLY)

	Prolabor-Political	Prolabor-Apolitical	Nonlabor-Political	Nonlabor-Apolitical	Total Sample
Catholic					
High education	47%	27%	23%	26%	32%
Low education	10	34	23	29	23
Protestant					
High education	29	12	35	24	25
Low education	14	27	19	21	20
	100%	100%	100%	100%	100%
No. of cases	(64)	(50)	(74)	(77)	(265)

A similar analysis of religion and education is also informative. Here we use figures for white workers alone since the Negroes were practically all Protestants and were heavily concentrated in the prolabor types. Table 6.15 summarizes the results. We reported earlier (Tables 6.12 and 6.13) that among the general types (whites only) most of the Nonlabor-Political UAW members were Protestant, while this was not true of the other three types, and that about eight of every ten *extreme* Prolabor-Politicals were Catholic, while seven out of every ten *extreme* Nonlabor-Politicals were Protestant. Here is a very strong suggestion of the role of religious affiliation in the development of a pro-labor political orientation; and when we consider further the traditional loyalty of urban Catholics to the Democratic Party and to labor union philosophy, the political behavior of those types with heavy Catholic proportions is quite comprehensible.

The figures of Table 6.15 now add the important information that the contrast between the prolabor and nonlabor political types in religious affiliation is found primarily among the *better educated* Catholics and Protestants. Indeed, it turns out that though the Catholics as a whole are more frequent in the Prolabor-Political type, those Catholics who have only eighth grade schooling are *not* more numerous but markedly less so in this type. Among Protestants, both the better educated and the less educated are represented a little more in the Nonlabor-Political type than in the Prolabor-Politicals (though this difference is confined to those past 40). It is similarly noteworthy that while the Prolabor-Apoliticals were found to have above average numbers of Catholics, this proves to be true only in respect to the less educated (and only the younger, less educated, furthermore). The proportion of *better* educated Catholics is slightly *under* the average for all types (and this relation is confined to the younger group—below 40 years of age). These same principal relations hold for Protestants in this type (the one minor exception is that it is the *older,* better educated who are particularly under-represented). It thus seems clear that education and religion need to be considered together in order to arrive at proper interpretations.

Moreover, other associated characteristics such as age and socio-economic status also enter into the relationships. However, successive divisions of our data in terms of these other variables reduce the number of cases to be compared to a point where conclusions become extremely shaky. Examples of the influence of third variables are reported in the preceding paragraph in the form of parenthetical inserts concerning age. One further illustration will suffice. The Prolabor-Political type was characterized above as having not more Catholics in general but more of the *better educated* Catholics. Additional analysis now shows that this is especially true of the better educated *younger* Catholics of *relatively high socio-economic* status and of the better educated *older* Catholics at the *middle and lower socio-economic* levels. Looked at the other way around, though only one-third of the total sample is in the Prolabor-Political type, one-half of the younger, better educated Catholics fall into this type. Likewise one-half of the older, better educated Catholics who are at medium or lower socio-economic levels are in this type. And over two-thirds of the young, better educated Catholics of high socio-economic status belong to this type.

Voting Behavior and Related Attitudes

The preceding sections of this chapter were largely devoted to a) a description of the answers to those questions that entered into our definition of the four types, and b) the social characteristics of the types. The variations in the answers to questions considered under (a), as stated before, were actually to be expected because they were used in selecting the types.

But what additional information is there about each of the types, information that was not used in categorizing the UAW members into the four groups, and that will provide us with further insights regarding these sub-groupings of auto workers? The first set of additional facts has to do with their voting behavior, and related features. While the election choices and similar characteristics of the voters in the sample were not directly used in our construction of the four types, these factors nevertheless are obviously associated indirectly with those questions that were used in the type definitions.

Table 6.16 presents the 1952 Presidential choices of each general type. It reveals substantial differences between the two types with a high labor political orientation, on the one hand, and the other two types, as well as some differences between the latter two types themselves. The fourth type (the Nonlabor-Apoliticals) were still preponderantly Stevenson voters—despite their non-labor political orientation—while the opposite was true of the Nonlabor-Politicals. Furthermore, we find that the bulk of the Eisenhower votes in the UAW membership came from those workers with a low labor political orientation but with a high political interest; in fact, they contributed nearly six out of every ten UAW votes for the Republican candidate.

TABLE 6.16

1952 PRESIDENTIAL VOTING BEHAVIOR
OF THE FOUR TYPES

	Prolabor-Political	Prolabor-Apolitical	Nonlabor-Political	Nonlabor-Apolitical
Stevenson	84%	74%	36%	59%
Eisenhower	6	6	61	25
Other; did not vote; refused to say*	10	20	3	16
	100%	100%	100%	100%

* Nearly all of these are non-voters.

Reasons for voting for Stevenson or Eisenhower. Among those UAW members who voted for Stevenson, the most frequent reason cited for voting for him, regardless of type, was that he ran on the Democratic ticket, or that they liked his platform. The percentage of Stevenson voters in each type giving this reason runs at about the same figure as for the total sample, 68 per cent. The type that might be expected to be low in the proportion of its Stevenson voters stating worker-oriented reasons (better for the working man, employment and security, etc.), namely the Nonlabor-Politicals, is actually the highest. Whereas 33 per cent of the Nonlabor-Apoliticals, 41 per cent of the Prolabor-Apoliticals, and 44 per cent of the Prolabor-Politicals, said they voted for Stevenson because he would be better for the working man, 56 per cent of the Nonlabor-Politicals gave the same reason. Generally the same relative differences prevail with respect to those reasons having to do with employment, security, and prosperity. This fact about the Nonlabor-Politicals might be another substantiation of the point made in other parts of this chapter, namely, that even though this type is by definition made up of workers with a low labor political orientation, it nevertheless has within it a number of

UAW members who see eye-to-eye with other members on many issues crucial to the union. Moreover, the proportion of Stevenson Nonlabor-Politicals indicating they voted for him because he ran on the Democratic ticket is as high as it is in the other types.

Although a small percentage of the Prolabor-Apoliticals and Nonlabor-Apoliticals mentioned civil rights when asked before the election to name issues personally important to them, none of them referred to this issue after the election in citing reasons for having voted for Stevenson. This is worth noting especially because 17 per cent of the Prolabor-Apoliticals are Negroes.[3] On the other hand, 4 per cent of the Stevenson voters in the Prolabor-Politicals and 5 per cent of them in the Nonlabor-Politicals did refer to civil rights. The explanation for the absence of references to civil rights by the Prolabor-Apoliticals (and the low percentage among the Prolabor-Politicals, for that matter, since they too have a high proportion of Negroes) is not self-evident, and only speculations can be made. Perhaps the answer is, apart from the possibility of limited articulateness in the interview, that in the UAW members' "priority list" of motivations for voting for their favored candidate, civil rights was given relatively little weight, especially in the case of the two apolitical types (none of the Nonlabor-Apoliticals mentioned it, either).

A comparison of the two extreme types with large proportions voting for Stevenson, that is, the Prolabor-Politicals and the Prolabor-Apoliticals, with their general type equivalents reveals 1) in the case of the extreme Prolabor-Politicals a sharp drop from the general Prolabor-Politicals in the percentage of persons giving the stereotyped, "pat" reason that he ran on the Democratic ticket; 2) contrariwise, among the extreme Prolabor-Apoliticals, the tendency to give such a reason was greater than among their general type equivalents. These two points are probably related to the wide difference in educational background of the two types.

For the two types with substantial numbers voting for Eisenhower, the Nonlabor-Politicals and the Nonlabor-Apoliti-

---

[3] In this connection, we plan later to present a detailed report on the Negroes in our sample, probably in the form of a research paper.

cals,[4] the most frequently stated reason for voting for him was "Needed a change." One-half of the former type, but only a little over one-third of the latter, gave this reason. However, the two types did not differ too much in the percentages stating that they were just voting against the Democrats. On the other hand, 10 per cent of the Nonlabor-Politicals, but *none* of the other type said they wanted to get rid of Truman.

The Korean War was apparently more important to the Nonlabor-Politicals than to the Nonlabor-Apoliticals, considering the fact that 22 per cent of the former, but only 9 per cent of the latter referred to it in giving a reason for voting for Eisenhower. This difference, as well as those reported in the above paragraph, is probably related to the fact that the Nonlabor-Politicals are more highly educated, and more of them consider themselves Republicans. These two facts together probably operate in the direction of making the Nonlabor-Politicals better able to articulate, especially on the issues emphasized in the Republican campaign itself. Analysis of the *extreme* Nonlabor-Politicals and Nonlabor-Apoliticals, who differ even more in education and self-designation as Republicans, supports this interpretation; the percentage of the extreme Nonlabor-Politicals stating each reason is higher than that of the general Nonlabor-Politicals, and the opposite is true for the Nonlabor-Apoliticals. That is, a smaller proportion of the extreme Nonlabor-Apoliticals than of the general type mention the usual Republican reasons.

Party Preference. The four general types vary considerably in their party choices, as shown in Table 6.17. A Democratic preference is highly associated with agreement on a labor political orientation, as the figures for the Prolabor-Politicals and the Prolabor-Apoliticals indicate. This is to be expected, partly because approval of the union's support for the Democratic candidate enters into the definition of our types. And a Republican preference is mostly to be found in the two nonlabor types, the Nonlabor-Politicals in particular having a much greater percentage of workers with Republican leanings than any other type. With the exception of only this one type, the Nonlabor-Political,

---

[4] Because of the extremely few numbers of Eisenhower voters in the two Prolabor types, no comparison is made here between the reasons given by those voters, and those by the Nonlabor Eisenhower voters.

TABLE 6.17

PARTY PREFERENCE AMONG THE FOUR GENERAL TYPES

	Prolabor-Political	Prolabor-Apolitical	Nonlabor-Political	Nonlabor-Apolitical
Democrats plus Democratic leaning	93%	91%	52%	75%
Republicans plus Republican leaning	2	3	28	11
Neither	5	6	20	14
	100%	100%	100%	100%

there is a close correspondence between the proportion of the members of each type calling themselves Democrats and the percentage of each type voting for the Democratic candidate for President:

	Per Cent Democrat	Per Cent of Voters for Stevenson
Prolabor-Political	93%	93%
Prolabor-Apolitical	91%	93%
Nonlabor-Political	52%	38%
Nonlabor-Apolitical	75%	74%

This one deviation in the case of the Nonlabor-Politicals is partly explicable in terms of the fact that relatively few of them considered themselves *strong* Democrats.

The two types with a low labor political orientation also have the greatest percentage of Independents with no leanings toward either of the two parties. This, too, is to be expected since support of the union's political program implies some degree of commitment to a particular party. In this connection, it should be remembered (see p. 40) that the Independents voted for Eisenhower two to one.

While the extreme Prolabor-Politicals and Prolabor-Apoliticals are understandably no more Democratic than their general types (since nearly all of the general Prolabors, to begin with, are Democratic, and hence little increase could be expected), the percentage of self-designated Democrats (and Independents with Democratic leanings) among the extreme Nonlabors drops considerably, in favor of Republican leanings and identification with neither party. This again suggests the close relationship between degree of support of the union's political program and identification with the Democratic Party. In neither of these two extreme types, however, does the proportion of Republicans exceed that of Democrats. To be sure, the percentages indicating "very strong" Democratic leanings are quite low in these two types.

1948 Presidential Choice. Among the differences separating the two Prolabor types from the two Nonlabor types is the fact that the latter types contributed nearly all of the votes shifting from Truman in 1948 to Eisenhower in 1952. While the vote of the two Prolabor types for a Republican presidential candidate increased from 3 per cent in 1948 to 6 per cent in 1952, the shift for the Nonlabor-Apoliticals was from 8 per cent to 25 per cent, and the shift for the Nonlabor-Politicals was from 25 per cent to 61 per cent. There is no need to elaborate on the proposition suggested here, namely, that the Nonlabor-Politicals constitute the greatest source of defection from the traditional pro-Democratic voting behavior of Detroit's workers. Of course, this proposition must be qualified by the fact that less than half of the Nonlabor-Politicals, however, voted a *straight* Republican ticket.

A second point brought out by comparison of the four types' 1948 voting behavior with that in 1952 is that only the two Political types included any voters for a third party candidate in 1948: 4 per cent of the Prolabor-Politicals and only 1 per cent of the Nonlabor-Politicals. These were almost entirely for Wallace.

A third point brought out by this comparison between 1948 and 1952 has to do with fact that while each type had an increase in the total percentage reporting that they voted, the type having the greatest increase in voting was the Nonlabor-Political group (who voted predominantly for Eisenhower); the type with the smallest increase occurred in the Nonlabor-Apolitical type.[5]

The most significant comparisons between the general and extreme types here are that a higher percentage of the extreme than of the general Prolabor-Politicals voted for Wallace (or

[5] This is in line with the findings on the national electorate, by Campbell, Gurin and Miller, which indicated that a large proportion of the people who had not voted in 1948 voted for Eisenhower (the most favored candidate of the Nonlabor-Politicals). Cf. their *The Voter Decides.*

some other "left-of-center" third party candidate), and that a much smaller percentage of the extreme than of the general Nonlabor-Apoliticals' voters cast their ballot for Truman, with a corresponding higher vote for Dewey.

1952 Gubernatorial and Senatorial Choices. While over 90 per cent of the voters in the two types with a high labor political orientation cast their ballots for the Democratic candidates for Governor and Senator, the other two types were not similar to each other in their respective percentages. 81 per cent of the Nonlabor-Apolitical voters, but only 57 per cent of these in the Nonlabor-Politicals, voted for G. Mennen Williams, the Democratic candidate for Governor; 76 per cent of the former, but only 55 per cent of the latter, chose Blair Moody, the same party's candidate for Senator. Although these percentages are higher than those for Stevenson, there is still the same general relationship between a Prolabor-Political orientation and voting for union-supported candidates.

While the Nonlabor-Politicals had a majority in favor of the Republican *Presidential* candidate, this was not the case with respect to their vote for the Republican candidates for Governor and Senator. This fact somewhat supports the proposition that among these union members, the vote for Eisenhower was in large part a vote for the personality and not for the party. The higher Williams and Moody vote among the Nonlabor-Apolitical members (as well as their majority vote for Stevenson) points to the possibility that this group might be pro-Democrat primarily for reasons other than any affiliation with their union, and that it constitutes a source for additional Democratic votes, given a concerted attempt on the part of the union and related groups to elicit such support.

As might be expected, the percentages of members in the extreme Nonlabor-Politicals and the Nonlabor-Apoliticals casting their ballots for the Democratic candidates for these two offices were lower than those of their general types, because, again, of the close relationship between degree of acceptance of a labor political orientation and actual vote for union-supported candidates.

Vote on Reapportionment Amendments. When asked before the election if they had heard about the issue of reapportionment, which was (and still is) highly important in the UAW's political strategy, 56 per cent of all the registered voters in our sample, it should be recalled, said that they had. However, the four types show wide variations in the extent to which each had some knowledge of the issue. It is clear that political interest, rather than labor political orientation, is the more determining factor here: 82 per cent and 74 per cent of the Nonlabor-Politicals and the Prolabor-Politicals, respectively, indicated that they had heard about it, in sharp contrast with 54 per cent and 43 per cent of the Nonlabor-Apoliticals and Prolabor-Apoliticals, respectively. The last line in Table 6.18 shows similar differences among the types.

TABLE 6.18

VOTE ON REAPPORTIONMENT PROPOSALS AMONG TYPES*

	Prolabor-Political	Prolabor-Apolitical	Nonlabor-Political	Nonlabor-Apolitical
For Proposal 2, against 3	45%	29%	22%	27%
For Proposal 2; no vote or no indication on 3	24	17	21	12
For 3, against 2	1	—	15	3
Other combinations	2	4	10	9
Not clear; don't know or remember how voted; no indication	28	50	32	49
	100%	100%	100%	100%

* Percentages are based on voters only.

How did they actually vote on the issues at election time? From the union's standpoint, a vote *for* Proposal 2 and *against* Proposal 3 was the preferable one; the least desirable was a vote in the opposite direction. The voting behavior with respect to this question (which was not used in constructing the types) clearly shows another aspect of the differentiating characteristics of the four types (Table 6.18). This issue, much more than that of voting for candidates, was a test of the influence of the union on the political behavior of its members. It is difficult to separate the actual influence of the union's political action efforts in

behalf of a Democratic Presidential candidate from the influence
of traditional Democratic party identification *per se* among the
workers, and of other similar forces. However, in this particular
case of reapportionment, 1) this issue was not considered popularly as a party matter (although it has implications, objectively,
for the distribution of power between the two parties) and 2)
the union itself campaigned vigorously for one of the two proposals and against the other. Thus the Democratic versus Republican labels were absent and the role of the union was prominent.

The Prolabor-Politicals stand out in their acceptance of their
union's political recommendation. And the Nonlabor-Politicals
have by far the highest percentage of UAW members (15 per
cent) voting against the union's stand, that is, they voted against
Proposal 2 *and* for Proposal 3. The fact that a higher percentage
of them voted in line with the union's recommendation (22 per
cent) than voted against it is offset by the fact that they have
the smallest percentage of all the types doing so.

It is obvious that a high labor political orientation does not
automatically guarantee a satisfactory performance by workers
on various specific matters that the union considers significant.
That is, from the union's own standpoint, such an orientation
is not enough. A considerable degree of interest in political
matters is also required to make workers with a high labor
political orientation into "ideal union members." The case in
point is that of the Prolabor-Apoliticals. Half of this group of
UAW members were unable to give an intelligent answer to the
question asking how they voted on the proposals. Moreover,
despite their high labor political orientation, only 29 per cent of
them voted on both proposals in accordance with the union's
recommendations, in contrast to the 45 per cent of the Prolabor-
Politicals.

The contrasts indicated above were, by and large, sharper
among the extreme types. All of the Prolabor-Politicals, for one
thing, voted on the issue, and of the 82 per cent who gave a
codable answer, all voted for Proposal 2; however, 35 per cent
made no reference to 3. 56 per cent of the extreme Nonlabor-
Politicals, on the other hand, clearly voted in opposition to the
union's stand (as compared with only 15 per cent of the general
Nonlabor-Politicals). A little less than half of each of the other

two types (higher than for their general types) voted clearly in accordance with the union's recommendation.

1951 Detroit Mayoralty Vote. As in the case of reapportionment, a vote for the union's mayoralty choice in Detroit might be considered a much more "pure" test of the union's effectiveness than a vote for the union's Presidential candidate. This is so because the Detroit municipal elections are run on a "nonpartisan" basis, with very little, if any, party labeling in the minds of the average worker during such campaigns.[6] While the two parties are not directly involved, or formally active, the union itself participates to a considerable degree. Hence, it may be presumed that voting behavior in such elections is a relatively direct reflection of union political loyalty and union effectiveness.

How does such loyalty reveal itself in each of our four types? The following table presents the marked differences among them, and also presents a further documentation of the differences in political interest as shown by the percentages not voting at all.

TABLE 6.19

1951 DETROIT MAYORALTY CHOICES AMONG THE FOUR TYPES*

Mayoralty Candidate	Prolabor-Political	Prolabor-Apolitical	Nonlabor-Political	Nonlabor-Apolitical
Union-supported	48%	16%	24%	5%
Union-opposed	31	37	57	69
Did not vote	21	47	19	26
	100%	100%	100%	100%
No. of cases	(90)	(67)	(66)	(65)

* Based on Detroiters only.

Decidedly the strongest support of the union-backed candidate comes from the Prolabor-Political type; it is the only type in which more Detroit UAW members voted for that candidate

---

[6] In other unpublished studies of two mayoralty elections in Detroit, it was found that at least 85 per cent of pro-Republican voters (as measured by Presidential choice) voted for the CIO-opposed candidate, while the pro-Democrats appeared to be much more evenly divided.

than for his opponent. Furthermore, three-fifths of all the votes for the union-supported candidate came from this one group, despite the fact that the Prolabor-Politicals make up only one-third of all the voters in the 1951 election. Clearly, the poorest supporter of the union-backed candidate is the Nonlabor-Apolitical type. Putting this in terms of votes for the opponent of the union-supported candidate, the difference between the types is primarily that between the two with a higher pro-labor political orientation, on the one hand, and the two types with the lower orientation.

A high labor political orientation alone, again, does not guarantee that a UAW member is going to vote in such elections; the Prolabor-Apoliticals make up 38 per cent of the sample's non-voters in the 1951 mayoralty election, although they constitute only 22 per cent of the total sample of Detroit voters. On the other hand, the two types with high political interest make up a smaller proportion of the non-voters than they do of the total sample.

Among the extreme types, we find the same relationships but to a more accentuated degree: the Prolabor-Apoliticals have the highest percentage of non-voters, the Prolabor-Politicals, the highest percentage voting for the union-supported candidate, and *all* of the Nonlabor-Apoliticals voting for the opponent.

The voting behavior of these types in Detroit's mayoralty election points up the importance of the issue of partisanship versus nonpartisanship in the local political scene. For some decades now, Detroit has had a presumably non-partisan structure in its municipal politics. Regardless of what the original intentions were for introducing the non-partisan system, there is no doubt that among the effects have been the weakening of worker interest generally in such matters, and also the reduction of the chances of success for candidates supported by labor organizations, even among those workers who do express an interest by voting. In more recent years, various groups in the city have been campaigning for a return of the two-party system *formally* into local politics. The absence of any *formal* party involvement in the local elections also means the absence of any locus of responsibility. The belief has been developed that the candidates are to be considered as "individuals," atttached to no definable groups or interests. Our data suggest the proposition that in partisan elections the worker judges the concrete issues and candidates in terms of his previous knowledge and familiarity with the traditional positions of the parties. Non-partisan elections fail to arouse the workers in the same degree, and provide less familiar bases for election choices. This generalization pertains especially to our Prolabor-Apolitical type, whose proportion of *non-voters* in the mayoralty election was particularly large in comparison to the proportion in the Presidential election, and whose proportion of votes *for the union-supported* candidate in the mayoralty election was much smaller than the proportion in the Presidential election. Party labels apparently do make a difference.

Differences between the parties. One more item should be added to our portraits of the four types with respect to voting behavior. It is of a somewhat more fundamental nature than the specific act of voting itself, and is pertinent to the general and much-discussed issue of the relationship of the labor movement to the present two-party system. We asked in the post-election interview:

> "Do you think there is any important difference between what the Democratic and Republican parties stand for, or do you think they are about the same?"

The importance of this question in our type analysis is seen especially in reference to the stratum of workers in any union with the characteristics of our Prolabor-Politicals (because of their greater articulateness, union participation and office-holding, etc.). It is assumed that these members will have a greater impact on the political decision-making that takes place in the union. The further assumption is that the greater the extent to which such workers believe that no important difference exists between the two major parties in the United States, the greater will be the chances of any attempt to establish a third, or "Labor," party. That is, the chances for a new pro-labor party would be increased if more of such influential union members believed that the Democratic Party is not essentially different from the Republican Party in regard to issues relevant to their status as workers and as active union members.

Viewed in this way then, how did the Prolabor-Politicals and the other three types (who presumably have less influence on the UAW's political decisions) answer the question put to them? Nearly all of each type gave a clear answer to the question and, of these, 75 per cent of the Prolabor-Politicals said there was a difference, in contrast to only 57 per cent of the Prolabor-Apoliticals, 50 per cent of the Nonlabor-Politicals, and 52 per cent of the Nonlabor-Apoliticals.[7] Thus, the Prolabor-Political type is more inclined to believe that there *are* important differences between the Republicans and the Democrats.

If the assumptions stated above are essentially correct, the implications of the figures presented here (which are confirmed in analysis of the extreme types) should be clear. In the political scene of Michigan, at least, the two major political parties are viewed as quite different by a key group of union members, the ones who most directly affect the political decisions of the union.[8] The party favored by this key group is, of course, the Democratic Party, as evidenced by stated party preference, and voting behavior, as well as by the fact that three-fifths of the Prolabor-Politicals believing that the two parties are different *spontaneously volunteered pro-Democratic remarks* when answering the question under discussion. It would appear, in other words, that the chances for the establishment (let alone the victory) of a new party on the initiative of the active members at the present time or in the immediate future are very slim indeed.

---

[7] If the "don't know" and "no answer" categories are included, these percentages decrease to 67 per cent, 49 per cent, 43 per cent, and 46 per cent, respectively. Even with these categories, however, the Prolabor-Politicals still mostly believe there is a difference between the two parties, and still to a greater extent than do the three other types.

[8] For an extended discussion of the need to reckon with functional groups when interpreting the findings of public opinion polls, see Herbert Blumer, "Public Opinion and Public Opinion Polling," *American Sociological Review*, 1948, 13, 542-54. "I think that it is . . . very clear that in the process of forming public opinion, individuals are not alike in influence nor are groups that are equal numerically in membership alike in influence . . . differences in prestige, position, and influence that characterize groups and individuals in the functional organizations of a society are brought into play in the formation of public opinion." Interesting evidence on the matter is discussed in the recent book, *Personal Influence* by Elihu Katz and Paul F. Lazarsfeld (Glencoe, The Free Press, 1955).

Of incidental interest here is the fact that among the Non-labor-Politicals, who had the highest percentage of Eisenhower voters and persons identifying themselves as Republican, slightly more pro-Democratic than pro-Republican remarks were volunteered when stating there was an important difference between the two parties. As is the case with many other items presented in this chapter, this fact suggests that this type is actually made up of two somewhat distinct sub-types, one of which is "on side" with the union with regard to specific issues but which nevertheless is not too keen about the idea of political action by their union—the other sub-type being not only against union political action but also not identified with worker-oriented issues. In this connection, it should be recalled that over half of all the Non-labor-Politicals declared themselves to have Democratic leanings, and only a little over one-fourth as having Republican leanings (see Table 6.16).

What sorts of images of the voting behavior of the types emerge from the above findings? Briefly, they are as follows:

Prolabor-Politicals: This type had the smallest proportion of undecided voters in the weeks before the election. Its actual vote for Stevenson was the highest of the types. Although they are slightly below the Prolabor-Apoliticals in their party identification as "Democrat or Strong Democrat," the leaning of their "Independents" toward the Democratic Party gives them a slight edge over the Prolabor-Apoliticals. They were the most definite in their support of the union's recommendations on the two reapportionment proposals; they made up the overwhelming majority of votes for the union-supported candidates for Mayor in 1951; and they more generally believe that there are important differences between the two parties. This group of UAW members, then, is the type most consistently in line with the union's political program.

Prolabor-Apoliticals: These UAW members had the highest percentage of non-voters in the 1952 Presidential and 1951 Mayoralty elections. They have the highest proportion identifying themselves as "Democrat or Strong Democrat." On the other hand, their votes for the union's recommendations on the reapportionment proposals and on the mayoralty election were quite low. Despite their high pro-labor political *orientation,* these auto workers *perform* quite poorly when it comes to following through on all or nearly all of the issues crucial to the union.

Nonlabor-Politicals: This type had the most supporters for Eisenhower—in fact, the only type with a majority for him. However, the majority in 1948 was for Truman, and for that matter, for the Democratic candidates for Governor and Senator in 1952, thus indicating that a large number of them split their ballots in the latter election. They have the highest proportion of all the types with Republican leanings, but still a majority of them have Democratic leanings. Their vote for the union's mayoralty candidate was no lower than that of the Prolabor-Apoliticals. But they had the highest proportion among the types voting against the union's recommendations on the two reapportionment proposals, although more of them voted in accordance with these recommendations than against. There appear to be two sub-types among these workers, one happening to view *certain* political and economic issues in the same light as the union but nevertheless believing that unions should not be in politics, the other being more consistently against the union on such issues. Nonetheless, together they constitute the key source of defection from the union's political efforts.

Nonlabor-Apoliticals: This type had the highest percentage of undecided voters before the election. In 1948, they supported Truman as much as did the two types with a high labor political orientation. They are predominantly pro-Democratic, though not very strongly so. They rank as the lowest of the types in support of the union's recommendations on reapportionment and the mayoralty election. Their voting behavior probably is not so much a manifestation of anti-union sentiments as it is of general political apathy.

General Attitudes Related to Political Behavior

Up to this point we have dealt with such matters as labor political orientation, political interest, social characteristics (age, religion, etc.), and voting behavior—all of great interest in gaining an understanding of the complex nature of the membership of the auto workers union. But perhaps of greater significance is the wider, somewhat more basic and subtle set of characteristics that can best be labeled "social psychological." We have reference to the UAW members' identification with their union (as apart from any labor political orientation); class identification; feelings of political effectiveness or impotence; authoritarianism; race attitudes; feelings of satisfaction with life and of social alienation ("anomie"); and the like. Many of these are dispositions pertinent to more general issues such as problems of "mass man"—apathy and democratic participation—and are not confined to questions of the composition of the rank-and-file of a major labor union such as the UAW. As we shall see, however, these two issues are highly related to each other.

Union Attachment. The question posed here is the interesting one of the relationship between the more narrow variable of attachment to the union in a relatively *structural* sense, i.e., without consideration of the union's more general program (including its political aspects), on the one hand, and a labor political orientation, on the other. Our index of attachment to the union was made up of the workers' responses to three questions dealing with expressed interest in the union, how often meetings are attended, and positions held in the union structure. Each of these will be reported upon with respect to differences among the types, and then the composite index itself will be similarly dealt with.

As the following table indicates, the differences among the types as to degree of interest in the union are essentially a matter of the pro-labor orientation of the members, i.e., nearly half of the two types with a high labor political orientation express a great deal of interest in the union, in contrast to much lower proportions of the other two types. In fact, the percentages of the Prolabor-Politicals and Prolabor-Apoliticals indicating a great deal of interest are three times as great as the percentage of the Nonlabor-Apoliticals indicating the same degree of interest. In comparing the Prolabor-Politicals and the Prolabor-Apoliticals with each other, however, we can see that the former type has the highest percentage (90 per cent) indicating *some* or a *great deal* of interest in the union. The lower figure for the Prolabor-Apoliticals (73 per cent) suggests that political interest (or more properly, the factors that affect such interest) has a positive relationship to the degree of union interest prevailing among workers with a high labor political orientation.

TABLE 6.20
INTEREST IN THE UNION AMONG THE FOUR TYPES

Degree of Interest	Prolabor-Political	Prolabor-Apolitical	Nonlabor-Political	Nonlabor-Apolitical
Great deal	49%	49%	27%	16%
Some	41	24	39	51
Little or none	10	27	34	33
	100%	100%	100%	100%

When we come to attendance at meetings, the similarities between the Prolabor-Politicals and the Prolabor-Apoliticals that obtained with respect to interest in the union disappear, as Table 6.21 indicates. The percentage of the Prolabor-Politicals attending at least one meeting a month, in fact, is more than twice that of the Prolabor-Apoliticals—as well as being equally great relative to the proportions of the two other types. The Prolabor-Apolitical type is, moreover, among the lowest attenders. Obviously, a high degree of expressed interest in the union is not necessarily associated with high attendance at its meetings.

TABLE 6.21
ATTENDANCE AT UNION MEETINGS AMONG THE FOUR TYPES

Frequency	Prolabor-Political	Prolabor-Apolitical	Nonlabor-Political	Nonlabor-Apolitical
At least once a month	41%	19%	20%	20%
At least 1-3 times per year but not once a month	43	28	37	30
Never; hardly ever	16	53	43	50
	100%	100%	100%	100%

The contrast among the four types is further documented by the data on positions held in the union and other organizations, as shown in Table 6.22.

TABLE 6.22

OFFICES IN UNION AND OTHER ORGANIZATIONS
AMONG THE FOUR TYPES

	Prolabor-Political	Prolabor-Apolitical	Nonlabor-Political	Nonlabor-Apolitical
Office in Union only	28%	5%	10%	7%
Office in Union *and* one or more other organizations	2	2	9	2
Office in other organizations than Union	13	7	10	10
No office at all	51	76	58	71
No indication	6	10	13	10
	100%	100%	100%	100%

The Prolabor-Politicals are the most active union members in terms of positions held in the union, and indeed, have the smallest percentage of persons with no position in any organization. It is also clear that the two types with high political interest are the most active in these terms. The figures for the Prolabor-Politicals also suggest that such a type need not be exclusively devoted to the union—that high interest, high meeting attendance, and high office-holding in the union are not necessarily accompanied by a corresponding *lower* interest, attendance, and office-holding, in other groups.

How do the four types compare with respect to the index that combines all three of the above items? The figures in Table 6.23 reveal that the Prolabor-Politicals are markedly different from the others in their attachment to the union. And a pro-labor political orientation does not by itself make for a high union attachment. Apparently a high interest in political matters generally, or that set of factors (education, age, occupation, etc.) affecting such interest, is also associated with a high union attachment among workers with a pro-labor political orientation.

Answers of the *extreme types* to the separate questions reveal, in the case of interest in the union, a much higher percentage among the extreme than among the general Prolabor-Politicals indicating a great deal of interest, and conversely, a much higher percentage among the extreme than among the general Nonlabor-Apoliticals indicating little or no interest in the union. In the case of attendance at union meetings, the contrasts among the extreme types are slightly greater than among the general types; in particular, the percentage of extreme Prolabor-Apoliticals attending at least once a month is nearly half that of the general Prolabor-Apoliticals. The figures pertaining to offices held in the extreme types show nearly half of the extreme Prolabor-Politicals (as compared with less than one-third of the general Prolabor-Politicals) holding some office in the union. On the other hand, the passive, apparently apathetic nature of the other type with a high pro-labor political orientation, the Prolabor-Apoliticals, is dramatically accentuated in their extreme type: 94 per cent of the extreme Prolabor-Apoliticals hold no office in any organization whatsoever! Indeed, a little less than one-third of the extreme Nonlabor-Politicals hold some office in the union, a proportion about two-thirds larger than that of the general Nonlabor-Politicals.

TABLE 6.23

UNION ATTACHMENT INDICES OF THE FOUR TYPES

Degree of Attachment	Prolabor-Political	Prolabor-Apolitical	Nonlabor-Political	Nonlabor-Apolitical
High	50%	32%	30%	25%
Medium	43	39	45	48
Low	7	29	25	27
	100%	100%	100%	100%

These data for both the general and the extreme types indicate again the crucial role of the social and psychological factors (such as age, ethnic or generation status, as well as ability to articulate and general political interest, etc.) that make for organizational participation in general. The two types with high political interest, for example, belong to more organizations and hold more offices in them, than the two types with low political interest. And of the two latter types, the Prolabor-Apoliticals are at the bottom—even when it comes to attendance and office-holding in the union.[9]

Class identification. As might be expected, the two types with a pro-labor political orientation also tend more than the Non-labor types to think of themselves as members of the working class. But as the following table shows, even the Nonlabor types are still preponderantly "working class" by self-designation.

TABLE 6.24

CLASS IDENTIFICATION BY TYPES

Class	Prolabor-Political	Prolabor-Apolitical	Nonlabor-Political	Nonlabor-Apolitical
Lower	2%	4%	—	3%
Working	80	81	66	70
Middle	18	15	33	27
Upper	—	—	1	—
	100%	100%	100%	100%

Perhaps the similarity between the two Prolabor types shown in Table 6.24 is to be expected, but if we consider that the Prolabor-Politicals are *dissimilar* to the Prolabor-Apoliticals in the variables ordinarily associated with class identification (such as income, occupation, and education), the close resemblance of the two types is all the more remarkable. The usual findings indicate that the lower the income, occupation, and education, the greater is the tendency to classify oneself as "working" or "lower" class. If this proposition were unqualifiedly correct, the Prolabor-Politicals certainly should have a lower percentage than the Prolabor-Apoliticals choosing these two classes, since they are markedly above the Prolabor-Apoliticals in income, skill-level, and education. The point is that they *don't* have such

[9] The fact that a sizable minority of the Nonlabor-Politicals are stewards and the like should not be surprising if we consider that the motives for attaining office in the union are not exclusively related to purely pro-union sentiments and certainly do not require pro-labor *political* sentiments. Cf. Leonard Sayles and George Strauss, *The Local Union* (New York: Harper & Brothers, 1953), pp. 83-88, for a discussion of types of stewards.

a lower percentage; in fact, they have quite similar percentages. In addition, the Nonlabor-Politicals, who are quite similar to the Prolabor-Politicals in these variables, nevertheless have a smaller percentage saying "working class" and a higher percentage saying "middle class." This set of self-designations as regards class by the Nonlabor-Politicals is understandable, in part, by reference to the fact that they do have more white-collar workers, and fewer Negroes and southern whites.

In other words, the above proposition concerning the relationship between variables like income, occupation, and education, on the one hand, and class-identification, on the other, holds true in all of the types *except* the Prolabor-Politicals. For example, the proposition would be that the higher the percentage of each type with nine or more years of schooling, the higher will be the percentage in each type claiming to be "middle class." The following table indicates that this is true in the case of three of the types, but *not* in the case of the Prolabor-Politicals.

TABLE 6.25

RELATIONSHIP BETWEEN EDUCATION AND CLASS
IDENTIFICATION IN THE FOUR TYPES

Type	% of Type with 9 or More Years Schooling	% of Type Saying "Middle Class"
Prolabor-Apolitical	37%	15%
Nonlabor-Apolitical	49%	27%
Nonlabor-Political	59%	33%
Prolabor-Political	75%	18%

Analysis of the extreme types reveal even stronger confirmation of this finding, which runs counter to usually accepted notions in the field of social stratification. The inference here is that a strong labor political orientation is intimately bound up with the subjective class-affiliation of better-educated workers.

Attitudes of Political Futility. As stated in Chapter 5, one of the most important factors in political behavior is the degree to which people feel that they "have some say" about the political process. If political interest is part of this behavior, it should not be surprising to find that the two types with little political interest should have the highest political futility. Forty-eight per cent of the Nonlabor-Apoliticals and 43 per cent of the Prolabor-Apoliticals do have high political futility as compared with 33 per cent of the Prolabor-Politicals and 35 per cent of the Nonlabor-Politicals. The figures for the latter two types suggest that a substantial proportion of even the politically interested auto workers nevertheless feel politically impotent insofar as their own individual efforts are concerned.

In only one extreme type did an increase in political futility over its correspondingly general type take place, and that, somewhat unexpectedly, was the Nonlabor-Political type. 55 per cent of this extreme type responded on at least three of the four statements in the direction of political futility. Apparently the two items responsible for this increase were 1) "The way people vote is the main thing that decides how things are run in this country," and 2) "People like me don't have any say about what the government does." This second statement was highly discriminating as between the four extreme types: only 12 per cent of the extreme Prolabor-Politicals agreed with this statement, in marked contrast to 43 per cent of the Nonlabor-Politicals, 50 per cent of the Prolabor-Apoliticals, and 58 per cent of the Nonlabor-Apoliticals.

Authoritarian Attitudes. Attention was called in the previous chapter to the findings concerning the authoritarian tendencies that constitute a challenge to democratic leadership in the union and in the general community. But do these tendencies distribute themselves evenly through the four types under consideration? Or are the authoritarian attitudes to be found more in some types and less in others? And which are these types? These questions are of more than academic interest, for in large measure they are related to the development of the labor movement and its impact on the socio-political structure of American society. The problem of democracy in a large-scale society like ours and, more concretely, in large-scale organizations like the union, is partly the problem of maintaining an adequate proportion of members who are capable of engaging in the market place of proposals and counterproposals, immune from the feeling that "the leader knows best," and from the temptation to condone, or resort to, desperate measures in times of social and political crises.

As the following table indicates, authoritarianism varies considerably among the four general types. We find that the Prolabor-Politicals are the only type with fewer authoritarians (those agreeing with at least four of the five statements used in the index) than non-authoritarians (those agreeing with no more than one of the five statements). And the Prolabor-Apoliticals have the largest proportion of authoritarians and the smallest proportion of non-authoritarians. This contrast certainly suggests that although workers may be similar in their labor political orientation, they need not be similar in certain fundamental social-psychological attitudes that in turn may be vitally intertwined with factors that determine their roles in mass organizations and mass society. Again, it should be stated that the Prolabor-Apoliticals have a high proportion of UAW members of a low educational and economic status, as well as of ethnic minority backgrounds, to which many of these attitudes are related.[10]

TABLE 6.26

AUTHORITARIAN ATTITUDES AMONG THE FOUR TYPES

	Prolabor- Political	Prolabor- Apolitical	Nonlabor- Political	Nonlabor- Apolitical
Authoritarian*	29%	40%	37%	36%
Non-authoritarian**	30	11	32	19

* 4 or more authoritarian statements accepted.
** 1 or less accepted.

In particular, political interest seems to be negatively related to the degree of authoritarian tendencies. Both the Prolabor-Politicals and Nonlabor-Politicals are higher than the two low political interest types in their percentages of non-authoritarians. But perhaps more significant is the fact that the Prolabor-Politicals by themselves stand out in their relatively lower percentage

---

[10] A study by Constance Tonat of a small, predominantly Polish UAW local, in a forthcoming M.A. thesis, reports that the older Poles tend to look to the native-born, younger Poles in the local for leadership, and are relatively inactive.

of authoritarians. While constituting 34 per cent of the entire sample, this type makes up 42 per cent of all the non-authoritarians.

Any interpretation of these characteristics should include a reference to the five items entering into the authoritarian index. While the percentages of each general type agreeing and disagreeing with each item are not presented here, the percentages of the extreme types accepting each of the five statements yield some further insight into the differences among the types. (Table 6.27).

TABLE 6.27

ACCEPTANCE OF EACH OF THE ITEMS IN THE AUTHORITARIAN INDEX AMONG THE EXTREME TYPES

	Prolabor-Political	Prolabor-Apolitical	Nonlabor-Political	Nonlabor-Apolitical
		% Agreeing		
The most important thing to teach children is absolute obedience to their parents.	35%	90%	47%	71%
Any good leader should be strict with people under him in order to gain their respect.	33	75	69	81
There are two kinds of people in the world, the weak and the strong.	53	97	74	81
Prison is too good for sex criminals; they should be publicly whipped or worse.	37	72	47	35
A few strong leaders could do more for this country than all the laws and talk.	27	55	27	65

The summarizing scores of these responses into authoritarian and non-authoritarian categories show that the percentage of authoritarians among the *extreme* Prolabor-Politicals is only half the percentage among the *general* Prolabor-Politicals, and that their non-authoritarians increase considerably (to 43 per cent). On the other hand, the opposite kind of shift occurs among the extreme Prolabor-Apoliticals: *none* of the extremes of this type turns out to be non-authoritarian, and nearly two-thirds of them are authoritarian.

As a matter of fact, only in the case of the Prolabor-Politicals
was there an increase from the general to the extreme type in
percentage of non-authoritarians *along with* a decrease in percentage of authoritarians. As indicated above, the opposite shift
took place among the Prolabor-Apoliticals; this was true also
of the Nonlabor-Politicals, while the Nonlabor-Apoliticals remained unchanged. What emerges from this is an image of the
Prolabor-Politicals as a special type within the UAW membership, characterized by a low degree of authoritarianism, compared
to the other members. The highly authoritarian character of the
Prolabor-Apoliticals, on the other hand, as well as their other
tendencies previously described, qualifies them for a highly
passive, dependent, and submissive role in the union's leader-
follower relationship, in contrast to the Prolabor-Politicals' more
active, positive leadership.

Attitudes on equality for Negro workers. By and large it
would appear that in the UAW ranks the issue of the treatment
of Negroes has been "settled", at least on the matter of acceptance of them as equals in the work situation. Only 15 per cent
of the total white sample, it should be recalled, voiced definite
objections to equal treatment in hiring and upgrading, while
54 per cent gave answers which were unambivalently in favor
of equal treatment of Negroes. However, there are some slight
deviations from these two percentages in the case of certain
types (Table 6.28).

TABLE 6.28

ATTITUDES ON EQUALITY FOR NEGRO WORKERS
IN EACH TYPE

Nature of Response	Prolabor-Political	Prolabor-Apolitical	Nonlabor-Political	Nonlabor-Apolitical
Fully for equality	57%	59%	47%	54%
Against equality	11	19	16	16

The patterns are not clear-cut. For example, the Nonlabor-
Politicals have the lowest percentage of persons in the "For
equality" category, but it does not follow that they also have the
highest percentage in the "Against equality" category. However,
we can say that: 1) these Nonlabor-Politicals tend to differ from

the Prolabor-Politicals and the Prolabor-Apoliticals in regard to their lower percentage of persons definitely approving equal treatment for Negroes; 2) the Prolabor-Politicals tend to differ from the three other types in regard to their lower percentage of persons definitely disapproving of equal treatment. In fact, only 23 per cent of all the non-equalitarians are Prolabor-Politicals, despite the fact that they constitute 31 per cent of the total white sample; only this type has fewer members, proportionately, among the non-equalitarians.

The two types with a pro-labor political orientation differ a little from each other with respect to their tendencies to reject the ideology of equal treatment of Negroes in the work situation —the type with low political interest being the more non-equalitarian. Of course, this point should be qualified by the fact that they have about the same percentages of people who are positive in their acceptance of the ideology. The lower percentage of Nonlabor-Politicals approving of equal treatment suggests that this type is less fully prepared to accept the union's official ideology on race relations. This deviation by itself might be a factor in the estrangement of a considerable minority of UAW members from allegiance to the union with respect to still other aspects of the UAW's program, and deserves more intensive study than we have been able to give it here.

The position of the Prolabor-Apoliticals in regard to their higher percentage indicating disapproval of equal treatment of Negro workers is further attested to by the data on the *extreme* types. More than 40 per cent of the extreme Prolabor-Apoliticals gave a definite "No" to the question involved, which is more than the proportion of the corresponding general type, and only a little over one-fourth gave a definite "Yes," which is less than half the proportion of the general Prolabor-Apoliticals.[11] All of the three other extreme types, on the other hand, registered a decrease in the proportion expressing non-equalitarian attitudes.

Satisfaction with Life and Feelings of Social Alienation. The four types distribute themselves among the three categories of

---

[11] This indication of strong anti-Negro feelings among extreme Prolabor-Apoliticals is possibly related to the fact that a very large proportion of them are Polish workers, who have been among the most prejudiced. See p. 180. Also cf. Widick and Howe, *The UAW and Walter Reuther,* especially Chapter 10.

satisfaction, referred to in Chapter 5 (p. 184), in the manner reported in Table 6.29. The figures indicate that whether they are looked at from the standpoint of percentages of highest satisfaction, or of lowest satisfaction, the two types characterized by a high interest in politics are, on the whole, the most satisfied with their life conditions. The relatively higher socio-economic standing of these two types, to a large extent, makes this finding understandable. Furthermore, the data on the extreme types reveal even greater satisfaction among the Prolabor-Politicals and Nonlabor-Politicals.

TABLE 6.29

DEGREE OF SATISFACTION WITH LIFE

	Prolabor-Political	Prolabor-Apolitical	Nonlabor-Political	Nonlabor-Apolitical
High	29%	22%	34%	28%
Medium	45	41	37	38
Low	26	37	29	34

The second form of personal adjustment used in the study has to do with feelings of "anomie," or social alienation. Here again, the Prolabor-Politicals stand out in their higher percentage of persons characterized by little alienation, and their smaller percentage of persons with highly alienated feelings (Table 6.30). In fact, the Prolabor-Politicals are the only type whose percentage of low alienation is greater than its percentage of

TABLE 6.30

FEELINGS OF SOCIAL ALIENATION AMONG THE FOUR TYPES

Degree of Alienation	Prolabor-Political	Prolabor-Apolitical	Nonlabor-Political	Nonlabor-Apolitical
High*	25%	42%	29%	32%
Low**	32	6	28	19

* At least 3 "alienation" statements accepted.
** No statements accepted.

high alienation. The table also reveals that, as in the case of other characteristics, the Prolabor-Politicals and the Prolabor-Apoliticals are widely divergent from each other with respect to the basic psychological attributes considered in this section of the chapter —despite their similarity in labor political orientation. Here, too, such factors as education, occupation, and ethnic status, play a key role in explaining such dissimilarities. The Prolabor-Apoliticals make up a little over one-fifth of the entire sample, but only 6 per cent of all the persons with low alienation; the Prolabor-Politicals, on the other hand, constitute a little over one-third of the total sample, but nearly one-half (48 per cent) of all persons with low alienation.

We can also see that these attitudes are somewhat related to degree of political interest; the two types with high political interest tend to have the lower percentages exhibiting high alienation. But analysis of the extreme types reveals that the Prolabor-Politicals are still quite different; while the average score of the extreme Nonlabor-Politicals on the five-item scale remains unchanged from that of the general Nonlabor-Politicals, that of the extreme Prolabor-Politicals drops considerably. Indeed, *none* of the extreme Prolabor-Politicals falls in the two highest scores of social alienation, but over one-fifth of the Nonlabor-Politicals do.

The data on political futility, authoritarianism, life satisfaction, and social alienation, among the four types give us the following "portraits" of each of the types:

Prolabor-Politicals: From a union standpoint this type represents the "ideal" member in respect to political action. According to our findings the members in this type present a distinctly favorable picture with respect to still other, more fundamental psychological tendencies. The general Prolabor-Politicals stand first or a close second on all the measures of basic attitudes studied in our analysis. The averages of the extreme Prolabor Politicals on every one of the scores confirm the picture of a group of workers characterized somewhat more than others by feelings of political effectiveness, nonauthoritarian attitudes, satisfaction with their conditions of life, and optimism. Because this group consists of so many union activists and participants in the general community life, the implications of this constellation of personal traits can scarcely be construed as other than favorable.

Prolabor-Apoliticals: Such a "syndrome" as described above definitely does not pertain to this second type. Obviously, a "good" rating with respect to a labor political orientation is not by itself an indication of non-authoritarian dispositions, or satisfaction with life, for example. This type, in fact, ranks last or next to last among the types on the measures of basic attitudes, when the averages for each measure are calculated. The total picture is one of a group of workers who, while believing strongly in union political action, do so in a somewhat passive, submissive and dependent manner. Additional information about this type, presented in previous sections of this chapter, confirms this interpretation, such as attendance at union meetings, positions held in the union, etc. These psychological traits are also involved in this type's low interest in politics and general community participation.

Nonlabor-Politicals: This type, generally speaking, ranks with the Prolabor-Politicals in its high standing on the four measures dealt with here. It, too, is first or second in its feelings of political effectiveness, democratic personality tendencies, life satisfaction, and little social alienation. However, we cannot assert with too much safety that the Nonlabor-Politicals are consistently comparable to the Prolabor-Politicals. While the extreme Prolabor-Politicals rate even better than their corresponding general type on all of the measures, the opposite is true for the extreme Nonlabor-Politicals on three of the four measures, political futility, authoritarianism, and social alienation. In fact, on the first and third of these measures, the extreme Nonlabor-Politicals drop to fourth position among the types.

Nonlabor-Apoliticals: This type remains consistently at the bottom (third or fourth) on the measures used here, no matter if we consider the general or extreme types. These UAW members have the greatest political futility, and this in large part explains their being in a low political interest category. A stronger acceptance of labor political action probably would affect this disposition, but perhaps it is equally correct to say that changes in their feelings of political impotence might affect their acceptance of labor political action.

Chapter Summary

In this chapter we have attempted to order our data in terms other than the usual breakdown by voting behavior. These terms have had to do with what we believe to be two of the key variables that are most pertinent in considering union members as voters, namely, degree of acceptance of a labor political orientation, and degree of active interest in the area of politics. Using these two variables, we divided UAW members into four "types." These types were then analyzed by reference to the questions used in defining them, the social characteristics of the members of each type, their voting behavior, and measures of several social-psychological attitudes. At the end of each section of the analysis we gave a summary for each type. What follows here, then, at the risk of over-simplification, is a "summary of summaries":

Prolabor-Politicals: By definition, these auto workers are above average in both their labor political orientation and their political interest. It is in this stratum of the union membership that the UAW receives its strongest support. According to our data, they are also the best educated, enjoy a relatively high income, and apparently have good jobs in the skill hierarchy of the automobile industry. A disproportionately large number of them are better educated Catholics.

Along with their having, understandably, a high Stevenson vote, there were few undecided voters among them before the 1952 election. Not only did they know the issues involved in the reapportionment vote, but voted best, in terms of the union's recommendations, compared with the other types. The support by this type of the union-backed mayoralty candidate was also the highest.

When we turn to the series of attitudinal measures, the Prolabor-Politicals are at the top (especially in the case of the *extreme* type) as compared with other types—whether it is a matter of union attachment (as defined by interest and participation in the union), feelings of political effectiveness, non-authoritarian attitude, life-satisfaction, or freedom from feelings of social alienation. Accompanying this set of attitudes is apparently a greater sense of "fair play" concerning the role of pressure groups in politics than is the case with any of the other three types.[12] Despite their relatively high education and income and skill-level, they tend strongly to consider themselves as members of the working class.

Prolabor-Apoliticals: While these UAW members are high in their labor political orientation, they are below average in political interest. Their attitudinal characteristics and voting behavior appear to flow largely from their low status as regards education, income, and occupation, as well from the related fact that they have a high proportion of women and of people from the major ethnic groups in Detroit.

The Prolabor-Apoliticals, furthermore, are characterized by a high proportion of non-voters, even though they tend to consider themselves strong Democrats. The type constitutes one of the key sources of failure of organized labor in Detroit and Michigan to win in the local "non-partisan" elections, and in such matters as the reapportionment issue.

As for their general attitudes, they make up the passive element in the union's loyal membership, as evidenced by their low degree of union attachment. Moreover, they tend to be with-drawn generally from active participation, organizationally speaking. Accompanying these dispositions is a high proportion of authoritarian attitudes, feelings of political futility, dissatisfaction, and social alienation, all of which fits with their lack of political interest as measured by knowledge of candidates and issues, etc. Finally, many of the white auto workers who do not conform to the union's official stand on racial equality are to be found in this type.

Nonlabor-Politicals: Here we have a group of UAW members who, while definitely interested in politics, are not prepared to accept fully the notion of active political participation by their union. Although we have not subjected this type to any more systematic detailed analysis than the other three types, our data concerning it suggest the existence of two somewhat distinct

---

[12] A separate study, by one of the authors, of all the UAW members attending the 1953 summer school at Port Huron, Michigan, indicates that these particular workers, all of whom can be considered active by virtue of the prerequisites for entry into the school, scored even lower than our Prolabor-Politicals on authoritarianism, political futility, and social alienation.

sub-types, one of them firmly attached to the union, exhibiting Democratic voting behavior and attitudes similar to the Prolabor-Politicals, but not completely trustful of union political action; the other quite different in that it consists largely of Republicans and Independents, members who are little interested in the union, and a small number who are definitely opposed.

In terms of their social characteristics, this type as a whole has the smallest proportion of women and of persons of ethnic minority status. They have more Protestants than the other types. Furthermore, they tend to be among the older, better educated, higher income workers.

The Eisenhower vote among Detroit's auto workers came mostly from this type, and they had the largest number of shifters from the Democratic column in 1948 to the Republican one in 1952. Most of them were well aware of the issues involved in the reapportionment election, and they had the highest vote against the union's stand on these proposals. Likewise, they had a high, but not the highest, vote for the opponent of the union-supported mayoralty candidate.

Despite their voting behavior contrary to the union's recommendations, their union attachment index is as high as the Prolabor-Apolitical type. In fact, they have twice as many holders of office in the union as the latter type. More than any of the other types, they consider themselves middle-class. While the *general* Nonlabor-Politicals are fairly low in authoritarianism, political futility, and social alienation, the *extremes* rank quite high on the last two of these measures.

Nonlabor-Apoliticals: This type, of course, is the very opposite of our first one, being below average both in its acceptance of a prolabor political orientation and in its degree of political interest. Here we have a group of old, long-time residents of Detroit; their education is relatively low, and so is their income.

This type had a rather high proportion of non-voters and the highest percentage of undecided voters before the election of 1952; they were the poorest supporters of the union on the reapportionment proposals and in the mayoralty election. They are the lowest when it comes to union attachment, and are characterized by a high degree of authoritarianism, political futility, and social alienation. The image conveyed by these characteristics is one of a group of men and women who, despite their long residence in Detroit (and thus presumably a greater opportunity for upward mobility), have not "made the grade," and consequently have given up in the race for status and success. Although not presented, our data concerning the low degree of their social participation (membership in organizations, etc.) confirm this image.

CHAPTER 7

Conclusions:
Union Members and the Future of Political Action

Union members and their families comprise one-third of all eligible voters in the United States. If they were to go to the polls and vote overwhelmingly in one direction, they could carry almost any national election. In an urban industrial center like Detroit, well over half of the potential voters are union members or persons in the immediate families of union members. Assuming that unions continue to work predominantly with and through the Democratic party, the fortunes of that party will rise or fall to the extent that union members and their families support labor political programs and leadership.

This confronts organized labor with a twofold challenge: On the one hand it must win and hold the political allegiance of its own members in ever-larger proportions; on the other hand, it must formulate programs and carry on activities in a manner that does not alienate many non-labor sections of the Democratic combination or cause a polarization of sentiment against the threat of "big labor". The future of a New Deal-Fair Deal type of Democratic party depends upon the ability of unions to make common cause with other groups devoted to similar objectives.

The UAW holds a key position among the forces that are shaping this political future. It is one of the largest and most vigorous unions, with heavy stress on political action and a history of successful cooperation with the Democratic party in Michigan and elsewhere. It appears likely to continue in the forefront, with some probability that it will exercise increased influence as a leading member-union within the AFL-CIO merger. Especially significant for present purposes, its members represent a major sector of mass production workers—and they will presumably behave on the political front not too differently from other millions in other unions. As a result of years of union educational effort and constant emphasis by the organization's leaders, however, they are probably a jump ahead in political understanding and readiness for political action. Consequently, what is found to be true of them, we believe, may be indicative of potential political behavior and attitudes in much wider labor circles.

In this chapter we want to speculate about these possible wider implications of our findings for a political psychology of American industrial workers. As a springboard into the broader interpretations, we shall first briefly restate our chief conclusions.[1]

In Regard to Auto Workers

1. On the whole, auto workers in the Detroit area were found to vote in agreement with union recommendations, to express trust in these recommendations, and generally to approve labor's political activities. There is no support here for a picture of top-level political maneuvering that lacks membership backing. To be sure, a small minority of the members stand opposed (15 to 20 per cent); slightly more (about 25 per cent) lack clear convictions and remain uncommitted, ready to sway with whatever pressures play most tellingly upon them in a particular campaign. The active majority sets the tone of prevailing sentiment in the union, however, and most of the wavering middle group goes along. Nevertheless, defections may occur when the opposing candidate or party has special appeal as in the case of Eisenhower.

---

[1] We shall not repeat detailed results and supporting data here. The principal findings have been summarized at the close of Chapters 2, 3, 5 and 6.

2. Not only are UAW members predominantly loyal to the union's political endeavors; at the same time, many more of them oppose than approve the political influence of business. They not only trust the voting recommendations of labor organizations much more than those of any other groups; they correspondingly *distrust* the recommendations of *business groups* and *newspapers* much more than those from other sources. Similarly, while a clear majority of auto workes declare that they would like to see unions have more to say in government, only one in five wants business to have more say; and more important, twice this number explicitly want business to have *less* say. The reasons auto workers gave for voting as they did in '52 and their statements about campaign issues further reinforce the conclusion that large numbers of them see the political world in terms of opposed goals and group interests as between orgoinzed labor and business. The unionism of these UAW members extends a long distance beyond simple and direct job-centered concerns; their predominant spirit fails to accord with the currently popular philosophy of emerging unity between labor and management, a doctrine of basic harmony and "dual allegiance." We will return to this point later.

3. In view of the union's active political campaigning the auto workers' degree of political interest and personal involvement in political action can be considered only moderate. Active forms of participation in the '52 campaign were infrequent and information regarding candidates and issues was distinctly limited. While workers gave a good deal of attention to newspaper, radio, and television during the campaign (TV was outstanding as a trusted source), while most workers reported that they talked with others about the election, and while almost all of them felt before the election that they cared "very much" which party would win, the entensive acceptance of defeat without negative feelings or words of regret would scarcely indicate any deep arousal or abiding political concern. Scores on an index of political interest based on replies to 14 questions suggest that most auto workers fall in the middle range rather than manifesting either very strong interest or notable lack of interest.[2]

---

[2] Statements similar to those in this paragraph could doubtless be made about most other sections of the population. Our findings do not mean that

4. Union efforts to "get out the vote" appear to have met with some degree of success. This we infer from the finding that registration among union members was no less than that for the Detroit area population as a whole. This contrasts with typical election figures which show smaller proportions voting among low income people including industrial workers. According to our figures, approximately one-fifth of the UAW members eligible to register did not vote in the presidential election. Non-voters (among those eligible) were especially numerous among auto workers of lowest economic status and most limited education and among the younger workers of middle or relatively high economic status. Somewhat paradoxically, most non-voters are about as interested in politics and as high in pro-labor political loyalties as are voters. Presumably, since their failure to vote is not traceable in most instances to special apathy or "off-sideness," it should not be too difficult for the union to get them to the polls with only slight additional stimulation.

The campaign on reapportionment of state voting districts—vigorously pushed by the union—highlights both the shortcomings and the achievements of the union's political communication with its members. The issue remained relatively unfamiliar and poorly understood: only 57 per cent of registered UAW members could clearly recall if and how they voted; but of those who *could* remember, 90 per cent voted in accord with the union's recommendation.

5. A substantial section of the UAW membership consists of those workers who are both politically interested and strongly pro-labor in orientation. These are the people whose full and

---

auto workers are *less* interested or concerned than are other citizens. On the contrary, to take one example, it was found in a nation-wide sample of voters in 1952 that 25 per cent said they did not "care very much which party wins the election" (A. Campbell *et al, op. cit.,* p. 36) while among Detroit auto workers only 17 per cent answered in this negative way. On this matter of political interest and many other points in our study, it is most important to recognize that we are discussing what is true of auto workers—whether the implications are favorable or unfavorable—without reference to whether other groups are better or worse. Thus, the fact that auto workers manifest a moderate amount of political interest, though with relatively few members actively involved in the campaign or intensely aroused, does not signify, any negative evaluation in comparison with other groups. It nevertheless, does point up a challenge, both for those wishing to see more grass roots political activity in labor and likewise for those who may prefer that working people remain indifferent and inert.

effective support the political action program has gained within the union. They are found to differ in significant ways both from the pro-labor group having little political interest and from the workers who are not pro-labor in regard to political matters.

First of all, this actively interested and on-side group—members who represent the best type of political participants from the union standpoint—tends also to display high interest and involvement in the union organization and activities apart from its political activities. They are also better educated than the average; they include more skilled workers; they have above average incomes; and they tend to be relatively young. The proportion of Negroes among them is greater than average; they have the largest percentage of fathers who were semi-skilled workers and the lowest percentage who were farmers; their parents were more frequently American-born than were those of other members and the foreign-born fathers came disproportionately from the British Isles and Canada. Among the smaller group of *extremely* pro-labor and politically interested, similar characteristics are present in even more pronounced degree. However, one important difference occurs in that a very high proportion of these members *most* active politically are Catholics, and few are Negroes.

These data carry a strong suggestion that existing trends toward increasing skill levels, higher income, greater education, and diminishing numbers coming from farm and foreign backgrounds do not pull workers away from union political interests and affiliations as is often alleged; on the contrary, these are the very characteristics that we find most associated with the combination of strong pro-labor orientation and lively political interest. These facts carry important implications regarding the future of labor in American politics, which are discussed later in this chapter.

6. Inquiry into several more general attitudes bearing on political outlook and behavior leads to the following conclusions:

a. Quite apart from union *political* activities, about one-third of the union members can be considered loyal, interested, active union participants; at the other extreme about one-fourth exhibit weak ties to the union and little emotional identification with it. The largest number are in between. In regard to *political* participation, the important point is that the members who are most closely attached to the union organization and most active in it tend also to be most on-side and most interested politically.

b. Feelings of political impotence, futility and skepticism occur commonly enough to suggest that such attitudes could have a serious negative effect on workers' political participation. For example, one-third of the UAW members agreed with the statement that "people like me don't have any say about what the government does," and only slightly over half the members thought that "there is any important difference between what the Democratic and Republican parties stand for." Individuals' feelings of political futility tended to be accompanied by relatively low degrees of political interest, further indicating that the sense of futility may constitute one factor in political indifference.

c. Authoritarian attitudes, insofar as they can be ascertained from a few simple questions, appear to exist to a disturbing extent among the workers interviewed. For example, 62 per cent agreed that "the most important thing to teach children is absolute obedience to their parents." The 40 per cent agreed that "a few strong leaders could do more for this country than all the laws and talk"; and people who are highly authoritarian tend also to have greater feelings of political futility and to take extremist partisan positions, denying the opposition (either business or labor) the right to support political candidates. At middle and higher socio-economic levels, the more authoritarian white workers also express more anti-Negro bias than do those less authoritarian; among those of low socio-economic status this relationship reverses, possibly because these poorer authoritarians may sympathize with Negro workers as fellow underdogs and may direct their hostility against persons who are better off.

d. The great majority of auto workers answer questions concerning their life and work in a manner signifying that they are reasonably content. Those who are more dissatisfied do not differ from others in their voting or their pro-labor political attitudes, but they are below average in political interest and feelings of political effectiveness. They likewise have more authoritarian attitudes.

e. A final attitude measure reveals feelings of social aliena-tion, pessimism, and despair on the part of a considerable segment of the auto workers. Indeed, the results reflect questionable enough conditions of personal morale or assurance about life to invalidate any complacent belief that all is well as to the mental health of present-day American workers. For example, 27 per cent say that "the lot of the average man is getting worse, not better" and 61 per cent believe that "these days a person doesn't really know who he can count on." The most "alienated" include disproportionately large numbers of non-voters and of Eisenhower voters. These results suggest that the political behavior of the socially alienated tends to run contrary to the prevailing norms of their fellow workers. Social alienation feelings also tend to go along with low political interest, attitudes of political futility, authoritarianism, and dissatisfaction with life.

7. The foregoing attitudes are by no means distributed at random among the union members. The *undesirable* types of feeling (political futility, personal discontent, authoritarianism, social alienation and despair) are much more common among those of poor education and low income. They may consequently be expected to decrease as a result of trends toward greater amounts of schooling and growing economic gains. Attitudes in generally *desirable* directions—opposites of those named above—are especially characteristic of the politically interested and pro-labor union members (the "pro-labor-politicals") described in paragraph 5.

Labor in Politics—Current Trends

In order to interpret the larger meaning of our findings it is necessary to reflect on major trends and problems pertaining to unions and union members in relation to politics. Even if we assume, as we are inclined to, that our results can be taken as approximately true, not only for auto workers but for great numbers of other urban industrial workers (as they are or as they are becoming), the challenging question remains as to what lies ahead. What significance has our study in relation to future developments? How stable are the political dispositions described? What probable trends can be inferred from an analysis of the changing conditions and influences which produce political effects of the kind under inquiry? In order to sketch an interpretative framework for considering these questions, we shall cut loose from our "data," though by no means ignoring the relevant facts.

We begin with the question whether union political action is of growing or diminishing importance. What pressures are operating on labor organizations to push them, or beckon them, into new types of political endeavors? Where is American unionism heading as far as political participation is concerned? A second set of queries, intertwining with the first, will focus on the minds of individual union members, to inquire what transformations may be in prospect there. Are working people being catapulted into a middle class world of respectability and plenty where labor unions are an anachronism? Or, if unions are still to have a place, what emerging expectations and desires must they attempt to satisfy—and with what implications in regard to the *political* functioning of unions.

First, then, what influences can be discerned that are making for (or against) increased union activities in the political arena? The fundamental fact, in our judgment, is that the current period is witnessing an accentuation of pressures and needs that impel unions toward greater political participation. To be sure, forces of this kind have constantly existed—and have led to labor political activities throughout union history—but not until the past decade or so have the influences accumulated to the degree now apparent.

Effects of the new conditions are attested by many well known events—the organization of CIO's Political Action Committee in 1944, the jolt to labor leaders when a Republican Congress was elected in 1946 and proceeded to enact the Taft-Hartley law, the American Federation of Labor's vigorous entry into politics with its Labor's League for Political Education (1948) and its endorsement of a presidential candidate in 1952 for the first time, except for the support of LaFollette on a third party ticket in 1924. During these last years labor unions have furnished no small part of Democratic party strength, both nationally and in many localities. In Michigan, for example, the UAW and other unions have worked closely with the Democratic organization, and are considered responsible in large degree for recent election successes of the party.

These are significant signs of change. And the underlying factors that brought them about seem unlikely to disappear in the forseeable future. These causes basically have to do with developments affecting the total economic and political organization of modern society. We wish here to stress two phases of the development that have a most direct and important bearing on the role of labor unions. One is the unprecedented growth of large-scale economic organizations and the dominant position these have come to occupy, not only in business and industry but also as they impinge upon politics, government, public opinion and the entire life of our society. Secondly, partly as a consequence of the organizational and pressure group developments and partly from other causes, there has also occurred an enormous increase in the scope and power of centralized government. It is unnecessary for present purposes to trace the historical roots of these changes. What is salient here is the fact that they have greatly altered the context within which unions must function.

In our type of society, with its relative freedom of association, its belief in disperson of power and avoidance of a monolithic state coordinating all activities and decisions, organized groups compete to advance their respective interests and to gain strategic positions from which they can more effectively influence social policy. These socially sanctioned procedures bring powerful organizations into opposition to other groups, leading to what has been described as government by pressure groups. The play of countervailing forces almost *demands* that each organization exert its influence in an effort to retain or augment its relative power.

Concretely, in the field of labor-management relations, this competition between large-scale organizations spreads from the direct economic dealings of collective bargaining to the political arena. Constant pressures operate from both sides to use the power of the State—through legislation, courts, and administrative decisions which will secure and enhance the welfare of the given organizations and help them to achieve their goals. Thus the entry of unions into politics on an increasing scale.

In addition to these factors of organizational power, other influences have been at work to intensify the problems and expand the scope of *government*. The expansion of governmental activities in turn makes it necessary for organized labor to assume a more active part in politics. The enlargement of governmental functions, including economic controls, has clearly occurred in response to the changing world (not as a socialist conspiracy!). One need merely pause to recall such changes—a world shrunken till nations are separated by only a few hours; ever closer interdependence of peoples and institutions; the harsh realities of two world wars, depression, a continuing cold war with the stupendous national defense needs it entails; the threat and the promise of atomic energy. . . . How could governments fail to extend the range of their functions and the exercise of their authority?

Government's intensified concern with all kinds of economic matters, including labor relations and the effects of unions, means that organized labor, too, is induced to give sharply increased attention to these governmental actions. Labor's active participation in politics becomes practically unavoidable.

A most important accompaniment of developments of the kind sketched has been the tremendous growth of organized labor since the 30's. The unprecedented increase in numbers has produced inevitable changes also in union problems, methods, and outlook. The auto workers' union is a prime example. Its meteoric rise from nowhere to a million and a quarter members typifies the revolution that has taken place on the American industrial scene. Paralleled throughout the major industries of the nation, these developments have brought unions to a point where it would be amazing, indeed, were they rigidly to follow the patterns and philosophies that proved natural and effective when organized labor consisted of scattered unions of craftsmen and limited numbers of less skilled workers in a relatively small range of industries.

At the same time, one must guard against exaggerating the differences that have occurred; there is certainly no sharp break from traditional trade union policies. Emphasis remains centered on the objectives of economic gains and control of working conditions—under a system of private capitalism. What, then, are the great changes in union orientation that we have referred to? The answer lies in several main characteristics of organized labor's growth and present situation.

1. In the first place, the sheer fact of size goes far to build up pressures for further political involvement. Large numbers of members mean, potentially at least, large numbers of votes and consequent political power. Under these conditions, it is surely more feasible, as well as more tempting, for unions to wade into political waters.

2. Along with unions' phenomenal growth of numbers and influence has come a not unnatural tendency for their leaders to aspire to elite positions of enhanced status and power, both for themselves and for their organizations. In part at least, opportunities for such recognition are to be achieved through political influence, governmental and community assignments, and a respected voice in public affairs.

3. A salient indirect consequence of union expansion arises from the renewed and intensified movement to regulate or control them. Under the new conditions of union strength, many sections of the public—and legislatures—are convinced that organized labor constitutes a threat to the general welfare and must be checked to prevent abuse of its "monopoly" powers. The Taft-Hartley Law nationally, and "right to work" laws in the states, give expression to these sentiments. The fact, and the prospects, of restrictive legislation almost compel unions to enter seriously into politics to combat policies which, as they see it, would cripple union organizations and undermine their effectiveness. Both in this connection and those that follow, the total context of contending pressure groups is a primary factor. Unions, like other groups, employ their political strength to defend themselves (notably against business and business-dominated organi-

zations) and to move toward their own organizational objectives.

4. Equally significant are the profound changes required in union strategy and outlook as their typical task has shifted from protecting and advancing the job interests of selected small sectors of the working population to that of making gains for the millions of workers throughout mass-production industries. When only a tiny fraction of working people were organized, their economic gains had little effect on the total economy. However, when wage increases and related benefits are won in key industries, quickly spreading to "pattern followers" over wide areas of the economy, the picture is entirely different. One important phase of this problem is the now familiar issue of the wage price spiral, the self-defeating character and the dangers of constant inflationary pressures. Labor leaders—and union members—show increasing concern over this question. And since means for inflation control are largely in governmental hands, unions of necessity get into politics in order to have a say on policies which they believe are basic to their ability to win economic gains that will not be cancelled out by "unjustified" rises in the cost of living.

5. But the attempt to combat inflationary prices is only one of numerous matters of public policy in which it becomes clear to unions that further gains for their members depend more upon governmental action then upon concessions that can be won from employers. Under existing conditions of unionism, in other words, the old union objectives of improving job opportunities, wages, working conditions, and status seem to call for new means. Utilization of labor's *political* power becomes no less "pragmatic," hard-headed and realistic than are the procedures of collective bargaining and the strike. Unionism certainly cannot now be interpreted (if it ever could be) as necessarily and exclusively "job conscious" or "job centered" in any narrow sense of those terms which would exclude political programs aiming to maintain full employment conditions, to secure better pensions, health insurance and unemployment benefits, to prevent employment discrimination, to strive for equitable taxation, aid to public schools, low cost housing—or whatever else union members as a whole may feel it worth struggling for.

While collective bargaining and "business unionism" will doubtless continue to occupy a large share of the time and resources of organized labor, this most assuredly does not mean that political activities are likely to be curtailed. Influences of the kind we have outlined seem destined to have more, rather than less, weight in the period ahead. As predictions go, we think it not particularly risky to say that organized labor will strive to play a much larger part in politics and government over the short-run future than it has in the past. What the longer-run future holds in store we do not venture to guess. But if labor unions continue to exist as an influential part of the institutional structure of a democratic society, it appears well-nigh inevitable that they will function prominently in political affairs.

Union Members and Political Action

Union members as individuals are, of course, also subject to the influences that have been listed. But there are additional important changes taking place among working people that could conceivably lead to far-reaching effects on the way they relate themselves to politics and to organized labor's role in politics.

Most challenging in this connection is the question whether industrial workers are becoming "middle class" in outlook as well as status and hence undependable as supporters of union political purposes.[3] The thesis that this is the case can be argued with considerable cogency. Certainly the tangible bases for distinctions between middle class and working class have been fast disappearing. They give promise of continuing to vanish. Working people have experienced spectacular improvements of em-

---

[3] "Middle class" is a questionable category for our purposes but no better term is available. It is used here and through the following pages to refer to the more traditional and conservative parts of the heterogeneous middle income population. Although large numbers of people at middle socio-economic levels are liberals, New Deal type Democrats, pro-labor in sympathies, we are not speaking of them when we refer to a middle class outlook. The reference is to the more individualistic (and Republican) sections of the middle class—the medium and upper range of white collar employees, small businessmen, professionals employed in business or self-employed, etc.

ployment relations and life conditions—to a point, indeed, that has caused one sociologist seriously to speak of the "professional-ization" of labor in Detroit.[4] Surely the conception of an exploited, submerged, and underprivileged industrial working class imbued with an "underdog" mentality, corresponds to no substantial reality in today's American society. Whether this rise toward "middle class-ness" means the decline of organized labor as a countervailing force against the power of business and wealth is quite another matter.

The general question here might be rephrased in this way: Can working people attain comfortable and respectable middle class planes of living and yet persist in their loyalty to organized labor and labor's political aims? More provocatively perhaps, the question could ask: Is there any ideological stopping place on the road upward from underdog to middle class status?

The essential fact with which to begin here is that decade after decade, almost year by year, wage earners are moving to higher levels, not only of real earnings, but also of education, leisure, health, economic security, status on the job and conditions of work. The present acceleration of technological change points to even greater alterations of the occupational structure, particularly the further elimination of the most routine and lowest level jobs in factory and office. Distinctions between skill levels and between manual and white collar jobs are growing dim and blurred.

There is little question that all these changes have vital implications for the social perspectives and political participation of the people involved. As working people rise to new levels of income and education; as they enjoy greater security and more leisure; as ever greater numbers occupy technical, skilled, and responsible positions; as they increasingly become home owners, suburbanites, stock holders; as the number of first and second generation immigrants continue to decline, and as all assume a more respected place in society, important shifts are bound to occur in their political orientation.

It is worth speculating a little about these impending shifts.

---

[4] Nelson Foote, "The Professionalization of Labor in Detroit," *American Journal of Sociology*, January, 1953, 371-380.

It would be most unwise to *assume* that they spell a conservative trend. Research like that of our study can furnish useful bits of information on these matters, but only as straws in the wind— perhaps we should say as benchmarks by means of which continuing inquiries may be able to establish trends. Clearly current evidence is dated. General interpretations must stretch beyond the time-bound descriptions of single studies. Yet, even research fragments have value in the absence of more adequate knowledge. In that spirit we shall refer to certain of our results as we now raise questions and venture possible answers as to where the political attitudes of working people may be going.

In our study, and in many others, it has been found that political inertia and indifference are associated with low socio-economic position. The auto workers who showed greatest political interest were better educated on the average and had higher level jobs and incomes than those with less political interest. The apathy and feeling of impotence among people of low status is based on a more fundamental attitude of incompetence and inadequacy in the political sphere. It is probable that as income and education improve, such a feeling of incompetence—a feeling of a lack of qualification for making judgments and for participating in politics—will decrease. Our data support this expectation, for example, in the findings on political interest. If we take those workers who, for the purposes of this discussion, can be considered the "under-dogs" in our sample, namely, those with a family income of $4000 or less and a low education (less than nine years of schooling), we find that only 13 per cent have a relatively high degree of political interest (above the middle range of interest), in sharp contrast to 52 per cent of the UAW members with $6000 or more family income and a better education.

As another example, consider the responses of these same two groups to the statement, "People like me don't have any say about what the government does." Three-fifths of our "under-dogs" (61 per cent) agree with such a sentiment, while one-fifth (21 per cent) of the opposite group feel the same way. These wide contrasts between the high and the low income-education workers show up in the many other measures we used in the study that bear on the point under discussion, such measures as their appraisal of chances for upward mobility, their social alienation, and their social participation.

On the basis of such data and reasoning, we can rather confidently anticipate that working people's interest and participation in politics will continue to increase. This will occur both because of greater feelings of political adequacy, more information, more appreciation of the rights and responsibilities of citizenship, and also because workers will increasingly perceive their own stake in political decisions. Unions, as well as political parties and other organizations, can be counted on to hammer home the idea that many of the worker's problems demand political solutions—and that their social and economic gains are jeopardized by unfavorable governmental actions at the hands of political "enemies." In short, industrial workers are developing greater political interest and involvement for precisely the same reasons that the upper classes have done so.

The directions that this growing participation will take can be analyzed with far less assurance. The moot question is: Will working people participate *as members of unions* or as members of the broad "middle class"? On the one hand we see factors that would push them toward conservative and non-labor oriented political objectives; on the other, there are influences that may prove supportive of pro-labor aims and continuing New Deal-Fair Deal types of social change. Which way the political winds of the future will blow depends on emergent forces only partly forseeable, including prominently the still-to-be-decided behavior of political leaders—those in the labor movement and those outside labor circles. What is most useful is not to attempt predictions but rather to note some of the important influences that political planning must take into account in its attempts to forecast and guide the course of labor in politics.

The *general direction* of the common man's political allegiance will be largely determined by the extent to which contemporary socio-economic changes bring (a) greater life satisfaction or greater discontent, and (b) increasing belief or disbelief on the part of working people that their problems and interests differ from those of businessmen, the wealthy, the upper middle class, and call for different governmental policies. We shall comment on these two basic sources of liberal-labor orientation and shall then note two or three other essential questions in regard to the emerging wants and expectations of workers that could pull them toward or away from the political leadership of organized labor.

Toward Contentment and Conservatism?

Assuredly, working people are becoming better off—as to income, security, occupational conditions and status. Therefore, they will be more satisfied with things as they are. Being satisfied, they will grow conservative. So runs the argument. Or, with a variation in key: The New Deal was sustained by adversity. Republicans returned to power as years of prosperity gradually covered over the bitter memories of the 30's. A resurgence of political liberalism or radicalism would require a period of "hard times." Assuming that the economy is kept on an even keel, labor political programs and liberal Democrats will hold no strong appeal for the contented middle class worker. All this may indeed prove to be the case. Or it may not.

It is true that election statistics and opinion surveys uniformly reveal a positive relationship between higher economic levels and political conservatism—for example, as represented in proportions voting Republican versus Democratic.[5] To cite a few illustrative figures, a careful nationwide survey[6] in 1952 found that income groups above $5000 voted 68 per cent Republican; those below $5000 were 53 per cent Republican. By occupational categories, managerial, professional and white collar people voted 68 per cent Republican in contrast to 43 per cent among manual workers. Corresponding figures for 1948 show larger differences: by occupational level, 68 per cent versus only 24 per cent. Similarly, a cross-section sample of the Detroit area population in 1951 yielded the following figures: upper socio-economic

[5] The facts on this point are incontrovertible. Confirmatory findings have been obtained in scores of studies, local and national. Results of studies in other countries are fully in accord with those of the United States.

[6] The survey was conducted by the University of Michigan Survey Research Center and is reported in Angus Campbell *et al, op. cit.* The percentages used here are derived from their tabulations, pp. 72 and 73.

class, 67 per cent Republican, middle group, 27 per cent; lower group, 17 per cent.[7]

It is noteworthy that the 1952 national sample reveals strikingly little variation among the different income groups *below* the $5000 level (constituting three-fourths of the total sample). The percentage of Eisenhower votes in the $4000 to $5000 bracket was, in fact, *less* than among those lower than $4000. This fact itself places a large question-mark beside any simple interpretations along the lines of the argument quoted at the beginning of this section. The thesis stated there would hold that the better-off "middle class" should have voted more Republican than the lower groups, say those under $3000 income. But in 1952 they did not.

Results from our study of UAW members partially fit into the pattern of higher socio-economic groups voting more Republican and partially run counter to it. Eisenhower votes were most frequent among the white collar and skilled auto workers living in upper income neighborhoods. However, among the much greater numbers of semi-skilled workers there is no such tendency; those living in higher income districts actually voted more strongly for Stevenson than did their fellows at lower levels (considering only white workers since no Negro workers lived in the better income districts). Moreover, as previously noted, the most pro-labor politically active group in the union includes a disproportionate number of better educated and skilled workers.

This leaves us with the puzzling question: Which of the contrasting patterns, a *pro*-labor or a *non*-labor political orientation, are wage workers more likely to follow as their economic lot improves? Available data, including our own, fail to answer the question. Our results do add a warning signal, cautioning against too ready acceptance of the more-money-more-contentment-more-conservatism formula. But the whole large issue is one to be examined in the light of all the general knowledge the social sciences can bring to bear. In these next pages we shall call attention to some of the general social-psychological considerations.

---

[7] Arthur Kornhauser, *Detroit as the People See It,* Wayne University Press, 1952, p. 206.

After all, is it true that social and economic gains necessarily make people more contented? Must it not rather be concluded that contentment depends on what people obtain *relative to what they want and expect?* In our society, desires have a way of outrunning the means for their gratification. It often happens that the more we get the more we want— and hence contentment elusively slips into the future. The middle-class way of life in America is almost synonymous with constant striving to become a *better* provider, to achieve *greater* success, to have a finer home, a still newer car, perchance to attain higher positions of responsibility, honor, and authority at work and in the community. Does this spell contentment? Or does the rise to middle class status mean rather an increase of *unsatisfied* aspirations? Even if the gap between middle-class and working people continues to narrow, there is surely no guarantee that this will cause those lower on the economic ladder to be more generally satisfied —whether they are called "working class" or by some other name. Indeed, their advances may intensify their discontent and their hopes for greater gains.

Significant but somewhat equivocal evidence on this issue is furnished by the index of "life satisfaction" used in the present study. When auto workers were classified into three socio-economic levels, the highest group—those closest to a middle class economic position—were the best satisfied. On the other hand, the large category of workers just below these, who have also advanced far toward middle class conditions, were the least satisfied. These results are open to different interpretations. On the one hand they can be construed as supporting the idea of growing contentment. The middle working group in this view is destined to grow better satisfied as it, too, rises one step further up the ladder. On the other hand, the interpretation could be that workers compare themselves with their fellow wage earners and experience satisfaction or dissatisfaction depending on whether or not they are better off than the others. The lowest economic group achieves satisfaction perhaps by refusing to enter the race. Under this conception, contentment occurs not as an outgrowth of social and economic improvements among workers in general, but rather is achieved by that *fraction* of workers who rise above their fellows—and by the least favored (the underdogs) who keep their sights down and quietly accept what their world provides. In any event, our data yield no clear support for the belief that the main body of working people grow more contented in proportion to their improved economic status. The findings do not remove the reasonable doubts suggested by the preceeding analysis.

The second link in the alleged sequence, the connection between contentment and conservatism, is open to equally serious questions. Are more satisfied groups necessarily more conservative and must discontent manifest itself in economic and political liberalism or radicalism? As a matter of fact, scores on our index of life satisfaction bore no relation to whether individuals voted Republican or Democratic and virtually no relation to their pro-labor or non-labor political orientation. More generally considered, a strong case can be made for the view that a given degree of personal contentment or discontent may take many different, even opposed, forms of expression, depending on the particular beliefs and social interpretations held by the individuals. Discontent may lead to anything from revolution to right-wing Republicanism. Contentment with things as they are may produce calm backing of the government in power or it may induce fanatic efforts to suppress real or imagined threats to the current happy state.

Important as prevailing feelings of satisfaction or unrest are, making either for maintenance of the status quo or for change and reform, they remain formless and unspecified except as they are given meaning and direction by the opinion-molding influences of the society. Are the "good times" and impressive rise in living standards credited to businessmen? To government? To organized labor? To impersonal forces of science and technology? And who is to blame for lags and lacks and continued insecurities? From what quarters is progress threatened? Against whom or what is the new-found prosperity to be safeguarded? Answers to such questions are multifarious and confused.

Yet it is the beliefs that come to be accepted on these matters that will go far to decide how the "middle class" workers will express their mixture of satisfactions, aspirations, and unrest. The outcome surely is not automatically settled by the augmented incomes, better jobs, and rows of model homes. In the final analysis, what counts most is the social-political *meanings* workers attach to their spiraling personal fortunes. And these meanings are being forged by the workers' day-to-day world—in part from their own immediate experience, the impact of events; but importantly, too, from the insights and understandings that are brought to them by print and air-waves, and perhaps above all by the words of their fellow-workers, neighbors, and leaders they personally know and trust. If they go conservative, it will not be because economic prosperity compels it but because liberal leadership—including prominently liberal leadership in organized labor—fails to reach them with convincing alternative social-political interpretations that fit their own fundamental needs.

Labor Views or "Middle Class" Views?

To speak of labor's becoming "middle class" usually implies that working people not only are reaching a higher *economic* level but that they are adopting the social philosophy and standards of the fairly well off white collar sections of the population. This may be happening; but we believe that any conclusion to this effect is premature. The future is still in the making. Whether the trend is for working people to assimilate a "middle class" conception of their position in society or an alternative that stresses distinctive and divergent goals remains a crucial question. Our study of auto workers contributes rather striking evidence that it is possible for wage earners to experience vast social and economic gains and yet remain steadfastly union oriented in their political views. This may well be the most significant of our findings.

According to our results, Detroit area auto workers are not going "middle class" in political outlook. They are predominantly oriented in agreement with the union; they approve of union political activities; they trust labor's voting recommendations and the great majority cast their ballots accordingly; they are inclined to distrust the recommendations of business groups and newspapers; they want organized labor to have a larger voice in government and they want business to have less influence; they are overwhelmingly Democratic and they look upon the Democratic Party as the party that protects and advances the interests of working people; they identify themselves as members of the "working class" rather than the middle class (78 per cent to 22 per cent). Details on these matters have been reported in earlier sections. But the essential facts warrant repetition here.

Projected upon a larger screen, what the facts suggest is that industrial workers who are members of a vigorous, politically aroused and relatively democratic labor organization which they believe works in their interests do not, even in a period of great prosperity, swing to a "middle class" ideology. With at least some degree of effectiveness, it appears, the union has given its members alternative pictures to those widely circulated through usual news and entertainment channels. The indications are that insofar as workers are kept in contact with an interpretation of society in terms of opposed economic interests and pressure groups, and insofar as they are alerted to the prevalent one-sided propaganda and use of public relations techniques by business and in behalf of business, most of them will look at their world from a labor viewpoint rather than as white collar Republicans. That this will continue to be the case among auto workers, and that it is potentially true for other unions, obviously cannot be asserted with certainty. We can only say that our present evidence points in that direction.

Choices of Political Directon: Collective versus Individualistic Answers

The central theme of the foregoing analysis is simply this: that future trends of union political action depend largely on working people's emerging (and still-to-be-determined) attitudes and guiding political philosophy. As we see it, there are two particularly vital choices in the making during the years just ahead. One is a key element in what we have called a "middle-class" versus a labor political orientation. It is the question whether working people will seek *individualistic* or *collective* solutions to their problems. The other basic choice has to do with how broad or narrow a labor union program will be favored.

It can be assumed that workers, however greatly they prosper, will continue to have problems and to experience unsatisfied desires—many of these in common with large numbers of their fellows. The typical "middle class" faith is that individuals can and should meet their problems and realize their aspirations individually, by exercise of personal initiative. Theirs is a world of abundant opportunity, as they see it (or try to make themselves see it), and the rewards in life belong to those who strive for them and demonstrate that they deserve them. Implications in regard to politics and government follow from this. In general, the philosophy favors policies of freedom and generous incentives for those on the upper rungs of the economic ladder, policies that serve the interests of these elite groups and those who identify with them; the less government "interference" with business the better; a minimum of expenditures for social welfare and public works, few economic controls, reduced taxation on wealth and corporate profits—in a word, a conservative Republican platform.

Organized labor has stressed an opposite philosophy. While adhering to a firm belief in private capitalism and individual freedom, unions have been concerned with protecting and winning economic gains for the less favored, for those who have little prospect of rising individually to higher economic positions. Accordingly, unions have generally advocated *collective* improvements for workers, including both improvements to be won directly from employers and those to be provided by extensive governmental actions in the areas of social security and medical care, progressive (versus regressive) tax systems, free education, regulation of business, public works programs, fiscal policies to maintain full employment, and similar measures to provide for the security and welfare of the common man. The crucial question is whether workers' support of collective welfare measures is weakening; whether the trend is toward an acceptance of economic and political policies oriented toward *individualistic* solutions. Will this type of philosophy prove more tempting to workers as they feel more secure in their jobs, as their status more closely approximates that of the white collar classes, as they become home owners, stock holders, suburbanites?

Obviously some important influences are operating toward such an outcome. Though the tendency is not apparent among auto workers, it could doubtless develop. On the whole, however, there are probably stronger reasons for anticipating no such swing. The concrete actualities of wage workers' position can hardly change in a manner that would elevate more than a small fraction of them to the psychological world of "unlimited" opportunity confronting the upper levels of white collar employees. There simply isn't "room at the top." The philosophy of *individual* success and *individual* freedom to advance is a philosophy for the few; it fails to fit the situation of the many. The mass of common people in an industrial society can be expected to remain responsive to economic and political interpretations that emphasize their *collective* strength, their *common* gains to be achieved through assertions of solidarity. Their life circumstances make it so.

Choices of Political Direction: Job-Centered versus Broad Social Goals

The second broad question of workers' political orientation is whether their interests as union members will be restricted to their own job-centered problems. Or will they wish to use their unions' augmented power and know-how to help achieve a variety of goals that spread out from the job into their entire lives? We called attention earlier to reasons for believing that an exclusively "bread and butter," business unionism limited to direct job interests does not meet the conditions and needs of labor in the present period, regardless of whether or not it did in the past. This is not to say that direct job interests are secondary. But it does assert that workers have important non-job-related wants which they may also expect their union to help solve. To the extent that they do look to their union for such help it means a widening of union political perspectives.

Job-related interests themselves have far-reaching ramifications. As unionists grow in their understanding of the forces affecting their incomes, security, status, and rights as workers, and the forces threatening the strength and security of their unions, they are almost inevitably impelled to see the need for exerting influence on governmental policies as well as carrying on direct dealings with employers. Even with respect to traditional union objectives, that is, we can expect members increasingly to look to *political* means, along with direct economic pressures, for attaining their ends.

But in addition, we wish particularly to direct attention to the political significance of other types of wants that may assume growing importance in the period ahead. Actually, there has always been much more of the non-economic, the idealistic and intangible, in union activities than meets the eye. Wages, hours fringe benefits are concrete and easy to publicize. Innumerable gains in employment relationships and working rules that protect feelings of human dignity, that give greater freedom and independence, that are demanded solely in the interests of fairness and decency—these often go unnoticed. Quite apart from the job, moreover, unions carry on a vast assortment of services for their members and engage in many community activities and in governmental and quasi-governmental programs at all levels, including an active part in international affairs. All these activities can be presumed to relate to needs and desires of union members, usually far removed from self-interested material gains. The conclusion for present purposes is that unions have no circumscribed area of "proper" union functions. They deal with whatever matters their members come to feel it desirable for them to deal with, under the impact of changing times and tensions and in response to the guidance of leaders alert to emergent needs and expectations.

Changes currently taking place seem likely to bring further shifts of union emphasis, leading to stronger accent, in political action and elsewhere, on intangible psychological goals along with the economic. With long continued prosperity and accelerating rates of production, further *economic* advances tend to be taken for granted. Wage earners are inclined to assume, union bargaining success being what it is, that they will go on sharing in the nation's material progress. Battles for further gains have, by and large, lost their excitement. Moreover, as workers become better off, moderate financial increments grow less urgent and less salient. Once basic necessities and means for decent living standards are achieved, the material needs play a less dominant part in behavior, permitting other, "higher" motivations to assert themselves—desires for status, for free self-expressive activities, for satisfying social relationships and a voice in decisions.

Clearly economic advances are not all that matters to workers and their unions. If this were the complete story, "why do not," to quote J. B. S. Hardman, "the opponents dispose of the disturbing movement by offering better bread and richer butter and more of both to the workers? Of course, by 'bread alone,' even if buttered, unionism could not survive, still less achieve its phenomenal growth and enhanced status in American society."[8]

In other words, besides the material gains, *status* and other intangibles are involved. This becomes especially important as the working population is made up less and less of men and women with an under-dog mentality. The egalitarian ideology of American society has much to do with this force in workers' lives and the functioning of their union, whether it be in the shop, the local community, or the country. The desire to be treated as an equal, or to be treated fairly, to receive some kind of recognition, the belief that these are *deserved* forms of treatment and consideration (an expectation not present in the under-dog), all these are increasingly a characteristic of larger segments of our society.

Furthermore, as a result of contemporary changes—above all the changes inherent in "automation"—it is safe to say that (in America at least) work is going to occupy a less prominent place in man's life in the future than in the past. Science and technology are transforming the world of work. Long hours, physical strain, monotony—as well as poverty—are disappearing. Where will this leave the industrial worker in relation to his union? Job problems will certainly still exist; workers will still look to the union for help in meeting them. But perhaps problems of how to center their lives meaningfully in leisure pursuits, and how to build a world in which they and their children can live rich and satisfying lives, will be equally pressing. The same is even more true for the ever-increasing numbers of retired workers. And working class wives. Unions are, of course, already moving into action with expanded recreational and educational

[8] *The House of Labor*, edited by Hardman and Neufeld, Prentice-Hall, New York: 1951, p. 58.

programs. Implications for political participation are no less important. People with leisure, and with better education and greater freedom from economic strain, can be expected not only to devote more time and interest to politics but also to develop broadened political aims relevant to their full life as whole men and women, with personal and social motivations which transcend the job and private economic advantage.

The essential psychological fact is that human needs are not neatly compartmentalized; there are no fences dividing people's interests as workers from their problems as consumers, parents, taxpayers, Americans in a divided world, wanderers in a confusing era of hitherto undreamed of opportunities and dangers for humanity. Among the tangled and contradictory values that characterize our times probably none are more important, and more neglected by "practical" politics, than the pervasive, vague, idealistic yearnings for social goals one can really believe in, goals shared by one's fellow men and worth working for with wholehearted devotion, purposes that give a sense of community and meaning to life. There is more than a little ground for suspecting that an enormous store of energy and enthusiasm can be channeled into imaginative political and social movements by labor groups if leaders will it so—or alternatively, by leaders utilizing other forms of organization. Sentiments of tremendous driving power go untapped that could be aroused by unselfish crusades for social justice, for efforts in the shop and in the community to establish conditions in which warm, satisfying human relationships and free, effective and signficant social participation can flourish.

Nor should we underestimate the force of altruistic impulses. To treat labor unionism solely in terms of workers' efforts to obtain advantages for themselves is to omit important parts of the picture. To no small degree the labor movement is built on deeply felt needs to make life better for *others*. The worker's own pay envelope and his own status count mightily, of course. But so, also, do his sympathies and poignant identifications with all those who need help and protection, all those who are *worse* off than he, the weak, the downtrodden, the unfairly treated. Even in this cynical age, it is impossible to deny everyday evidences of self-sacrificing dedication to "causes," acts of

genuine charity, operations of tormented consciences that find
no peace so long as fellow human beings are mistreated or
deprived of their rights, outpourings of indignation against
misuse of power even where it is remote from one's own affairs.
Unionists may or may not believe that "charity begins at home"
but surely few would hold that it ends there.

We well recognize that labor union history has taught
unionists to shy away from all this "idealistic" talk. Their job,
they believe, is to fight doggedly for immediate "practical"
objectives in the here and now. They have learned to be extremely wary of the dangers lurking in reform programs, radical
ideologies, and policies advocated by starry-eyed intellectuals.
But the opposite danger is likewise very real. Concentration on
job-centered material gains for special groups easily evokes
charges of sheer opportunism and anti-social self-seeking. Great
increases of union strength have brought correlative fears of their
power. When they appear to use that power irresponsibly, that
is, when they act without sufficient regard for the public interest
and with inadequate recognition of the varied non-job-related
wants of their own members, they place enormous obstacles in
the way of consolidating their potential support both among
middle class groups and within the lukewarm and unconvinced
sections of their own membership.

Union activities on the *political* front are particularly vul-
nerable. There the union can least afford to open itself to suspi-
cion that it is trying to use political influence for narrow paro-
chial advantage. Only by espousing the cause of workers and
common people generally can labor hope to be politically
effective at the national level. This requires a broadening of
union political horizons far beyond wages and shop problems.
Only by following this course do unions avoid being political
targets for non-union political publics. These pressures from
outside the union cannot but have their impact on the rank and
file as well as on union leaders. Moreover, we can look for such
effects to increase as wage earners move upward in economic
status and education, and are further integrated into middle class
communities.

UAW political activities reflect the influence of all these
factors making for union programs characterized by a broad

social orientation. There is a definite touch of idealism and social reform in the auto union's politics. This adds special significance to our finding that, in the main, members accept and go along with this brand of political action. And yet a large part of the support is passive and unenthusiastic. Many members are indifferent and a sizable minority are opposed. A question of first importance, looking to the future, is whether the unaroused and unconvinced members would join more heartily into the program if they saw it even less as an extension of the union's fight for direct economic gains (growing decreasingly vital?) and became convinced that it is genuinely inspired by broad-gauge concern for fuller, happier lives and a better world —for themselves and their families, to be sure, but also importantly for the millions who are *worse* off and in *greater* need. The question has even sharper point when asked in reference to the family members of unionists and in reference to the vast numbers of low-income white collar workers and middle class people who are wavering between the appeals of business and Eisenhower Republicans, on the one side, and unions and New Deal-Fair Deal Democrats on the other side.

Too often this whole question is treated as if the objectives of self-interest and of reforms in the interest of all working people were alternatives. Obviously unions can and do work for both. But an unending dilemma of relative emphasis does exist. There are innumerable combinations and intermediate positions between the one extreme of exclusive concern with the union's own job-centered advantages and the opposite extreme of going all-out for grand programs of social change. Unions are forced constantly to decide and re-decide how much to emphasize each and how to fit the parts together.

To the extent that the preceding analysis holds water, it suggests that future trends will be toward wider union political perspectives. But certainly there is no settled answer. The vitally important thing is for people, in and out of unions, to keep asking the question and weighing all relevant evidence that bears on it. And the most important evidence consists of their own preferences in the light of their own situations. People's values and desires over the changing years *could* incline union political action more toward expanded, reform-oriented goals, with the general public interest in view, or toward more restricted objectives that have special importance for unions or for particular industries. Only time will tell which is to prevail.

Our study of auto workers contributes principally in a negative way on this entire issue. That is, the responses show a lack of enthusiastic involvement or deep emotional commitment, an absence of the "higher," more idealistic forms of political motivation. In the opposite direction, as has been pointed out, many auto workers express feelings of political futility and impotence, personal discouragement, social alienation, and authoritarian attitudes. We have no reason to suppose that these negative attitudes are any more common among Detroit auto workers than in other comparable groups. Indeed, one may suspect that the picture is usually more unfavorable elsewhere since UAW educational and political activities are among the best. But the fact remains that the union's political program, however liberally conceived by the top leaders, has not engendered much zeal among the members. This is not said in criticism. Few people in our society, whatever their station in life, glow with political fervor.

We note the fact in respect to auto workers solely to call attention to the untapped possibilities, the unfilled *needs* of people for social endeavors in which they might fervently believe and eagerly participate. The question is whether labor political activity, even as imaginative and vigorous as that of the UAW, in its determination to be practical and effective, fails to stir workers beyond rather passive and superficial acceptance of the immediate political job to be done. Our query is whether there are reservoirs of potential crusading spirit and devotion to social justice and human rights that may give new life to labor's political role in the years ahead.

Reading through our interviews, even those with strongly pro-labor unionists, produces an impression that this political business is relatively remote and unimportant; that it is necessary, perhaps, to try to keep things from being worse (war, depression, weakening of unions, for example) but rarely do the responses reveal a positive spirit of pride or adventure or "mission" in what labor is doing, rarely any sense of dedication to helping build a new world. This is especially significant, we repeat, in view of the fact that UAW leadership is in the very forefront in these matters. Certainly the negative emphasis of these last pages does not detract from the outstanding political achievements of the union and the extent of membership support its activities have won. Indeed, it may be deemed unreasonable, when there is so much on the credit side, to point to what has *not* been accomplished. After all, large-scale labor participation in politics is young. It has made tremendous progress. Give it time.

Precisely because we accept this viewpoint, it has seemed most important to ask what further strides may be needed during these coming years, keeping in mind the changing patterns of life conditions, motivations, and social-political pressures we have sketched. Despite the auto union's political vision and skill, and its demonstrated success, challenging opportunities and needs exist for developing still stronger and more enthusiastic participation. Such developments may or may not occur in directions suggested by our analysis. The important thing is that shortcomings as well as elements of strength be examined and that all promising paths to full and enthusiastic democratic political involvement be explored.

Business versus Labor Influence on Political Beliefs

In considering alternative paths that labor political action may travel, we have several times referred to the decisive importance of the underlying structure of expectations, values, and beliefs that are held. The directions in which people seek political solutions for unsatisfied wants are defined by the accepted thought patterns of the times and by the social interpretations circulated and popularly approved within their groups. But the formation of opinions is complicated by the fact that divergent and contradictory views compete with one another. Individuals are exposed to an unending series of influences that tend to mold their opinions and their underlying aims and values in subtle, unnoticed fashion. It would be hard to maintain that these influences are balanced, that all sides are fairly presented in a manner that leaves people free to make up their minds. Many a person who protests most loudly that "nobody's going to tell me how to vote" is, in fact, induced to vote exactly as some newspaper or commentator wishes, without ever realizing what has happened.

What workers want and believe and act on inevitably reflects, in part, what they read in the daily papers and hear over the air, what they learned in school and what their children learn, what their neighbors, preacher, and corner grocer have to say. Since newspapers, magazines, radio, and television are controlled with few exceptions by persons having the viewpoint of business and the well-to-do, it is natural that they exert their influence predominantly toward preventing changes and ideas which run counter to business values and desires. They attempt to create and strengthen a faith among working people that the best solution to their problems lies in individual effort and loyal support of business leadership.

The crucial question is what counter-measures organized labor can and will take to offset the predominantly business-oriented presentation of the news, ideas, and interpretations. Will influence exerted by business in shaping public opinion through control of mass media and through pressures on schools, writers, clergymen, and other opinion leaders be felt as a serious threat to labor unions and their political programs? Will this aroused concern, if it grows, lead labor organizations to more vigorous attempts to combat one-sided influences by providing their own members, and the public generally, with other information and alternative views more favorable to union efforts and to social change in the interest of working people as the union sees it? What these questions mean to suggest is the probability that sophisticated labor and business leadership will increasingly perceive their long-run power relationship as determined in great measure by public opinion (including workers' opinions) and its political expression; that consequently they will carry on the struggle to achieve their respective goals largely through contending efforts to win moral approval and support in the public mind.

The serious problem for organized labor is whether continued reliance on the collective bargaining process, without much greater attention to public opinion and political influence than has been common, might mean that bargaining itself will become less usable for their purposes, tending more and more to be conducted within an atmosphere and a legal framework thoroughly in accord with management views and devoted to preserving management powers in an unmodified form. Collective bargaining, backed by the strike, is only as dependable as the state of opinion, law, and politics permits it to be. The position unions come to occupy over the next few decades will in all probability be determined more by events on the broad ideological and communications front, in politics broadly conceived, than by developments in the direct dealing between management and labor. The crucial question will persist: Who controls the social controls?

It is these considerations that are neglected in the persuasive case that has been argued by some liberal economists for "limited function" unions "integrated" into the pluralistic society. According to this conception unions should operate solely as bargaining agencies operating in the area of employment relations. No attention is paid to the unbalanced state of communications controls and social influence in the society, and the implications for unions. But if the dissemination of ideas, the inculcation of basic value premises, the control of rewards and penalties for thinking "right" or "wrong" are predominately under business influence, how do opposed views get an adequate hearing unless labor unions refuse to be "limited" or "integrated" into the going system with the going rules and power relations unchanged —or changed in ways unfavorable to labor? A "free pluralistic society" may become a pious phrase if there are no effective offsetting interest groups to challenge domination by corporations and their allies in shaping opinion on the social-political front. This counter-influence function could conceivably be taken over by new organizations but it is difficult now to picture an effective political organization representing broad labor interests that does not rest largely on labor union support.

All this points to the probability that the main body of American organized labor will feel compelled to engage in extensive programs of political education and political influencing. A major part of the effort will necessarily have to do with union members themselves, both because it is essential for unions to hold their loyalty and enthusiasm in the face of pervasive counter-pulls and likewise because of the enormous indirect effect that members' relations to the union are bound to exert on the general public. These indirect effects are of two kinds: (1) the personal influence of unionists on the attitudes of their family members, relatives and neighbors; (2) the picture that the union's way of dealing with its own members conveys as a demonstration of union-policy-in-action in regard to democratic process and individual rights, interest in goals beyond the pay envelope, and concern with the *public* welfare.

The successful accomplishment of these objectives is a most formidable assignment. Unions have the problem of so conducting their political education that it arouses positive, active enthusiasm among potential supporters while at the same time doing what it can to avoid alienation of middle class voters and unionists who are not "on side." Union political education confronts not only the obstacles of widespread indifference and the resistance created by opposed opinion-influencing agencies, but also the deeply ingrained belief that unions belong in the factory and should stay out of politics, and the even firmer adherence to belief in individual independence in politics, typified by the familiar "nobody can tell me how to vote." A profound change is occurring, too, in that the old stirring symbols of concrete evils to be destroyed by militant labor action have lost their force. The fight against starvation, long hours, intolerable working conditions; the battle for a "living wage" and "the right to organize"—for most workers these no longer represent vital issues. New moral justifications are needed, emotionally potent convictions, which by the nature of the changing times, will be more abstract and require more sophisticated understanding of society's—and working people's—problems.

These considerations, we believe, will more and more call for a freely inquiring, non-manipulative type of union political education, on pragmatic grounds even where the leadership may not be so inclined by reason of its own social values. Education of this kind must be mainly *self-education*. If workers are to become effectively and satisfyingly involved, they first have to understand what goes on, where their own interests as unionists and as members of the larger society lie. Working people will move toward solutions to their problems to the extent that they and their chosen leaders learn to inform themselves and to participate democratically in deciding the direction they, and our society, must take.

If unions come to define their political role in some such fashion, it leaves them with disturbing questions. One question in particular, that we have not hitherto mentioned, presents serious unresolved dilemmas. It is the problem of how fully union political activities are democratically controlled and how far unions can and should go in protecting the rights of political dissenters in the union. Unfortunately, the argument for union democracy and respect for the rights of individual members vis-à-vis the union organization is frequently employed by opponents of unions as a high-sounding justification for restrictive measures aimed at crippling union political activities. Yet above and beyond all partisan misuse of the issue, a problem of grave importance does exist. It is not solely a matter of restrictive laws and attacks by anti-union crusaders who find it suits their purposes to become defenders of union minorities. Both phases of the problem are important: on the one side, actual and threatened curtailment of union political freedom imposed from outside; and on the other side, the difficult task of insuring genuine democratic decision-making and justice for dissenting members, while at the same time preserving the organization's effectiveness.

The argument against use of union dues for political purposes has already borne fruit in provisions of the Taft-Hartley Law restricting such spending[9] and, more recently, in such state laws as the Catlin Act in Wisconsin which prohibits a wide range of union activities in elections, including even the discussion and publicizing of elections and candidates. Similar bills have been proposed in other industrial states such as Ohio and Michigan.

If our analysis of the imbalance of opinion forming forces in society is correct, vital need exists for labor unions to have full opportunity to express and effectively support their views in opposition to those of other influential groups. It is precisely

[9] At the time of this writing, the UAW was engaged in a court suit brought by the Department of Justice arising out of the appearance of a candidate for federal office on one of the union's television programs. Subsequently, the charges against the union were dismissed by the court (February, 1956).

here that the dilemma arises. On the one hand, there is the question whether democratic doctrine can be reconciled to the employment of dissenting members' dues for political purposes that run contrary to the wishes of those individual members—in an organization to which the individuals must belong for other reasons. This question persists even though the use of funds may be approved by an overwhelming majority of the members. But on the other hand, we have the question whether it is not right and necessary for a democratic majority to be free to act. For example, it is generally agreed that unions can properly decide by majority vote whether to accept or reject an employer's bargaining offers, to strike or not to strike, and almost no one would now contend that the dissenters from such decisions should be entitled to refuse the use of their dues money to implement the will of the majority. Where is a line to be drawn between such core economic activities of the union and political types of action which a majority may also approve as being in the interests of the organization and its members? Admittedly these are difficult questions. We do not ask them with any thought of giving answers. We do believe it is most important that the questions be insistently asked. The problems are ones that must be faced by unions themselves as well as by all other segments of society concerned with labor's role.

Among the several aspects of the complex question, three principal elements can be distinguished. One has to do with internal union democracy. It is clear that unions differ greatly in the degree to which their decisions are democratically made. UAW-CIO, we believe, is one of the most democratic. But to the extent that a union fails to maintain adequate membership control, the conduct of its political program poses acute questions beyond those already mentioned. Shall the union officers in these instances be free to use union funds politically in any manner they decide? How can the political rights—in this case perhaps of the majority—be guaranteed? Is government regulation necessary? Or will unions themselves be sufficiently concerned with maintaining public approval and solidarity within the union so that they will work toward acceptable solutions assuring full democratic participation by members?

A second thorny division of the general question raises the

issue of compulsory union membership. Specifically, in the present connection, it asks whether involuntary membership will be deemed compatible with *political* action by unions. Should the unions (in case individuals are more or less compelled to belong to them) be limited to certain forms of political action, and should the limitions be self-determined and self-imposed or should they be enforced by law? And, third, if compulsory membership through union shop agreements is approved by majorities of workers, as is widely the case, and if union political activities increase in importance as we have predicted, will it prove desirable and feasible for unions to set up any special provisions for political dissenters?[10]

These questions clearly have important bearing on the future of labor in politics. While this is not the place to weigh the pros and cons nor to attempt answers, the problems are noted here as concrete examples of the difficulties that unions must overcome as they move further into politics, seeking to marshall the full political strength of their membership and, simultaneously, to give convincing evidence, both to their members and to other segments of society, of their genuine devotion to democratic ideals and the public interest.

The total picture that emerges from our study and from the reflections in this chapter remains sketchy but we believe it is clear and meaningful in its main outlines:

(1) *The possibilities.*

It appears that broad union political objectives of the kind represented by the UAW *can* win extensive approval and support among union members. Auto workers in the Detroit area stand as evidence.

As to the future, it is highly probable that improved socio-economic conditions and other influences will make for increasing political *interest.* While the *direc-*

---

[10] As one illustration of an attempt to deal with the problem of political dissenters in unions, it may be noted that in Great Britain the law provides that union members can file individual requests for exemption from the payment of contributions to the "political fund" of their union and that they are thereupon relieved from making such payments.

tion those interests will take is uncertain, it cannot be assumed to be toward non-labor, conservative goals. It is extremely doubtful that the changing social conditions often held to presage a swing of industrial workers toward "middle class" and conservative positions will in fact produce these effects. Both our findings and our speculative analysis lead to the conclusion that it is quite possible for wage earners to experience great social and economic gains and yet remain definitely pro-labor.

During the years ahead, furthermore, our analysis suggests that the trend may be toward a type of political program that is broad in scope, aiming to satisfy workers' varied tangible and intangible wants and at the same time keeping the *general* welfare prominently in view.

(2) *The obstacles.*

Even with a vigorous, effective political program, large numbers of members continue to be indifferent, uninvolved, lacking enthusiasm and conviction. A significant, though limited minority, is actively opposed to labor political action. Many members exhibit deep feelings of political futility, frustration, and social alienation. (On the whole, these negative dispositions are most characteristic of older and less educated workers; consequently passage of time may be expected to reduce their seriousness.)

Other leading obstacles to be surmounted include these: Many unionists hold firmly to traditional job-centered unionism and are correspondingly suspicious of any extensive labor participation in politics. Serious fears and criticisms of labor's power (and abuses of power by officials) occur among some union members and more widely among other groups whose cooperation and goodwill are indispensable to labor. Interlacing with the doubts, resistances, and hostilities, and in some degree accounting for them, are the preponderantly business-oriented influences shaping public opinion in a non-labor direction.

(3) *The challenge of the undetermined future.*

In the face of the complex cross-cutting influences it is obviously not predictable whether union political action will flourish or decline. The best our analysis can do is underscore leading factors to be taken into account in the ongoing studies that are needed to trace changing trends and to guide the policies of those seeking to influence the trends. Our empirical research and our more general analysis both suggest that labor political action will tend to increase and grow in importance. But this will depend in large measure on the efforts and effectiveness of those desiring and those opposing such developments. The future *could* go against an expanded role for labor in politics. There *could* be a revived insistence on limited, job-control union philosophy. Or unions *could* follow roads that lead to management-dominated unions or to government domination. Significant forces press toward each of these outcomes. That is why we emphasize the *challenge* of labor's political future.

Perhaps nowhere is there greater understanding of the challenge and more resolute determination to meet it than in the auto workers' union. Yet even in the ranks of that organization we have seen that much remains to be accomplished. This provides some measure of the enormity of the challenge for less politically advanced segments of organized labor—and by the same token it suggests how doubtful the outcome.

APPENDIX A

The Interview Questionnaires

I. Pre-Election Interview

1a. First, let me ask: Are you a registered voter? ____Yes____No
IF YES, GO TO Q. 2

1b. IF NO: Could you tell me why you have not registered?
w____Too young   x____Not a citizen   y____Residence Requirements   z____Other answer: (If not clear or complete, ask: How
do you mean? Why was that? Would you tell me a little more
about that?

IF 1b ANSWERED w,x,y, GO TO Q. 26
IF 1b ANSWERED z, ASK 1c THRU 1f

    1c. Do you know how a person registers, that is, how to sign
up to be able to vote? (If necessary: What do you have to
do to register?)

    1d. Did you think about registering for the November election?
____Yes____No (If Yes) How does it happen you didn't
go ahead and register?

    1e. Did anyone talk to you about registering? ____Yes____No
(If yes) Who?

1f. Have you ever voted? _____Yes_____No (If yes) When was
   the last time you voted?_____

GO TO Q. 26

IF YES TO 1a

2. Would you say that you personally care very much which party
   wins the presidential election, or that you don't care very much?
   _____Care _____Don't care
   Why do you feel that way?
   _____
   _____
   _____

3. Generally speaking, do you usually think of yourself as a Repub-
   lican, a Democrat, an Independent, or what? _____Rep _____Dem
   _____Ind _____Other: (_____)
   (If Rep or Dem) Would you call yourself a strong (Rep or
   Dem), or not a very stong (Rep or Dem)? _____Strong _____Not
   very strong
   (If Independent or Other) Do you think of yourself as closer to
   the Republican or the Democratic Party? _____Rep _____Dem
   _____Neither

4a. What would you say are the main issues or things being talked
   about in the presidential campaign?
   _____
   _____
   _____

4b. What issues or things being talked about are the most important
   ones to you?
   _____
   _____
   _____

5. We're interested in how many people know who the candidates
   are for President, and for Governor and Senator in Michigan.
   Would you tell me who the candidates are:
         For President? _____
         For Governor of Michigan? _____
         For Senator here in Michigan? _____

6. I'd like to ask you about the good and bad points of the two
   candidates for president. Is there anything in particular about
   Stevenson that might make you want to vote for him? (What
   is it?)
   _____
   _____
   _____

7. Is there anything in particular about Stevenson that might make you want to vote against him? (What is it?)

----

8. Is there anything in particular about Eisenhower that might make you want to vote for him? (What is it?)

----

9. Is there anything in praticular about Eisenhower that might make you want to vote against him? (What is it?)

----

10. Where would you say you get most of your information about candidates and what they stand for?

----

11. Do you think you will vote in the coming election—that is, are you:
    _____sure you will vote _____pretty sure _____might not vote _____do not intend to vote
    (If might not vote) Why do you think you might not vote?

GO TO Q. 12
(If not intend to vote) Why is it you do not intend to vote?

If you *were* going to vote, how do you think you would vote today for President—for Stevenson, the Democratic candidate, or for Eisenhower, the Republican candidate? _____Stev _____Eisen _____Other _____Undecided

GO TO Q. 20
IF SURE OR PRETTY SURE OR MIGHT NOT VOTE ON Q. 11:

12. Now, just to make it definite—if the elections were being held today, which way would you vote for President—for Stevenson, the Democratic candidate, or for Eisenhower, the Republican candidate?

_____Stev _____Eisen _____Other _____Undecided

| Skip to Qs. |
| 17 Thru 19 |

IF STEV, EISEN, OR OTHER ON Q. 12, ASK 13 THRU 16:

13. Just to make sure that I have your ideas straight now, would you tell my why you are going to vote for_____as President?

_____

_____

14. Is there a chance you might change your mind and *not* vote for _____? _____Yes or Maybe _____No
    (candidate)
    (If yes or maybe) What sort of thing might make you change your mind?

_____

_____

15. Has there been any time when you thought you might not vote for_____?
    (candidate)
    _____Yes _____No _____Can't recall
    (If yes) Why were you doubtful?

_____

_____

    Can you recall how long ago it was that you had these doubts?

_____

16. Are you personally doing anything to help_____ (candidate) get elected, like talking to people, or anything like that? _____Yes _____No
    (If yes) What are you doing?

_____

_____

_____

GO TO Q. 20 THRU END

IF UNDECIDED ON Q. 12 ASK 17 THRU 19

17. (If undecided on 12) How does it happen that you're not sure which man to vote for as President?

18. Has there been any time when you thought you *did* know who you were going to vote for in the coming election? _____Yes _____No _____Can't recall

(If yes) Who was it? _____Eisen _____Stev _____Other
What made you change?_____
_____
_____
_____

How long ago did you get doubtful about voting for?
_____
_____
_____

19. If you *had* to make up your mind *today*, would you prob-
    ably vote for Eisenhower or for Stevenson? _____Eisen
    _____Stev _____Other _____Still undecided
    (If Eisen, Stev, or other) Why do you think you would
    vote that way?
    _____
    _____
    _____

CONTINUE WITH Q. 20 THRU END

FOR ALL REGISTERED VOTERS, ASK Q. 20 THRU END:

20. Now, as one of the last questions, would you tell me: Do you
    think it will make a great deal of difference to the country
    whether the Republicans or the Democrats win the election, or
    won't it make much difference which side wins?
    _____Great deal of difference _____Not much difference

20a. (If great deal of difference) In what way would it make a
     difference?
     _____
     _____
     _____

20b. (If not much difference) Why do you feel that it won't make
     much difference?
     _____
     _____
     _____

21. Which way are you going to vote for Senator—for Potter, the
    Republican candidate, or for Moody, the Democratic candidate?
    _____Potter _____Moody _____Other _____Undecided
    (If undecided) If you *had* to make up your mind *today*, would
    you probably vote for Potter or for Moody?
    _____Potter _____Moody _____Other _____Still Undecided

22. Which way are you going to vote for Governor—for Williams,
    the Democratic candidate, or for Alger, the Republican candi-
    date?
    _____Williams _____Alger _____Other _____Undecided

(If undecided) If you *had* to make up your mind *today,* would you probably vote for Williams or for Alger?
____Williams ____Alger ____Other ____Still Undecided

23. Within the past few weeks, have you talked politics with anyone? ____Yes ____No
(If yes) Who did you talk with? (Ascertain relation to respondent)

_____

_____

_____

24a. Have any other people or organizations been in touch with you about the election—have they sent you things in the mail, handed you leaflets, phoned you, asked you to meetings, talked to you in person or anything like that? ____Yes ____No

IF NO, GO TO Q. 25; IF YES CONTINUE AT 24b

24b. Which ways have they been in touch with you—by mail, leaflets, talked to you, or what? (check under column 24b in Table, and ask 24c, 24d, and 24e for each one checked)

	24b	24c	24d	24e
	(Check below to show answer to 24b)	Was it about registering, or in favor of a particular party or candidate? (Record "R" or "PC" or "R & PC")	(For ones checked under 24b) What people or organizations (sent you things in the mail), (handed you leaflets), etc.?	(For each answer in 24d) How do you feel about having them (send you things in the mail), (hand you leaflets), etc.?
Sent things in the mail				
Handed Leaflets				
Phoned				
Meetings				
Talked in Person				
Other (Specify):				

25. Have you heard about any proposal to vote on reapportionment in Michigan? ____Yes ____No Comments:

25a. (If not mentioned in 25) Have you heard anything about Proposal 2 or Proposal 3? _____Yes _____No   Comments:

25b. (If yes to 25 or 25a) How are you going to vote on this? (If vague—for example, "I'll vote for it," "I agree," etc., ascertain what Respondent agrees with, or is voting for. How do you mean? Which way are you going to vote for it? In what way do you agree?)

_____

_____

_____

Now, would you give me just a few facts so we can know something about all the people we talk to:

26. What year were you born?_____

27. How long have you lived in Detroit?_____

28. How many grades of school did you finish? (Circle answer)
    1   2   3   4   5   6   7   8   9   10   11   12   13   15   15   16

29. Is your religious preference Protestant, Catholic, or Jewish?
    _____Protestant _____Catholic _____Jewish _____Other (Specify
    _____) _____None

30. What is your occupation? I mean, what kind of work do you do? (Be specific). (If retired, what *was* main occupation)?

31. Do you belong to a labor union? _____Yes _____No
    (If yes) Are you an officer in your union, on any committee, or anything like that? _____Yes _____No
    (If yes) What do you do? _____

32. M_____   F_____

33. W_____   N_____

Address _____

Interviewer _____

Interview Number _____

II. Post-Election Interview

1. a. How do you feel about the way the election came out? (How do you mean? What other feelings do you have about it?)

    _____

    _____

    _____

   b. Are you glad or sorry that Eisenhower won?
      Glad_____ Sorry_____
      RESPONDENT'S COMMENTS:

   c. Would you tell me why you are glad (sorry)?

    _____

    _____

    _____

2. a. Now that the Republicans won the election, do you think it will make a great deal of difference to the country, or won't it make much difference?

Great deal of difference........ Not make difference........

RESPONDENT'S COMMENTS:

(If great deal of difference) in what ways will it make a difference?

(If not make difference) Why do you feel that it won't make much difference?

----

3. We know that a lot of people intended to vote but weren't able to. How about you: did you vote or not?

Voted........ Did not vote........

(IF *VOTED* on Q. 3, ask 4 through 8—*IF DID NOT VOTE*, skip to 9)

IF VOTED:

4. a. Now, would you tell me how you voted this time: Who did you vote for for President—for Eisenhower, the Republican candidate or for Stevenson, the Democratic candidate?

Eisen........ Steve........ Other answer:

b. And who did you vote for for Governor—for Williams, the Democratic candidate, or for Alger, the Republican candidate?

Williams........ Alger........ Other answer:

c. And who for Senator—for Potter, the Republican candidate, or for Moody, the Democratic candidate?

Potter........ Moody........ Other answer:

5. a. What would you say was the main reason why you voted for........................(Eisenhower or Stevenson)?

----

b. Was there any other important reason why you voted for ....(Eisenhower or Stevenson)?

----

6. a. How long before the election did you decide that you were going to vote for........................(Eisenhower or Stevenson)?

----

b. (IF IN LAST TWO WEEKS BEFORE ELECTION) Why did you wait till then to decide?

_____

_____

_____

7. Had you ever thought during the election campaign that you might vote for_____(Stevenson or Eisenhower, whichever *not* voted for?)
    Yes_____ No_____
    (IF YES) Why did you decide *not* to vote for him?

_____

_____

8. a. Did you vote on the question of reapportionment in Michigan —you know, on Proposal 2 and Proposal 3?
      Yes_____ No_____ Don't remember or Not sure_____
      (IF YES OR NOT SURE) How did you vote on it? (If vague, which proposal did you vote for? Against?) (Record how voted on *each* of the two proposals, using R's way of referring to them—i.e., either by proposal number or by names of groups backing each.)

_____

_____

_____

   Why did you vote that way?

_____

_____

_____

   b. Does it make any difference to you that Proposal 3 won instead of Proposal 2?
      Yes_____ No_____
      (IF YES) How do you mean?

_____

_____

_____

(IF NOT MENTIONED IN 8a):

   c. Do you know what groups or organizations were for Proposal 2? (Who?)

_____

_____

_____

   d. Do you know what groups or organizations were for Proposal 3? (Who?)

_____

_____

_____

SKIP TO Q. 11

IF DID NOT VOTE: (9 through 10)

9. a. If you had voted, would you have voted for Eisenhower, the Republican candidate, or for Stevenson, the Democratic candidate?

Eisen_____ Steve_____ Other answer:

   b. What is the main reason why you would have voted for _____(Eisen or Steve)?

_____

_____

   c. Was there any other important reason why you would have voted for?_____(Eisen or Steve)?

_____

_____

10. a. What was the main reason why you didn't vote? (How do you mean? etc. Get a clear picture)

_____

_____

(IF BECAUSE NOT REGISTERED) What was the reason you didn't register to vote? (How do you mean? etc.)

_____

_____

   b. Some people feel bad about not voting and some don't feel that it matters. What about you—how have you felt about not voting in this election?

_____

_____

FOR ALL:

11. a. Did any other members of your family living here with you vote for President? Which ones?

Wife_____ Husband_____ Others (relation to R):_____

_____

_____

   b. Did your wife (husband) vote for Eisenhower or for Stevenson?

Eisen_____ Steve_____ Other answer:

   c. And your_____(ASK FOR *EACH* RELATIVE NAMED IN 11a)—did he (she) vote for Eisenhower or for Stevenson

Relation to R_____Eisen_____ Steve_____
Relation to R_____Eisen_____ Steve_____
Relation to R_____Eisen_____ Steve_____
Relation to R_____Eisen_____ Steve_____

12. a. Did you personally do anything to help get_____
(Eisen or Steve) elected—like giving money for his campaign,
telling people why they should vote for him, handing out
leaflets or buttons, or anything like that?
Yes_____ No_____
(IF YES) What did you do?

_____

_____

(IF NO) Why was it you didn't do things like that?

_____

_____

13.   Do you think there is any important difference between what
the Democratic and Republican parties stand for, or do you
think they are about the same?
Different_____ Same_____

R'S COMMENTS:

14.   In the weeks before the election, did you talk with any people
about the election and the candidates? Yes_____ No_____
(IF YES) What people did you talk with? (Get their relation
to R.)

_____

_____

15. a. Were there any particular people you know personally whose
ideas you wanted to hear before you decided how you would
vote?
Yes_____ No_____ Other answer:
(IF YES) What people were they? (Get relation to R.)

_____

_____

b. Were there any particular *groups* or *organizations* whose ideas
you wanted to get before you decided how you would vote?
Yes_____ No_____ Other answer:
(IF YES) What groups or organizations were they?

_____

_____

_____

16. In the days before the election, did you know whether most of your friends and people you work with were for Stevenson or Eisenhower? (Which one?)
Steve_____ Eisen_____ DK_____

R'S COMMENTS:

17. a. In election campaigns, different groups work for one candidate or another. Are there any groups on this list (HAND R CARD #2) that you particularly trust—that is, you'd be more likely to vote for candidates they recommend? (Which group?) (SHOW CARD AND READ WHOLE LIST BEFORE GETTING THE RESPONSE.) (Check under col. a)

	a. Trust	c. Not Trust
Business groups	_____	_____
Church groups	_____	_____
Labor groups	_____	_____
Veterans groups	_____	_____
Daily newspapers	_____	_____
Fraternal organizations (like Masons, Knights of Columbus, Elks)	_____	_____

b. (ASK FOR *EACH* GROUP NAMED BY R.) Why is it that you particularly trust recommendations by_____ (each group named?)
_____(name of group trusted)_____

_____(name of group trusted)_____

c. Are there any groups on the list that you don't trust, that is, you'd be more likely to vote against candidates they recommend? (Which groups?) (check under col. c above)

d. (ASK FOR *EACH* GROUP NAMED BY R.) Why don't you trust_____(each group named)
_____←(name of group not trusted)_____

_____←(name of group not trusted)_____

18. a. In the last few weeks before the election, did you listen to radio or TV programs by the candidates? Yes_____ No_____

(IF YES) How often would you say (About how many times a week?)
_____

_____

_____

Could you tell me who you heard speak? (What other candidates did you hear?

----

b. Did you listen to radio or TV speeches about the election by people who were not candidates?
Yes_____ No_____

(IF YES) Could you tell me who some of the speakers were that you heard?

----

c. Did you listen regularly to any news program or commentators?
Yes_____ No_____

(IF YES) Who? (Or what programs—name or hour and station)

----

19.   In those last weeks before the election, did you read about the candidates and the election in the daily newspapers?
Yes_____ No_____

(IF YES) What newspaper did you read? (INTERVIEWER: Do *not* read list)
_____Detroit News
_____Detroit Times
_____Detroit Free Press
_____Others (Specify): _____

20.   Did you read about the candidates and the election in any magazines or other papers?
Yes_____ No_____

(IF YES) What magazines and other papers did you read?

----

21.   As you know, many groups and organizations get in touch with voters before the election: What ways were any groups and organizations in touch with you? (Read each item below

separately; if YES, check under 21a, and ask 21b,c,d, for that item.)

	21a	21b	21c	21d
	Check below if YES to item in first column	Which party or candidate were they for?	(For ones checked under 21a): What people or organizations (sent you things in the mail), (handed you leaflets), etc.?	(For each answer in 21a): Do you think it is a good thing or not for them to ---- (send you things in the mail, hand you leaflets, etc.? Ask separately for each item checked in 21a)
Did they send you things in the mail?				
Did they hand you leaflets?				
Did they phone you?				
Did they talk to you in speeches at meetings?				
Did they talk to you in person?				
Were there any other ways? (SPECIFY):				

22. a. Now, here is a list of all these things I've been asking about. (HAND R. CARD NO. 1) Which one of these would you say was the most *important* in giving you information and ideas about the candidates and the election? (Read the 7 items aloud and then ask:) Which one of these was most important in giving you information and ideas? (Record answer in column a)

(a) Most Important		*(b)* Trust Most	*(c)* Trust Least
....	Newspapers	....	....
....	Magazines and other papers	....	....
....	Radio	....	....
....	TV	....	....
....	Leaflets and things sent by mail		....
....	Personal talks	....	....
....	Speeches at meetings	....	....

b. Which of these on the list would you say you *trust* most? (Record in col. b)

R'S COMMENTS:

c. Which of these do you trust *least*? (Record in col. c above)

R'S COMMENTS:

23. a. During the Presidential campaign, many labor unions were for Stevenson, and many businessmen and business groups were for Eisenhower. Do you think it was all right for the unions to work to get Stevenson elected, or that it was not all right? All right........ Not all right........

R'S COMMENTS:

Why do you feel that way?_____
_____
_____
_____

(IF ALL RIGHT ON 23a) Were there any things the unions did in the election campaign that you didn't like? Yes........ No........

(IF YES) What things?_____
_____
_____
_____

b. As you know, many businessmen and business groups were for Eisenhower. Do you think it was all right for businessmen and business groups to work to get Eisenhower elected, or that it was not all right? All right........ Not all right........

R'S COMMENTS:

Why do you feel that way?_____
_____
_____
_____

(IF ALL RIGHT ON 23b) Were there any things that businessmen and business groups did in the election campaign that you didn't like?
Yes_____ No_____
(IF YES) What things?_____
_____
_____
_____

24. a. Would you like to see labor unions have *more* to say or *less* to say about things the government does that are important to working people?
    More_____ Less_____
    R'S COMMENTS:

    b. Would you like to see businessmen and business groups have *more* to say or *less* to say about things the government does that are important to working people?
    More_____ Less_____
    R'S COMMENTS:

25. Now I'd like to ask you another kind of question. Here are things that some people say and we want to find out how other people feel on these things. I'll read them one at a time and you just tell me offhand whether you *agree* or *disagree*.
    (READ EACH ONE CLEARLY AND REPEAT IF NECESSARY. Record any comments)

	Agree	Disagree
a. There's little use in writing to public officials because often they aren't really interested in the problems of the aveage man. Just offhand, do you agree or disagree?	_____	_____
b. Nowadays a person has to live pretty much for today and let tomorrow take care of itself.	_____	_____
c. The way people vote is the main thing that decides how things are run in this country.	_____	_____
d. These days a person doesn't really know who he can count on.	_____	_____
e. In spite of what some people say, the lot of the average man is getting worse, not better.	_____	_____
f. People like me don't have any say about what the government does.	_____	_____
g. It's hardly fair to bring children into the world with the way things things look for the future.	_____	_____

h. The most important thing to teach children is absolute obedience to their parents.

i. All candidates sound good in their speeches, but you never can tell what they will do after they are elected.

j. Any good leader should be strict with people under him in order to gain their respect.

k. There are two kinds of people in the world, the weak and the strong.

l. Politics and government are so complicated that the average person can't really understand what's going on.

m. Prison is too good for sex criminals; they should be publicly whipped or worse.

n. A few strong leaders could do more for this country than all the laws and talk.

26. Next, I have a few questions that ask how you feel about things in your life. First, there is this pretty general question:

a. On the whole, how satisfied would you say you are with the life you have? Which one of these answers here (HAND R. CARD No. 3) comes nearest to telling how you feel about your life? Would you say you are
    _____Completely satisfied
    _____Well satisfied
    _____Neither satisfied nor dissatisfied
    _____A little dissatisfied
    _____Very dissatisfied

b. Do you worry a lot about the future?
    Yes_____ No_____

c. Do you often feel restless, wanting to be on the move doing something, but not knowing what?
    Yes_____ No_____

d. Taking your life as it is now, do you feel that you have as much chance to enjoy life as you should have?
    Yes_____ No_____ Other answer:

e. Do you feel that you are accomplishing the sorts of things you would like to in your life?
    Yes_____ No_____ Other answer:

f. How do you feel about your chances for getting ahead? (How do you mean?)
    _____
    _____
    _____

g. What would you say "getting ahead" means to you?_____

27. a. Do you think there is any danger of a bad business depression and unemployment in the next few years? Would you say there is:
A very great chance____, some chance____, or no chance at all____?

b. Do you think the government can do things to keep the country from having a depression, or can't it do anything to stop it? Can____ Can't____ Other answer:

28. a. Do you think there is any danger of another world war in the next few years? Would you say there is:
A very great chance____, some chance____, or no chance at all____?

b. Do you think the government can do things to keep from having another world war or can't it do anything to stop it? Can____ Can't____ Other answer:

29. (WHITES ONLY) Do you think Negro and White workers should be treated equally in hiring, promotions, and lay-offs or not?
Yes____ No____
Could you tell me more on how you personally feel about that? (How do you mean? In what way?) _____

30. Now, would you tell me just a few facts so we can know something about all the people we talk to:

a. Do you have a group of friends you see fairly often?
Yes____ No____

(IF YES) How often do you get together or do things with them? (Number of times a week or number of times a month)

b. What people are they—people that live around here, people you work with, people you see at church, or what?

c. How much did this group talk politics before the election?

_____

_____

_____

d. Do you have relatives you see often?
Yes_____ No_____
(IF YES) How often do you get together or do things with them?

_____

_____

31. a. Do you belong to any organizations or clubs like these? (HAND R. CARD NO. 4 and ask about *each* item on *your* duplicate card[1]): Do you belong to any_____? (Record group *number* in column a and ask b,c,d, and e for that organization. After completing for *that* group, ask about each other group on list.)

b. Get name of organization and record in column b.

c. About how often do you go to its meetings? (Record in column c)

d. How do you feel about belonging to this group? Do you have: (1) a *great deal* of interest in it, (2) *some* interest, or (3) *little* or no interest? (Record 1, 2, or 3 in column d and record comments)

e. Were you ever an officer or on any committee? What was it? (Record in column e)

(a) Group No.	(b) Organization's Name	(c) To Meetings	(d) Interest	(e) Offices
____	_____	_____	_____	_____
____	_____	_____	_____	_____
____	_____	_____	_____	_____
____	_____	_____	_____	_____

32. If you were asked to use one of these four names for your

---

[1] The card contained the following list:
1. Lodges (Elks, Moose, Masons, Knight of Columbus, etc.)
2. Veterans organizations (VFW, American Legion, Amvets, etc.)
3. Church
4. Church groups (clubs, etc.)
5. Parent-Teacher Association
6. Neighborhood groups
7. Sports and athletic clubs
8. Political groups
9. Labor unions
10. Social groups (dances, cards, parties, etc.)
11. Any others (nationality groups, etc.)

social class, which would you say you belonged in: the middle
class, lower class, working class or upper class?
Middle......... Lower......... Working......... Upper

33. a. Where were you born? (Country if foreign born; or which
state if in US):

_____

_____

_____

b. Where did you live most of your life while you were growing
up?

c. Was it on a farm........., in a small town........., a medium-sized
city........., a big city.........?

34. What was your father's occupation? (What sort of work did
he do?)

_____

_____

_____

35. Was your father a Republican, a Democrat, or what?
Rep......... Dem......... Other:

36. What country was your father born in? _____
What country was your mother born in? _____

37. Are you married, widowed, separated, divorced, or single?
Married......... Widowed......... Separated......... Divorced.........
Single.........
(IF NOT SINGLE) Have you been married more than once?
Yes......... No.........

38. Do you own this house or are you renting?
Own......... Rent......... Other......... (explain) _____

39. a. How long have you lived in this house?_____
b. Where did you live before?_____
(IF IN DETROIT, what part of Detroit? Ask street and inter-
section):

_____

_____

_____

40. Do you own an automobile? Yes......... No.........
(IF YES) What make is it?_____ Year_____

41. a. What kind of work do you do on your main job? (BE
SPECIFIC!) (Just what do you do? If retired or unemployed,
record that fact, but also ask: What kind of work *did* you do?)

_____

_____

_____

b. How long have you been doing this kind of work?_____
c. What is the hourly wage rate on your job? (Weekly rate if
on salary) _____

d. How long would it take a new man to learn your job?

----

e. Would you tell me which of these answers (HAND R. CARD NO. 3) comes nearest to the way you feel about your job? Would you say you are: (read list)

------Completely satisfied

------Well satisfied

------Neither satisfied nor dissatisfied

------A little dissatisfied

------Very dissatisfied

42. (IF MARRIED WOMAN) What kind of work does your husband do on his main job? (BE SPECIFIC!) _____

43. a. Would you look at this card and tell me which of these is nearest your total family income this year? (HAND R. CARD NO. 5) I mean your family living here with you.

------Under $2,000	------$ 5,000 to $ 6,000
------$2,000 to $3,000	------$ 6,000 to $ 8,000
------$3,000 to $4,000	------$ 8,000 to $10,000
------$4,000 to $5,000	$10,000 or more

b. How many are there in your family who live on this income?

----

c. What is your own income from your main job this year?

(If c is *same* as a, SKIP to Q. 44; If c is *less* than a, ask d,e,f.)

d. Do you have any other jobs? (What other jobs?)

----

e. Does anyone else in your family work_____ that is, your family living here with you?_____ Who?

----

f. What other income does your family have—that is, your family living here? (Get source)

----

44. Last of all, now a question or two on how you voted in the past. In 1948, you remember that the candidates for President were Truman, Dewey, Wallace and some others. Do you re-

member for sure whether or not you voted in that election?
Voted_____ Didn't vote_____ D.R._____

(IF VOTED) Which one did you vote for?
Dewey_____ Truman_____ Wallace_____ DR_____
Other (specify) _____

45. (FOR DETROIT VOTERS ONLY) Do you remember if you
voted in the election for Mayor last year between Cobo and
Branigan?
Voted_____ Didn't vote_____ D.R._____

(IF VOTED) Who did you vote for, Branigan or Cobo?
Cobo_____ Branigan_____ D.R._____

46. M_____ F_____
W_____ N_____
ADDRESS _____
INTERVIEW NO. _____ TRACT NO. _____
INTERVIEWER _____
DATE _____

APPENDIX B

Sampling Procedure and Errors of Sampling

The population from which the sample was drawn was composed of the mailing list of all UAW locals located in Detroit, Highland Park, Hamtramck, Inkster, Lncoln Park, Dearborn, Ferndale, Royal Oak, River Rouge, and Wyandotte, Michigan. These communities comprise the heart of the Detroit Metropolitan Area and contain the bulk of its population. The UAW mailing list is not quite synonymous with current membership as it is not completely up-to-date; it includes some persons who live outside the area, others who have moved, and still others who have left the union; it also excludes a few union members living in the Detroit Metropolitan area who belong to locals outside this area. Then, too, the list included a few names of persons who are not members of the union, but who receive union publications. However, none of these sources of error appeared too serious; the mailing list was the most satisfactory way in which we could locate union members.

It was planned to select 1,500 names as a random sample of the lists of the UAW members located in the above-mentioned areas. The original list of approximately 290,000 persons was recorded on an addressograph tape. The drawing of 1,500 names was accomplished by marking every 194th name on the list. When a name was drawn, a card was made out for that individual giving his address as well as his name. In this manner, 1,499 names were actually drawn. The street address of each person to be interviewed was coded by census tract. Census tracts are small areas of a few square blocks, and the coding by census tract enabled us to group addresses in the same general locality. In this way each interviewer could be given an assignment which enabled him to seek several interviews within an area of a few blocks.

Interviewing began on October 20, 1952. Over 800 of the 1,499 interviews were assigned within the first few days of interviewing. The assignment of the remaining interviews was distributed over the next ten days. When the first interviewers reported back after their original assignment, it was immediately apparent that some of the addresses were out-of-date or otherwise incorrect. In cases where the respondent could not be found at that address, or the doorbell indicated a different name, the interviewers were instructed to obtain a forwarding address from the neighbors. This was effective only in a limited number of cases.

Another serious problem was the large number of "not-at-homes." The interviewer was seldom fortunate enough to contact a respondent at the first call. Repeated call-backs were necessary. After three call-backs, spaced at different times of the day, the interviewer was instructed to return the incomplete interview to the office. In many cases, four and five call-backs were made before attempt to establish contact was abandoned. All interviewing was terminated on Monday, November 3, the day before the election.

TABLE A.1

DISPOSITION OF INTERVIEWS

		Pre-election Interview		Post-election Interview
Total Sample		1499		487*
Potential Interviews		1169		453
Obtained	828		351	
Not obtained	341		102	
Refusal	98		58	
Not at home	243		44	
Not Potential		330		34
Dead	11		1	
In Army	8		2	
Language	10		0	
School; ill; vacations; etc.	26		0	
Unlocatable	275		31	
Known to have moved	225		16	
Wrong address, could not be located	50		15	

* In addition to these 487 cases, interviewed in the pre-election phase and post-election sample, a less systematic supplementary sample was assigned for post-election interviews, to be used as a check on the main sample. The supplementary sample is described in the text.

Refusal to be interviewed presented still another problem. When the interviewer returned reporting a refusal, he or she was questioned whether he thought sending another interviewer would possibly succeed. Most persons who refused to be interviewed refused before the interview had even commenced. There were a few persons who insisted on terminating the interview before the interview was completed. These persons were called on the telephone by a member of the survey staff and their further cooperation was asked. In several cases the interview was completed over the telephone. Table A.1 shows the disposition of the 1,499 interviews attempted in the pre-election sample.

Although 1,499 names were selected, it turned out that only 1,169 of these persons were potentially available for interview. 330 persons representing 22 per cent of the total sample either could not be located because they had moved, or had a wrong address, or were dead, in the Army, could not speak English, or were temporarily away—at school, or in the hospital, or on vacation. Of the 1,169 potential interviews, 341, or 29 per cent were not obtained. Ninety-eight of these were refusals and 243 represented persons who were not at home, even on the 3rd, 4th, or 5th call-back, although we did ascertain that they lived at the address to which the interviewer was sent. Thus 828, or 71 per cent of the 1,169 possible interviews were obtained.

During the course of the first interview another type of effort was made to obtain a correct address. A list of "moves" was sent to the UAW headquarters for checking with the locals. In only about ten cases was the local able to supply a correct address for the interviewee. Evidently even the local union could not keep abreast of the constant movements of its members. Presumably the local list was up-to-date, but actually it is most difficult if not impossible to keep track of all the workers, many of whom are unmarried and who live in rooming houses. The large number of "not-at-homes" (243), in spite of repeated calls, is also an indication of the daily movement and mobility of these persons.

A subsample of the original sample was chosen for the second interview. This subsample was based on the results of the first interview. Completed first interviews were categorized into "Stevenson intent," "Eisenhower intent," "undecided," "refused to say," "not registered" (though eligible), and "ineligible to register." The ineligible to register group was not assigned for second interview. One hundred per cent of all other categories except the "definite Stevenson intent" were assigned for post-election interview. Of the 439 persons expressing firm intention to vote for Stevenson, a random sample of 167 was selected for the second interview since it was judged unnecessary to have our sample retain so large a number of members who were committed to the union-supported candidate. In order to have our results adequately represent these members in proportion to their true numbers, however, all of our statistical tabulations used weighted figures that restore the 167 to their original magnitude of 439 by multiplying all subdivisions of the 167 by a weighting factor of 2.63 (i.e., the ratio of 439 to 167).

A basic sample of 487 individuals (unweighted figures) was assigned for the post-election interview. The disposition of these cases is shown in Table A.1. The post-election interviewing began in late November 1952 and ended early in February 1953.

In addition to the basic sample, we chose a sample of 49 of the original "refusals" (50 per cent of the total), 62 of the "not-at-homes" (25 per cent), and 50 of the "unlocatables" for attempted post-election interview. It was hoped that enough of these interviews could be completed to yield a crude indication whether the cases missed in the pre-election sample would substantially have changed our results. Only 67 of the supplementary interviews were completed and these have not been included in any of the analyses reported. Informal comparisons were carried out, however, which suggest that responses of the 67 cases do not differ greatly from those of the basic sample. For example, the basic sample showed 20 per cent not voting or refusing to report; the supplementary sample has 24 per cent. Of those reporting, the percentage of Stevenson votes in the main sample is 74 per cent, in the supplementary sample 73 per cent. A few other comparative figures follow:

	Basic Sample	Supplementary Sample
Glad that Eisenhower won	37%	42%
Did member help in campaign	27	18
Business political recommendations trusted	7	7
—not trusted	35	37
Labor political recommendations trusted	49	40
—not trusted	12	21
All right for unions to work for Stevenson	78	72
Should unions have more influence on government	55	48
Should business have more influence on government	19	16

The supplementary sample is very similar to the basic sample in such characteristics as age, sex, race, education, occupational classification, and years in Detroit; differences are well within the margin of chance variations. Altogether, the evidence from the supplementary sample tends to agree closely enough with the main body of data to indicate that sampling errors were not serious. The percentages of responses remain remarkably similar.

Check on Accuracy of the Sample

Certain other sources of data enable us to check the representativeness of our sample in respect to a few characteristics. The two sources used are the U. S. Census[1] and a study conducted by the Detroit Area Study of the University of Michigan.[2] Comparisons of the three population surveys are shown in Table A.2. On the whole,

[1] U.S. Bureau of the Census, *U.S. Census of Population: 1950, Vol. II, Characteristics of the Population,* Part 22, Michigan Chapter C, U.S. Government Printing Office, Washington, D. C., 1952, pages 317-318.

[2] *A Social Profile of Detroit: 1952.* University of Michigan, Detroit Area Study, Ann Arbor, 1952.

326 *Appendix B*

a satisfactory degree of correspondence is shown. The one sizable discrepancy occurs in respect to age; our interviewing included somewhat too few young workers and too many older workers.

TABLE A.2

COMPARISON OF THE SAMPLE WITH OTHER POPULATION DATA

	This Study	Detroit Area Study[1]	U.S. Census[2]
Sex—			
Male	89	87	91
Female	11	13	9
Race—			
White	81	°	83
Non-white	19		17[3]
Religion—			
Catholic	42	46	°
Protestant	51	50	
Other and none	7	4	
Age—			
Under 25	7	°	13
25-54	71		71
55 and over	22		16
Median income	$4706[4]		$4404 ("Operatives")
			$5582 ("Craftsmen and Kindred Workers")
Median school years completed	9.4	10.1	

° No data available.

[1] Data from the Detroit Areas Study, loc. cit.

[2] U.S. Bureau of the Census, loc. cit.

[3] As this figure was obtained by inference, it must be further explained. The census shows 335,726 persons employed in manufacturing of motor vehicles and motor vehicle equipment. Of these, 45,547 or 14% were Negroes. But this is not a fair sample of *unionized persons* in the auto industry. Data by industry and occupation group were not given by color. However, the assumption was made that virtually no Negroes were employed in the auto industry in the "Professional, Technical, etc.," "Managers, Proprietors and Officials," "Clerical, etc.," and "Sales" categories. Therefore, the 61,692 persons in these categories are deducted from the 335,726 we find Negroes to be 17% of the remainder. It also might be pointed out that the remainder, about 274,000 persons comes close to the number of persons from which we drew our sample.

[4] The median income reported here is consistent with the results found in the Detroit Area Survey of 1953. In that survey it was found that the median income of all Detroit families in 1952 was $5,028; of "operatives" (mostly production workers) $4,404; and "craftsmen and kindred workers" $5,582. As our sample contained mostly operatives with some craftsmen, the results of the two sample surveys seem very similar.

Guide for Estimating Size of Sampling Errors

The comparisons of percentages throughout the report must be interpreted with a degree of caution because of the sampling errors involved with limited numbers of cases. In general, we have not called attention to differences unless the odds are at least 9 to 1 against their being mere chance occurrences due to sampling errors. For most of the comparisons in the report, the probability that the differences are "statistically significant" is much greater, reaching at least the 95 per cent level (odds of 19 to 1).

The following sampling error table provides a rough guide for the reader who wishes to evaluate the percentage differences:

APPROXIMATE SIZE OF PERCENTAGE DIFFERENCES REQUIRED BETWEEN TWO PERCENTAGE FIGURES IN ORDER THAT THE DIFFERENCE BE SIGNIFICANT AT THE 95 PER CENT LEVEL

Size of the two percentages to be compared:	*Number of individuals in each of the two groups on whom the percentages are based*			
	50	100	200	400
Approx. 10% to 20% (or 80% to 90%)	14%	10%	7%	5%
Approx. 20% to 30% (or 70% to 80%)	17	12	8	6
Between 30% and 70%	20	14	10	7

The use of this table can be illustrated by an example. Suppose we wish to compare two subgroups, each containing approximately 100 persons. In one group, 68 per cent answer in a given way while in the other 83 per cent answer in this way. Is the difference large enough to be statistically "significant"? Since these percentages are in the neighborhood of the 70 to 80 per cent range, we consult the middle row of entries in the above table; and since each percentage is based on roughly 100 cases, we look under the column headed 100. The sampling error thus located, in the second row and the second column is 12 per cent. Since the difference between the two obtained percentages (15 percentage points) exceeds the 12 per cent, the probability is greater than 95 per cent that a true difference exists in the direction shown.

Sampling errors for differences of percentages that involve other combinations than those represented in the table can be roughly approximated by interpolating between the nearest figures given in the table.

APPENDIX C

Construction of Indexes and Ratings

Index of Socio-Economic Level

This index made use of three items: occupation, median income of the census tract in which the respondent lives, and whether he owns or rents his home (or room). The index was constructed to give a rough measure of occupational level and material plane of living. It omitted educational and cultural indicators and also direct reports of income though these are, of course, associated factors.

Four levels were defined as follows:

1. *High* (relative to our total sample)

    All workers owning home located in the highest one-fifth of census tracts by median income of residents.

    White collar workers residing in the upper three-fifths of census tracts.

2. *Medium plus*

    Manual workers owning homes in the second highest fifth of census tracts or renting in the highest one-fifth.

3. *Medium minus*

    Manual workers owning homes in the middle fifth or renting in the second highest fifth.

4. *Low* (relative to our total sample)

    All workers living in the lowest two-fifths of census tracts. The numbers in each of the socio-economic categories are these:

	Unweighted Numbers	Weighted Numbers*	Per Cent by Weighted Numbers
Level 1	74	105	20%
2	79	134	26
3	86	123	23
4	93	161	31
	332	523	100%
Unclassified	19		

* For explanation of weighting, see p. 324.

Rating of Labor Political Orientation

Responses to questions used in obtaining this index were scored in the following manner (positive scores meaning pro-labor and negative scores the opposite):

	Score
Was it all right for unions to work to get Stevenson elected?	
Yes	+1
No	−1
Was it all right for business groups to work to get Eisenhower elected?	
Yes, without *also* saying yes for unions	−2
Groups whose political recommendations are particularly trusted—	
Business groups	−1
Labor groups, without also saying business groups	+2
Labor groups and also business groups	0
Do *not* trust labor groups	−2
Want unions to have more or less say in government?	
More	+1
Less	−1
Want business to have more or less say in government?	
More	−2
Less	+1

Answers scored in this way can produce a total score from −9 to +5. These raw scores were translated into derived positive scores, running from 0 to 8. The distribution of these scores and their meaning are discussed on pages 115-117.

Raw Score	Derived Score
−9 to −4	0
−3	1
−2	2
−1	3
0	4
1	5
2	6
3	7
4 or 5	8

Rating of Political interest

This rating is explained on pages 123-137, where the 14 questions that enter into the rating are separately dealt with. In scoring, one point was allowed for each answer indicative of political interest, with a score of "2" assigned on one question (see page 129), thus yielding a total possible score of 0 to 15. The raw scores were again translated into derived scores, as follows:

Raw Score	Derived Score
0 to 5	0
6	1
7	2
8	3
9	4
10	5
11	6
12	7
13 to 15	8

The distribution of scores is shown on p. 136.

Rating of Attachment to the Union

This rating is based on three questions, scored as indicated below.

	Score
In listing organizations he belong to, does he mention the union and, if so, what degree of interest does he express?	
Does not mention belonging	0
Expresses little or no interest	1
Expresses some interest	2
Expresses a great deal of interest	3
Reported attendance at union meetings	
Never or hardly ever; less than once a year	0
Fairly often; once every 2 or 3 months	1
Often; most of the time; once a month or more	2
Has he held union office or committee assignment?	
Yes	1
No	0

The total scores range from 0 to 6. These are further explained and the distribution of scores is reported on pages 146-148.

Ratings of Four General Attitudes—

>Political futility
>Authoritarian attitudes
>Satisfaction with life
>Feelings of social alienation

The remaining ratings were all obtained from "agree-disagree" responses to the list of statements included in Questions 25, 26, and 41 of the post-election interview. Each item was scored 0 or 1, the latter for a reply indicative of the attitude being rated. The specific items, the scoring and the distribution of total scores are explained in the body of the report, as each of the attitude measures is presented—

>Attitudes of political futility   pp. 155-156.
>Authoritarian attitudes   pp. 167-168.
>Satisfaction with life   pp. 182-184.
>Feelings of social alienation   pp. 189-190.

APPENDIX D

Supplementary Tables

TABLE D.1

REASONS FOR APPROVING OR DISAPPROVING UNION'S SUPPORT OF STEVENSON

Do you think it was all right for unions to work to get Stevenson elected or that it was not all right? *Why do you feel that way?*

Reasons	Stevenson Voters	Eisenhower Voters	Did Not Vote	Total Sample
All Right				
Unions have been helped by Democrats; Unions made gains under Democrats; Stevenson pro-labor	26%°	19%°	16%°	23%°
They have a right; it's their privilege	13	18	23	15
Unions are for the people; for the working man	20	°°	11	15
Business does the same thing	10	2	3	7
Stevenson the best man; Unions thought he was the best man	4	2	8	4
Unons should support him	2	—	1	2
All right, with qualifications (e.g., "O.K., but shouldn't try to influence people's vote")	2	7	3	3
Miscellaneous, indefinite and unclassifiable	12	8	2	10
Not All Right				
Unions should not be in politics; don't like my money being used that way; don't believe in pressure groups	3	13	10	6
People should be allowed to make up their own minds	1	8	1	3
Miscellaneous, indefinite and unclassifiable	3	12	3	5
No. of cases	(170)	(116)	(65)	(351)

° Percentages in this and the following tables do not total 100% even though some respondents gave more than one reason since many respondents gave no answer. Percentages in all the tables of post-election responses are weighted as stated in the footnote on p. 29.
°° Less than 1%.

TABLE D.2

REASONS FOR APPROVING OR DISAPPROVING BUSINESS SUPPORT OF EISENHOWER

Do you think it was all right for businessmen and business groups to work to get Eisenhower elected, or that it was not all right? *Why do you feel that way?*

Reasons	Stevenson Voters	Eisenhower Voters	Did Not Vote	Total Sample
All Right				
It's their privilege; they have the right; if they want Eisenhower, let them work for him	31%	24%	34%	30%
Republicans and Eisenhower for business; business look for their own interest; thought Eisenhower the best man	20	21	16	20
If it's all right for unions, also for business	21	11	4	16
All right, with qualifications (e.g., "O.K., but shouldn't try to influence people's vote")	3	2	1	3
Miscellaneous, indefinite and unclassifiable	7	21	8	10
Not All Right				
Business should not be in politics	2	5	—	3
Business is anti-union; against the workers	3	—	4	2
Business went too far; put too much money into campaign	3	—	1	2
Business not for the interests of everybody; not for the country	1	1	4	2
Shouldn't tell me who to vote for	*	4	1	1
Miscellaneous, indefinite and unclassifiable	3	2	—	3
No. of cases	(170)	(116)	(65)	(351)

* Less than 1%.

TABLE D.3

REASONS FOR TRUSTING OR NOT TRUSTING VOTING RECOMMENDATIONS BY LABOR GROUPS

Why is it that you particularly trust (or don't trust) recommendations by *labor groups?* [For complete question, see Interview II, Question 17.]

	Stevenson Voters	Eisenhower Voters	Did Not Vote	Total Sample
Trust; would more likely vote for recommended candidate:				
They know who has done most for workers; for the poor man; for workers	26%*	3%*	16%*	20%*
My class of people; I'm a labor man, represent my interests	18	—	5	12
They pick pro-labor candidates; pick good candidates	3	2	7	3
Union leaders elected democratically; express will of workers; responsible to membership	4	—	—	3
Honest; truthful; give accurate information on candidates	2	2	5	2
What labor does is good for the country	1	1	4	1
Other reasons	1	**	—	**
Don't trust; would more likely vote against recommended candidates:				
All reasons	1	22	1	6
No. of cases	(170)	(116)	(65)	(351)

* In Tables D.3 through D.8, percentages total less than 100% since the table is limited to those respondents who indicated trust (or lack of trust) for the particular group and who expressed a reason for their trust or distrust. The overall count of persons expressing trust and distrust of the different groups is summarized on page
** Less than 1%.

TABLE D.4

REASONS FOR TRUSTING OR NOT TRUSTING VOTING RECOMMENDATIONS BY BUSINESS GROUPS

Why is it that you particularly trust (or don't trust) recommendations by *business groups?*

	Stevenson Voters	Eisenhower Voters	Did Not Vote	Total Sample
Trust; would more likely vote for recommended candidates:				
What's good for business is good for country; country built by business; what they do helps us	2%	7%	4%	3%
Smart men; know how to run things; know what we need	1	2	3	2
Other reasons	—	2	—	*
Don't trust; would more likely vote against recommended candidates:				
Selfish; only want to make money; only for candidates who are just pro-business	11	6	7	9
They favor anti-labor party; are anti-labor; don't represent workers' interests; they don't have same interests I have	16	2	4	11
For the money-men; the rich; Wall St.; capitalists	6	2	4	5
Other reasons	4	—	1	3
No. of cases	(170)	(116)	(65)	(351)

* Less than 1%.

TABLE D.5

REASONS FOR TRUSTING OR NOT TRUSTING VOTING RECOMMENDATIONS BY NEWSPAPERS

Why is it that you particularly trust (or don't trust) recommendations by *daily newspapers?*

	Stevenson Voters	Eisenhower Voters	Did Not Vote	Total Sample
Trust; would more likely vote for recommended candidates:				
Do a fair job of reporting news; give facts on both sides; non-partisan; get most of my information from them	*	11%	7%	4%
Other reasons	—	4	—	*
Don't trust; would more likely vote against recommended candidates:				
Biased; not truthful; not responsible	18	6	14	15
Too pro-Republican; controlled by Republicans; always smearing Democrats; with the wrong party or side	10	4	1	8
Aligned with business groups; for the big guys	8	2	3	6
Anti-labor; don't represent labor	7	—	1	5
For themselves only	4	*	1	3
Advertisers control policy	3	—	1	2
Other reasons	1	*	3	1
No. of cases	(170)	(116)	(65)	(351)

* Less than 1%.

TABLE D.6

REASONS FOR TRUSTING OR NOT TRUSTING VOTING RECOMMENDATIONS BY CHURCH GROUPS

Why is it that you particularly trust (or don't trust) recommendations by *church groups?*

	Stevenson Voters	Eisenhower Voters	Did Not Vote	Total Sample
Trust; would be more likely to vote for recommended candidates:				
Not one-sided; honest; truthful; try to do right; for the best; good people	12%	8%	12%	11%
Wouldn't lead me astray; can rely on church; pick good people	8	5	3	7
Not selfish; for the good of people; not involved in politics	4	5	7	5
Other reasons	4	4	—	3
Don't trust; would be more likely to vote against recommended candidates:	2	4	3	3
No. of cases	(170)	(116)	(65)	(351)

TABLE D.7

REASONS FOR TRUSTING OR NOT TRUSTING VOTING
RECOMMENDATIONS BY VETERANS GROUPS

Why is it that you particularly trust (or don't trust) recommendations by *veterans groups?*

	Stevenson Voters	Eisenhower Voters	Did Not Vote	Total Sample
Trust; would more likely vote for recommended candidates:				
Patriotic; fought for the country; know about war	5%	4%	1%	4%
I'm a member; was in service	3	—	5	3
Not selfish; represent best interests of people; interested in total country; in good government; pick good men; try to do right	3	6	—	3
They know what they're talking about	2	2	3	2
They have my interest at heart	2	2	3	2
Other reasons	10	3	1	7
Don't trust; would more likely vote against recommended candidates:				
All reasons	—	3	1	*
No. of cases	(170)	(116)	(65)	(351)

* Less than 1%.

TABLE D.8

REASONS FOR TRUSTING OR NOT TRUSTING VOTING
RECOMMENDATIONS BY FRATERNAL ORGANIZATIONS

Why is it that you particularly trust (or don't trust) recommendations by *fraternal organizations?*

	Stevenson Voters	Eisenhower Voters	Did Not Vote	Total Sample
Trust; would more likely vote for recommended candidates:				
They're truthful; men of integrity; high standards	4%	2%	5%	4%
Of same religion as mine; made up of church members	3	2	1	2
Other reasons (e.g., "non-partisan")	2	9	3	4
Don't trust; would more likely vote against recommended candidates:				
All reasons	°	—	1	°
No. of cases	(170)	(116)	(65)	(351)

° Less than 1%.

TABLE D.9

FEELINGS REGARDING THE ELECTION OUTCOME
(Post-election Interviews)

How do you feel about the way the election came out?

Responses	Stevenson Voters	Eisenhower Voters	Did Not Vote	Total Sample
Favorable				
Needed a change	*	13%	10%	5%
The people's choice; the will of the majority	2%	8	19	4
Eisenhower a good man; will do a good job	*	7	11	3
Means end of Korean War; end of war generally	1	2	4	2
Miscellaneous, indefinite and unclassifiable	10	62	30	24
Unfavorable				
Would rather have Democrats; always been a Democrat; made gains under Democrats	13	—	3	9
Republicans not good for unions; Democrats are for the worker; Republicans for the rich, etc.	6	—	1	4
Stevenson woud have made a good President	5	—	—	3
Don't like it, *but:* Give Republicans (Eisenhower) a chance; Eisenhower's OK; too soon to say	12	—	4	8
Don't like it, *but:* It's what the people wanted; we must go along with the majority	13	—	3 .	9
Don't like it, *but:* Republicans will have to do their best; won't be too different from Democrats; not afraid of Republicans	5	—	—	3
Don't like it, *but:* Guess we could use a change	5	—	—	3
Don't like it, *but:* Eisenhower seems favorable to labor	2	—	—	1
Miscellaneous, indefinite and unclassifiable	20	2	15	16

TABLE D.9 (Continued)

Responses	Stevenson Voters	Eisenhower Voters	Did Not Vote	Total Sample
Neither Favorable Nor Unfavorable				
Don't like it, but:				
Don't really care; indifferent	4%	—	8%	4%
Don't know yet; have to wait and see	3	*	—	3
Miscellaneous, indefinite and unclassifiable	4	7	5	5
No. of cases	(170)	(116)	(65)	(351)

* Less than 1%.

TABLE D.10

REASONS FOR FEELING GLAD OR SORRY
THAT EISENHOWER WON

(Post-election Interviews)

Are you glad or sorry Eisenhower won the election? *Would you tell me why you are glad (or sorry)?*

Responses	Stevenson Voters	Eisenhower Voters	Did Not Vote	Total Sample
Glad				
Eisenhower the man for the job	6%	23%	18%	12%
Needed a change; Democrats in too long	3	23	10	9
Eisenhower a great military man; great general; will end Korean War; end of war generally; more experienced in world affairs	3	18	10	7
Eisenhower will appoint good men; favorable reference to appointments	2	6	—	3
Republicans will reduce prices; taxes; national debt	*	7	1	2
Means an end to corruption and graft	—	9	—	2
Good to have Truman out; other unfavorable references to Truman	1	2	5	2
Miscellaneous, indefinite and unclassifiable	3	25	11	9
Sorry				
Democrats more pro-labor; I'm a union man; looks bad for workers; Republicans for the rich	14	—	4	9
Had it good under Democrats; I'm a Democrat; liked the New Deal	7	—	1	5
Just don't like Republicans	5	—	3	4
Stevenson the better man; Eisenhower not qualified	5	—	3	3
Reference to depression, unemployment fears	4	—	3	3
Worried about Taft and/or McCarthy; men behind Eisenhower	3	—	—	2
Miscellaneous, indefinite and unclassifiable	5	—	1	4

TABLE D.10 (Continued)

Responses	Stevenson Voters	Eisenhower Voters	Did Not Vote	Total Sample
Neither Glad Nor Sorry				
Guess it will turn out OK; Eisenhower might be OK	9%	*	1%	6%
Too early to say; wait and see	5	3	7	5
It's the people's choice; must go along	6	—	1	4
Miscellaneous, indefinite and unclassifiable	3	2	4	3
No. of cases	(170)	(116)	(65)	(351)

* Less than 1%.

TABLE D.11

REASONS FOR THINKING THAT THE ELECTION OUTCOME WILL (OR WILL NOT) MAKE MUCH DIFFERENCE
(Pre-election Interviews)

Do you think it will make a great deal of difference to the country whether the Democrats or the Republicans win the election, or won't it make much difference which side wins? *In what way would it make a difference?* Or: *Why do you feel that it won't make much difference?*

	Vote Intention				
	Steven-son	Eisen-hower	Unde-cided	No Answer; Refuse to Say	Total Sample
A Great Deal of Difference					
Pro-Democratic or Anti-Republican					
Republicans might bring depression; unemployment	20%	—	6%	8%	15%
Republicans not for workers; anti-labor	10	1	—	3	8
Democrats best for country; better conditions	8	—	—	5	6
Democrats are for labor	5	—	4	3	4
Republicans are for rich	5	—	6	3	4
Gov't. and things generally bad under Republicans	4	1	4	—	3
Specific benefits from Democrats (Prosperity; standard of living; civil rights)	3	—	2	3	2
Republicans make war more likely; not want a military President, etc.	3	—	—	—	2
Other specific points against Republicans	2	—	2	5	2
Total Pro-Democratic or Anti-Republican	59	2	25	30	46
Pro-Republican or Anti-Democratic					
Republicans will end war; better foreign policy	○	15	—	3	3
Republicans will clean up corruption	○	9	—	—	2
Other specific benefits by Republicans (cut taxes; oppose socialism, fresh ideas, etc.)	○	16	—	—	3
Total Pro-Republican or Anti-Democratic	1	41	—	3	8

TABLE D.11 (Continued)

	Steven-son	Eisen-hower	Unde-cided	No Answer; Refuse to Say	Total Sample
			Vote Intention		
Other reasons and "don't know" just how; indefinite and unclassifiable	13%	14%	14%	14%	13%
Total number saying "a great deal of difference"	73	57	39	46	67
Not Much Difference					
Not be any significant change either way; neither bring depression nor stop war	6	11	4	—	6
The two parties are about the same	3	8	12	11	5
First years not make much difference; one man can't change things	5	10	—	—	5
Other reasons and "don't know" why; indefinite and unclassifiable	7	9	31	11	9
Total number saying "not much difference"	21	38	47	22	26
No answer; unclassifiable as to much difference or not	6	5	14	32	7
	100%	100%	100%	100%	100%
No. of cases	(486)	(118)	(49)	(37)	(690)

* Less than 1%.

TABLE D.12

REASONS FOR THINKING THE ELECTION RESULTS WILL (OR WILL NOT) MAKE MUCH DIFFERENCE

Now that the Republicans won the election, do you think it will make a great deal of difference to the country, or won't it make much difference?

(If "great deal of difference") *In what ways will it make a difference?*
(If "not make much difference") *Why do you feel that it won't make much difference?*

	Stevenson Voters	Eisenhower Voters	Did Not Vote	Total Sample
A Great Deal of Difference				
Pro-Democratic or Anti-Republican				
Republicans might cause depression; cut wages; will change social benefits	13%	°	18%	11%
A difference for labor; Republicans will curb labor	14	°	4	10
Had it good under Democrats; worse under Republicans; Republicans' past record not good	5	—	1	3
Republicans a rich man's party	4	—	—	3
Unfavorable reference to cabinet appointments	2	—	—	1
Pro-Republican or Anti-Democratic				
End of Korean War; Peace	3	13	3	6
Republicans will lower taxes; prices	4	7	5	5
Republicans will stop Russians; will have better foreign policy; will stop giving money to foreign countries	4	5	1	4
End of corruption; no more scandals	—	10	1	2
Other pro-Republican comments	2	17	1	5
Miscellaneous, indefinite and unclassifiable	14	12	19	15
Won't Make Much Difference				
No difference right away; can't tell yet	6	13	7	8
Republicans have to be good; will try to do good	6	2	3	5
World conditions unaffected; no change in foreign policy; won't stop war; threat of Russia unaffected	5	4	1	4

TABLE D.12 (Continued)

	Stevenson Voters	Eisenhower Voters	Did Not Vote	Total Sample
Won't be much change; no difference between parties	4%	4%	4%	4%
Republicans can't change policies in effect for 20 years; economic structure already set going	5	2	—	3
Republicans won't bring depression; won't hurt labor	3	2	1	3
Party is not the important thing; country too big to be affected by one party or another	°	3	7	2
Taxes can't be cut	2	2	—	2
Miscellaneous, indefinite and unclassifiable	9	15	10	10
No. of cases	(170)	(116)	(65)	(351)

° Less than 1%.

Index